# MAKING MINDANAO

PATRICIO N. ABINALES

# MAKING MINDANAO

## COTABATO AND DAVAO IN THE FORMATION OF THE PHILIPPINE NATION-STATE

ATENEO DE MANILA UNIVERSITY PRESS

To Julia Nuñez and Jorge Abinales,
and to Donna Jeanne Amoroso
with love and gratitude

ATENEO DE MANILA UNIVERSITY PRESS
Bellarmine Hall, Katipunan Avenue
Loyola Heights, Quezon City
P.O. Box 154, 1099 Manila, Philippines
Tel. 426-59-84 / FAX (632) 426-59-09



Cover design by Fidel Rillo

The National Library of the Philippines CIP Data

Recommended entry:

Abinales, Patricio N.
Making Mindanao : Cotabato and Davao in the formation of the Philippine nation-state / by Patricio N. Abinales. – Quezon City : ADMU Press, c2000
1v

1. Southern Mindanao – History – Politics and government. 2. Cotabato – History – Politics and government. 3. Davao – History – Politics and government. 4. Political development. I. Title.

DS688.M2 959.9'73 2000 P0020000011
ISBN 971-550-349-7 (pbk.)

# CONTENTS

# TABLES

# ABBREVIATIONS

| | |
|---|---|
| AFP | Armed Forces of the Philippines |
| BSBI | *Bringing the State Back In* |
| CNI | Commission on National Integration |
| CPP | Communist Party of the Philippines |
| FMSJR | Federated Movements for Social Justice and Reforms |
| JUSMAG | Joint U.S. Military Advisory Group |
| KM | Kabataang Makabayan |
| LASEDECO | Land Settlement and Development Corporation |
| MAP | Muslim Association of the Philippines |
| MDA | Mindanao Development Authority |
| MIM | Muslim Independence Movement |
| MINSUPALA | Mindanao-Sulu-Palawan Association |
| MNLF | Moro National Liberation Front |
| NLSA | National Land Settlement Authority |
| PACD | Presidential Arm for Community Development |
| PC | Philippine Constabulary |
| PVL | Philippine Veterans' League |

# PREFACE

This book is a revised version of the dissertation I submitted to the Department of Government and the Southeast Asia Program at Cornell University. It attempts to place the history of southern Mindanao—specifically Cotabato and Davao—at the center of Philippine political development. It suggests that to understand such development, studies should not be focused solely on principal metropoles like Manila, but also need to incorporate tales from the peripheries. Only by interweaving these stories can we take the next crucial step in writing the country's full political history. The book is also a narrative of the connections the Philippine state has had with local power in these provinces. While the conventional, and popular, interpretation emphasizes subjugation (by Manila) and resistance (by Mindanao), the histories of Cotabato and Davao show a more intricate relationship that this formula often obscures.

I had a personal reason for working on this topic. I grew up in a province in the northwestern part of Mindanao which, since the late 1960s, has become noteworthy as an area of outmigration. Using college as an excuse, I left my hometown with little intention of going back. Manila's purported cosmopolitanism was simply too tempting to resist. And for nearly two decades, I became more Manileño than Mindanaoan, as annual visits home became increasingly perfunctory (my family remains in Ozamiz). This changed in 1987. The assassinations of two friends, the uncertainties of a political life after Marcos, and a spur-of-the-moment application for a one-year fellowship at Cornell's Southeast Asia Program led me to reconsider my plan to stay in Manila politically and intellectually. Going to Ithaca, New York, altered my life's goals considerably.

The dissertation was conceived while Benedict Anderson and I were trudging through two feet of snow. Ben turned to me and suggested that instead of studying my "friends" in the Philippine communist movement, I should consider where my parents came from and why their families moved to Mindanao. After all, as Ben gently reminded me, very little had been written about Mindanao compared to the attention given by both Filipinos and non-Filipinos to the rest of the archipelago. Acting the dutiful graduate student, propelled as well by a growing curiosity about my alienation from home, I followed Ben's advice. By the time I completed my course work, I was committed "to work on Mindanao."

The first impulse, of course, was to plunge into the literature on the MNLF rebellion and discern new ways of investigating it. This phase would inform the research proposal I submitted to the Social Science Research Council in 1991. Fieldwork, as has become a truism, has a way of altering one's original ideas. After six months of searching for local materials, interviewing "resource persons," and just hanging out with old and new friends in Cotabato, Cagayan de Oro, Davao, Ozamiz, and, oh yes, Manila, I felt increasingly drawn to Mindanao's complex past. By the time I went back to Ithaca, I was certain that I wanted to write a political history of not my home province, after all, but Cotabato and Davao.

I hope readers will find the analyses and reevaluations presented here helpful in understanding *and* appreciating southern Mindanao's role in our history as a nation and as a people. Those wanting further verification, or seeking to challenge my arguments are welcome to look at the primary and secondary documents I collected during my fieldwork. I donated most of them to the Ateneo de Manila University library a few years back. I do not believe that scholars—even in their active years—should hold on to their data as if these were private property. They should be accessible to others, especially in the societies studied. Only then can a meaningful debate be sustained beyond the boundaries of American institutions of higher learning and be participated in by Filipinos.

In the pursuit of this project, I was privileged to have Benedict Anderson, Vivienne Shue, Martin Shefter, and Takashi Shiraishi as my academic advisers. Ben helped me overcome my political and intellectual provincialism with his incessant prodding for more information about the Philippines. His ability to provide alternative explanations and his propensity to think comparatively have been a source of inspiration. Vivienne pushed many of her students to probe deeper into the dynamics of peasant societies, Chinese politics, and state-society relationship and assured me that "history" is political science. The ideas and approaches that Ben and Vivienne taught me are evident in this book. These two mentors have my eternal gratitude. Martin Shefter is one of those rare Americanists who encourage their students to look at American politics from a comparative perspective. His work on American political development and his class on social change in the United States inspired the sections on the American colonial state. Takashi Shiraishi was most concerned with the structures of the state and how these changed over time as the state tried to subdue communities in southern Mindanao. The issue of state and violence in Mindanao that this book tries to address was inspired by his constant inquiries and I am grateful to him.

The book's Southeast Asian inclinations were strongly influenced by the work of Ben and Takashi as well as that of O.W. Wolter, Audrey Kahin, the late George Kahin, and Saya Shiraishi. Francisco Nemenzo, Ernesto Corcino, Rudy Rodil, Felipe Miranda, and Resil Mojares in the Philippines, and Alfred McCoy, Mike Cullinane, Julian Go, Paul Hutchcroft, and Mark Thompson elsewhere played important roles in shaping my comparative and historical outlook.

At Cornell, I came to value the collegiality and friendship of Mary Callahan, Vince Boudreau, Donna Amoroso, Carol Sy Hau, Coeli Barry, Thanet Aphornsuvan, Elizabeth Remick, Michelle Mood, Steve Van Holde, Sunny Vergara, Mike Montesano, Jim Ockey, Geoff Robinson and Pete Zinoman. My respect for my cohorts grows as I watch them continue to engage their respective countries, areas, and regions of interest meaningfully. Carol Arguillas, Ting Tiongco, Estella Estremera, Judith Bayug, the Ridao family, Mike and Marilou Costello, Ruffa Guiam, Bebot Rodil, and Miguel Bernad helped me get reacquainted with Mindanao. In Manila, Tesa Encarnacion, Ed Tadem, Maricor Baytion, Susan Fernandez, Marites Vitug, Laura Samson, Cynthia Bautista, Maricris Valte, and Bobi Tiglao have been considerate intellectual and personal companions, making life in the "imperial capital" more fun and interesting. I would also like to thank the staff of the Xavier University's Research Institute for Mindanao Culture, the UP Third World Studies Center, *The Mindanao Cross, The Mindanao Times,* and the Lopez Museum for their generous help with sources.

The Cornell Southeast Asia Program accepted my application for the year-long Fellowship for Southeast Asians in 1988 for the first year of graduate school. The Department of Government then provided me with generous teaching assistantships and summer support. Funding for the dissertation research and write-up was provided by grants from the Social Science Research Council and the Mellon Foundation Write-up Fellowship, respectively. I thank all these institutions for their assistance. I also wish to thank Esther M. Pacheco of the Ateneo de Manila University Press for agreeing to publish *Making Mindanao,* as well as the anonymous readers who gave invaluable comments on the manuscript. Ma'am Esther and her staff have been very patient with the revision process, and I hope I was able to live up to their expectations.

My parents, Julia Nuñez and Jorge Abinales, allowed me to chart an intricate pilgrimage starting with a stint in the local seminary. I hope my current status, though, can make up for not fulfilling a commonly held dream in rural Ozamiz, that of seeing the eldest son ordained as a priest. Donna Amoroso's thoughtful commentaries were matched by a rigorous dissection of the book's writing style. I am especially grateful for her contributions to chapter 3; her work on Malaysian history and postwar nationalism provided the comparative foil that made me rethink my analyses of the Magindanao elite. Also, I could not have finished either the dissertation or its revision without her intellectual and personal presence. To these three kindhearted folks, I dedicate this book.

Kyoto, Japan
July 2000

CHAPTER 1

# State Formation and Local Power in a Philippine Periphery

In late 1974, the Moro National Liberation Front (MNLF) rebellion erupted in the Muslim provinces of Mindanao, hampering the consolidation of the Marcos dictatorship and steadily sapping its energy and resources. The war also left Mindanao intensely fragmented and volatile, and paved the way for the rapid expansion of a fledgling communist insurgency in the Christian provinces of the island (Gowing 1979, 234–35; Jones 1989, 133–44). These movements failed to accomplish their respective projects and have declined at present, but the state still contends with their legacies, notably the resilience of centrifugal forces that appear to undermine the full integration of Mindanao into the Philippines (Canoy 1989). Scholars point to rapid economic change in a frontier zone and its impact on fragile relations between indigenous Muslims and Christian settlers as root causes of the conflict that has engulfed over half of the island. These reasons, however, provide only partial (and inadequate) understanding of the emergence of religious nationalism and communism in Mindanao. Communalism, in particular, is often considered a primordial force, but as a source of identity, it can be constructed, invented, and changed. Likewise, intense economic change caused by capitalist expansion may lead to increased class tension and open conflict. In other circumstances, it may break down class solidarities, complicate rather than polarize conflict, and even avert social strife.

I would suggest that Mindanao's communal enmity and economic transformation originate actually from a more fundamental process: the manner in which the modern state was constructed and the nature of its relations with both indigenous and settler societies. This study is about state formation and the way the organization of politico-administrative authority defines the political life of an area. Because the modern Philippine state originated not in national, but in colonial form, this study returns to the American colonial era to trace the process of state formation in this southern periphery of the Philippines. It also traces the ties that evolved between local state authority and the different societies under its domain, as well as its intricate ties with the colonial/national center in Manila.

Rejecting the use of identity politics and economic change as dominant independent variables, this study will attempt to answer the following questions: First, how did the construction and metamorphosis of the state in Mindanao reshape social and political life there so that communal and social differences became emphasized rather than attenuated? Second, given the persistence of such differences, how was the state—in both colonial and postcolonial forms—able to keep southern Mindanao stable until the late 1960s? What cemented the area to the larger colonial/national body politic even as anticenter sentiments were allowed to flourish?

## Identity Politics, Economic Change and Southern Mindanao

Scholarship on Mindanao has always accepted communal and religious differences as principal factors in separating communities. It is not surprising, therefore, that when the MNLF rebellion erupted, it was interpreted within the framework of historic ethnoreligious conflict (Tan 1977; Gowing 1979; George 1980; Ahmad 1982, 4–10; Mercado 1984, 151–75). Events themselves reinforced this interpretation. The MNLF's success as a separatist movement hinged on its warning that the Marcos dictatorship was launching a vigorous, systematic effort to destroy the Muslims as a community. Domestic and international support reinforced this notion by equating the oppression of the Muslim "people" with the eradication of Islam (Misuari c1980; Asani 1979). The result was the mustering of a popular army almost overnight that fought the military on near-conventional terms. Yet, four years after it erupted, the MNLF was in disarray. It broke into several factions as the different tribes within the Muslim community came into conflict with one another over questions of leadership and the direction of the revolution (Molloy n.d., 17–18, 20–21 ). At the same time, members of the old "Moro elite" who had joined the rebellion now abandoned the MNLF and mended ties with the dictatorship. These elites invoked "traditional authority" within their respective communities and tried to regain from the MNLF the right to be spokesmen of the Muslims when dealing with the state (Alonto 1977; Ahmad 1982, 17, 20). These developments, as well as pressure from the international Islamic community, forced the MNLF to the negotiating table where its relative inexperience at political arbitration kept it perennially outmaneuvered by the government. While the MNLF outlived Marcos, it was never able to recover from these schisms and its power and influence continue to decline. Of late, Muslim separatism has been resurrected in the Abu Sayyaf and the Moro Islamic Liberation Force (MILF), whose commitment to an independent Islamic state represents a politicized Islam in contrast with the more secular, communalist MNLF (Turner 1995, 1–19).

Studies on the origins of the MNLF tend to validate the mobilizing and unifying power of "primordial ties" when communities are affected by profound economic and political change (Brown 1988, 54–5; Brass 1991, 64; Smith 1981, 134–35, 141–47). The MNLF's swift decline, however, exposed the fragility of communal identity as both primordial tie and mobilizing symbol (McKenna 1992, 11). There was, in fact, little basis for unity among Mindanao Muslims aside from Islam (Majul 1973, 26; Gowing 1979, 4–6). Notably, Muslim communities spoke related but mutually unintelligible languages and differed socially and politically in significant ways (Madale 1984, 180–81). The so-called Bangsamoro was subject to "several attachments and loyalties simultaneously" that affected its members' behavior during crisis situations (Hobsbawm 1990, 123–24; Majul 1985, 13).The Moro elite's breakaway and capitulation, for example, was caused by its anxiety that the rebellion's populist slant would destroy social distinctions within the Muslim communities. It was also the result of opportunist calculations by these elites that casting their lot with the state rather than the rebellion could better preserve their local preeminence (Che Man 1990, 127–29).

There is another weakness in using the politics of identity as the dominant explanation. As this study will show, the role of Islam in southern Philippine politics antedates the MNLF's radical mobilization. Communal identity had long been used, but for precisely the opposite purpose: to keep the Muslims "integrated" into the larger Philippine body politic through the co-optation of "brokering" Muslim elites. Scholars argue that state leaders engaged in "nation-building" in Mindanao with the intention of destroying Muslim minorities through assimilation into the dominant Filipino culture (Brown 198, 8). In fact, these leaders *preserved* communal differences as part of the process of nation-building and state construction, engaging, like Jomo Kenyatta, in ethnic juggling in order to frustrate separatist appeals and provide access to the state for loyal Muslim allies (Mayall and Simpson 1992, 8). Identity politics could thus be used by revolutionaries and separatists, but also by Muslim elites who prized their participation in Philippine politics and the state. "Confessional allegiance" can lead to separatism; it can also enhance state-building (Mayall and Simpson 1992, 19–20). By determining the historical foundations of this Muslim identity and tracing changes in its form and substance, we can account for its invocation by competing actors.

Scholars have persuasively shown, across different regions and at different times, that states can play significant, if not decisive roles, in the formation of communal ties. In certain cases, where there were none, such ties have even been created or invented.[1] Where communal ties exist but have negligible influence, conditions can arise for people or political forces to find new significance in them. This is true particularly of postcolonial states whose origins, official domains, structures, and practices often correspond imperfectly with the social milieu upon which they stand (Smith 1981, 137). Finally, the meanings attached to communal ties can be changed by the interaction of particular states and indigenous groups (Brass 1991, 254).

We need to examine exactly how the state affects the emergence and transformation of communal identities and how these, in turn, shape and reshape state-society ties. In this reappraisal, therefore, the importance of the state's relation to the Muslims and related symbols like nationalism becomes central (Gellner 1983, 4; B. Anderson 1994, 163–86). I will show that throughout most of the American colonial period and the first twenty-five years of the Philippine republic, state-Muslim interaction in Mindanao was premised on keeping Muslims distinct but at the same time formally integrated into Philippine territory. This framework continued well into the late 1960s when changes within Mindanao and on the national political scene reconfigured social relations and redefined Muslim identity, this time along more conflictual lines. Further substantiation of this general trend will be one object of this study.

Turning to the other Mindanao rebellion, that of the Communist Party of the Philippines (CPP), the role of the state can also be found alongside, and occasionally precipitating, conventionally cited factors. Studies of Mindanao's political economy have highlighted how transnational capital broke down the relative isolation and social tranquility of frontier communities and created a rural proletariat. They have also attempted to show how commercialization hastened class disparities within these communities and begot a mass of poor peasants who, together with the rural proletariat, became the potential mass base of the revolution.[2] I do not find this argument persuasive. In fact, it was not the capitalist transformation of the Mindanao countryside that was directly responsible for the extraordinary growth of Filipino communism. That growth can instead be traced to a strongly interventionist state whose military forces were committed to destroying the MNLF and protecting the state's massive development projects (Demegillo 1979). One of the more serious consequences of this was the militarization of Mindanao society, particularly among the poorer urban and rural communities of the island. It would be within these mercilessly assaulted communities that the first successful underground networks of the CPP would grow (Davis 1987, 149, 156). The party could easily attract fresh recruits from the victims of these brutal changes, individuals whose family, clan, and class ties were shattered by militarization. It is noteworthy that CPP organizers were especially successful in slum areas that served as haven for refugees and casualties of war removed from their social and solidary ties (Hackenberg n.d.; *Mindanao Focus* 1990, 5–26).

The revolution in Mindanao was, in a way, the "offspring" of the state, born of the Marcos dictatorship when the state reached its most centralized form (Tiglao 1988, 67–68). As long as Marcos resorted frequently to coercion, the CPP never lacked new members. The party's growth in Mindanao was so phenomenal that by the last years of the dictatorship, it outpaced all other areas where the revolution had gained ground. Once the dictatorship collapsed, however, crisis ensued within a CPP grown reliant on polarized politics. The party, especially in Mindanao, was overwhelmed by internal debate over the failure of revolution and the new, seemingly weakened state. Like the MNLF, therefore, the once-vaunted communist movement in Mindanao declined in power and influence in the 1980s.

This scenario confirms Skocpol and Goodwin's (1994, 259–78) observation that "[p]olitically exclusionary authoritarian regimes in the postcolonial world have been the ones most likely to generate broad, cross-class political support for revolutionary movements." The CPP expanded enormously because the shift to authoritarianism polarized Philippine society and simplified political battles. Once the dictatorship was overthrown and a weakened state form supplanted it, the revolutionary movement also began to unravel. This pattern has not been adequately examined by scholars interested in the Philippine communist movement. It is, however, key to understanding the spectacular communist expansion in places like Mindanao, as well as the CPP's dramatic decline and perhaps downfall (Porter 1989).

So far, I have argued for the significance to both Muslim and communist rebellions of their encounters with the state. This is a state that, at its weakest, was able to maintain social peace and stability and keep the upper hand over its adversaries. In its authoritarian form, in contrast, this state stimulated formidable opposition. Only a study of state formation and transformation, of the state's relationship with the various Mindanao communities, will better contextualize the two rebellions and lay the basis for understanding their eruption and decline.

## State Formation in Postcolonial Societies

In *Bringing the State Back In* (BSBI), Evans et al. (1985, 351) identified state formation as a "frontier" of state theory about which little had yet been written. They argued that investigation into how states are constructed would likely reveal "differentiated instances of state structures and action." Studying states within a temporal context allows us to understand how they emerge, consolidate, change, and even break down. The use of history affords the opportunity to tease out variations not only between state forms but also within a single state through stages of development (P. Anderson 1989). State formation is not a uniform process but an intricate procedure that reveals a diversity of experiences: the disparate ways in which states are imagined, the different forms they take when constructed, and the various mutations they undergo as they develop or deteriorate.

Being aware of and devoting proper attention to the past can check the tendency to seek explanation solely in contemporary factors. It also prevents potential reification of the state (Tilly 1975, 8). States do not appear out of nowhere; they are institutions whose shapes are determined by their histories. As observed by the editors of BSBI, however, state formation remains an underexplored field. Tilly's pioneering effort is limited by his European focus, and the editors have correctly pointed out that scholars have yet to "[pull] together research findings from studies of diverse parts of the world" to produce broader comparisons (Evans et al. 1985, 362; Tilly 1990, 192–225). There is good reason to remedy this deficiency. The few studies of postcolonial state formation to date reveal a richness that could immensely expand and deepen our knowledge of states. Lisa Anderson's (1986, 270–79) comparative study of Tunisia and Libya shows that understanding contemporary states requires an understanding of the construction of their colonial forebears. Writing about Indonesia, Benedict Anderson (1990, 96) notices that "the policy outcomes of the New Order [regime] are best understood as maximal expressions of state interests; and that the validity of this argument can usefully be gauged by reflecting on the history of the state in Indonesia." Finally, in Crawford Young's remarkable comparative sweep of the different colonial experiences within Africa, and between Africa and other areas of the postcolonial world, tracing root causes of current crises leads one back to colonial origins. States in postcolonial societies may have new facades, but digging deeper into their pasts, we inevitably encounter the skeletal frame of their modern political and administrative institutions: the colonial state.

When an alien institution imposes its will on indigenous communities under pretexts of racial or cultural superiority and introduces massive economic change to make their colonies' human and natural resources serve the demands of a growing world capitalist order, the colonial state defines the parameters within which subsequent postcolonial nation-states found their existence. Despite the anticolonial rhetoric intrinsic to nationalist movements in postcolonial societies, in reality, after gaining power, new leaders pattern the ideas, structures, and even routines of new states on colonial prototypes. The curse of the modern postcolonial state is that it is the progeny of its vanquished opponent. Crawford Young's (1994, 9–10) description of the African colonial state applies, to a greater or lesser degree, to other colonial situations as well:

> The colonial state in Africa lasted in most instances less than a century—a mere moment in historical time. Yet it totally reordered political space, societal hierarchies and cleavages, and modes of economic production. Its territorial grid—whose final contours congealed only in the dynamics of decolonization—determined the state units that gained sovereignty and came to form the present system of African politics. The logic of its persistence and reproduction was by the time of independence deeply embedded in its mechanisms of internal guidance.

The urging of the BSBI editors for more attention to state formation becomes doubly significant when we factor in these colonial origins. Studying postcolonial state formation involves tracing continuities and discontinuities between colonial and national state forms. It will also facilitate broader cross-regional comparisons between Western and non-Western societies, a goal the BSBI editors articulated ten years ago.

The paucity of state formation studies has another important dimension: the lack of investigation into what is happening on the local level. The important contribution of the scholars cited earlier is limited by their focus on the center alone. State formation, however, is a process that takes place all over the map as the state seeks to establish its authority in the territory it claims as its own. Making the study of postcolonial state formation more meaningful entails devoting some attention to arenas outside the centers of state power. For while the center may lay out the grand plans for building a state, it is in areas beyond the capital where most of the actual process takes place. John Furnivall's (1939, 1–137) detailed study of how a colonial official installed British imperial authority in southern Burma, then a far-flung outpost of the empire, demonstrates the extreme difficulty of building states outside the capital. Unfortunately, Furnivall's work on colonial state formation at the local level remains unique; no state theorist has picked it up or attempted to conduct inquiries of the same breadth and focus as this colonial bureaucrat-scholar. State formation in non-Western societies is, therefore, a frontier area for state theory in more ways than one. We need to go beyond the current state (back to colonialism) and the capital (out to the provinces) to build a base for broader comparison.

## A Second Look at the Postcolonial State's Capabilities

The other area in which postcolonial states contribute to the general theory is the exercise of state capabilities. State theory is sometimes criticized for its tendency to reify the state by treating it as a unitary organization with the inherent ability to stand above and dominate societies under its rule (Skocpol 1979, 14–18). Scholars cognizant of such criticism have attempted to develop new typologies to avoid the perils of reification while accommodating new empirical findings. One such effort has been to characterize states as either "strong" or "weak," based on how effective they are in projecting and exercising power vis-à-vis societies they govern. Joel Migdal (1988, 37) argues that most postcolonial states have failed to exercise their capabilities effectively. He notes that for these states to govern, they must reach accommodation with "a melange of fairly autonomous social organizations" that form weblike networks in society. States are forced to rely in particular on societal strong men both to ensure a modicum of stability and to gain access to the general population. This accommodation is detrimental, according to Migdal (1988, 31–32), because states end up compromising their capabilities and conceding power and initiative to strong men. In the final analysis, dreams of extraction and appropriation, coercion and regulation, and ultimately the attainment of legitimate status are all foiled. Comparable conclusions have been reached by Merilee Grindle and Atul Kohli regarding Mexico and India. Grindle (1977, 179) argues that Mexican politics have generally functioned as a "system of accommodation and payoff." State leaders at the federal level have to negotiate constantly with strong men in order to implement agricultural development projects at the local level. And in most cases, these projects do not achieve their intended goals. Kohli (1990, 385) maintains that the onset of the Indian state's problems of governability coincided with the declining capacity of the Congress Party to stem power struggles among bosses at the regional and local levels. He observes that two trends—"the growing democratization of traditional power relations in the civil society, and the failure [of Congress] to create a rational basis for generating new leadership through formal political institutions—are at the heart of the increasing authority vacuum in Indian politics." As difficulty in maintaining harmony within the system escalated, the party system also began to break down, creating a crisis of rule.

This theoretical argument highlighting the strengths of society to explain the feebleness of most postcolonial states has even been extended to countries purported to be paragons of state strength (Migdal 1988, xiv). In China, according to Vivienne Shue, state power is constantly subverted by societal forces organized in weblike structures. The strength of these networks is demonstrated by the pressure they put on local communist cadres who become part of the community conspiracy to limit state exactions (Shue 1988; Lewin 1988, 72–82). Similar reexamination of the social basis of both the South Korean developmentalist state and its North Korean opposite indicate that "the concrete processes of social and political change have not been determined simply by the state's directives but have been intimately shaped by the specific ways in which individuals, groups or social classes have reacted to state actions and to their experiences of social change" (Koo 1993, 231).

The fundamental contribution of this argument is its ability to restore the significance of a complex society to the understanding of state politics. Societal considerations had never actually been removed from the picture, but had been marginalized by the inordinate attention given to institutions. Now the weakness of many postcolonial states is traced to their inability to exercise absolute control over social forces. States exist not above or over their respective societies. There is no pristine all-powerful state in most societies, something that is particularly apparent in the postcolonial world. Jean-Francois Bayart (1993, 220–21) argues that the state

> operates as a rhizome rather than a root system. Although it is endowed with its own historicity, it is not one-dimensional, formed around a single genetic trunk, like a majestic oak tree whose roots are spread deep into the soil of history. It is rather an infinitely variable multiplicity of networks

> whose underground branches join together with the scattered points of society. In order to understand it, we must do more than examine the institutional buds above ground and look instead at its adventitious roots in order to analyze the bulbs and tubers from which it secretly extracts its nourishment and its vivacity.

Migdal, Kohli, and Shue (1994) have reached similar conclusions and have proposed a "state-in-society" formulation to help understand the manifold variations in state capabilities. They also maintain that the asymmetry of state capabilities becomes more apparent when one examines the various levels of the state's infrastructure. They propose that the study of state-society relations should focus not just on what is happening in the capital, but also on what is evolving in the outskirts. This disaggregation of states into their vertical and horizontal divisions enables one to examine "key building blocks of states and societies and the sorts of interactions among social forces leading to various patterns of domination." What becomes apparent eventually are the "multiple arenas of domination and opposition":

> Officials at different levels of the state are key figures in these struggles, interacting—at times, conflicting—with an entire constellation of social forces in disparate arenas. Any individual part of the state may respond as much (or more) to the distinctive pressures it faces in a particular arena as it does to the rest of the organization (Migdal et al. 1994, 9).

Weakness in structure and capability thus can be seen in more vivid manifestation in the periphery. Here, powerful social forces reign supreme, capturing the state and its resources and making its agents perform according to their wishes. State leaders do attempt to overwhelm these forces; in postcolonial societies, these efforts routinely come to naught. These "strong societies" are simply too powerful for the state. In the final instance, the state retreats and is further weakened.

The conceptual attraction of this "strong society-weak state" argument (and its more recent amendment, the "state-in-society" perspective) is diminished by one fundamental drawback. The argument is critical of the formalism of earlier studies of states and institutions, but perpetuates the error itself. In its attempt to explain why weak states litter the postcolonial world, the perspective uncritically accepts the formalist assumption that state actors are different from and perennially in discord with their societal counterparts. Even the state-in-society revision, while grounding the state in a social context, retains its distinction as a state in that context. It concedes power to society over the state, but still posits the latter's existence with its own boundaries.

In this formal division of state and society, the strong society-weak state perspective overlooks one fundamental feature of many postcolonial weak states: a considerable blurring of what is official and what is not and how the lack of a clear divide weakens state capabilities. In reality it is difficult to distinguish between citizen and bureaucrat, party official and local warlord, police officer and local smuggling kingpin. Bayart (1993, xvii) observes that the vagueness of what is official and what is not explains why, in the 1976 draft of their constitution, Nigerian leaders matter-of-factly defined political power as "the opportunity to acquire riches and prestige, to be in a position to hand out benefits in the form of jobs, contracts, gifts of money, etc., to relations and political allies." In Mexico, regional leaders like Ignacio Pesqueira of Sonora acted like local despots and at the same time swore allegiance to preserve the Mexican government (Acuna 1974, 136–37). Studies of local bosses and warlords in Southeast Asia also show how profound the ambiguity is and how little separates the personal/private from the official/public (Ockey 1992; Sidel 1995).

Authors like Migdal (1988, 255) do not go far enough when they describe the strong man as being "wedded to state resources and personnel to maintain local control and to gain new resources to enhance that control." They remain circumscribed by a formalist differentiation between state and society and thus lose the opportunity to examine the interdependence of state and strong man. To the extent that postcolonial states incorporate and thus legitimize traditional authority, the strong man's very basis of power is bound up with the state (Azarya 1988, 6–7). His power may consist largely of controlling "critical resources, such as land, credit and jobs," as well as in dictating "the rules of behavior for much of the population" (Migdal 1988, 257). But he is also the state's representative who convinces, cajoles, and often coerces the communities under him to comply with state directives. In short, strong men are self-aggrandizing individuals whose search for power requires that they be part of the state. They make no distinction between their personal goals and their public responsibility and thus undertake the representation, defense, and implementation of state interests, even if they are discriminating about it. Working both spheres, they are petty Louis XIVs: in their realms, they are the state.

This amended image of postcolonial strong men actually approaches Shue's description of "Janus-faced" Chinese communist cadres and their imperial predecessors, the scholar-gentry. Shue (1988, 79) argues that in rural areas, these cadres "act at once as agents of the state and defenders of their regions [and] they frequently adopted a dual role not unlike that of certain segments of the old regime elites." *Pace* Shue, however, I argue that being Janus-faced is not always contentious and pressure-laden. On the contrary, strong men also seek integration in their own person—the better to bring benefits to their communities, as well as limit state encroachment (Shue 1994, 75–76). Recognition of this collaborative interlacing of state and society brings us next to the question of what strong men actually do politically: the issue of governance.

## Modifying State Weakness through Accommodation and Governance

There is no denying that strong man-centered politics are far from "the modern norms of what a state should do" and that the inability to exercise their capabilities aggravates the weakened conditions of postcolonial states (Migdal 1988, 255). Yet this interpretation leaves a central question unanswered: Why have these supposedly weak states not broken down and splintered into many pieces? Or to put it another way, why do social forces, presumed to be antistate, stop short of "smashing the state" and content themselves merely with undermining it? The likely response of authors like Migdal is that the survival of weak states is due to accommodation with social forces. The state-society relationship, accordingly, is a series of compromises by which the power of social forces is recognized in exchange for access to the communities of a given society. This explanation, however, leads to only one outcome: a resilient society able to undermine the incursions of the state and weaken it. It cannot explain why these states are still standing, and how, despite looking like dilapidated machines, they still seem able to rule.

Precisely because of their condition, weak states are a bundle of contradictions. We find clear evidence of enfeebled capacity, but also signs of actual governance (Azarya and Chazan 1987, 106–31). At the local level strong men embody that contradiction, suggesting that accommodation works both ways. It is not just a one-way street with the state making most of the concessions; strong men also sacrifice part of their autonomy and privilege to serve the state. Their power blends their own personal wealth and private retinues of armed men with the titles they are granted for representing the state. In her study of a Taiwanese strong man, for example, Johanna Meskill (1979, 260) conveys this mix of the personal and official: "[it] was of the essence of the Taiwanese strong man that he represented a local, but economically differentiated, group and that he combined personal prowess, local prestige, wealth, and at least marginal legitimacy in the eyes of the government." One could add that marginal legitimacy almost always includes the possession of official titles. Thus strong men regard their leadership as a dual one: enhancing an already-established place in the community by representing the state. Adding an official designation magnifies the strong man's power, but it also requires him to fulfill, even if inadequately, certain functions of the state.

We need, therefore, to modify such terms as accommodation and compromise to include more than the idea of state weakness, the failure to accomplish some of the features associated with modern states. They also embody what strong men/state actors understand governing to be. We can say that corruption, patrimonial plunder, electoral fraud, and clan-based politics are at one and the same time signs of weakened states and the accepted conventions of governing. They are not part of the entitlements of being official; they are what is official. Such a dual elaboration of state capabilities is the outcome of the ambiguous border between state and society (Tilly 1984, 13).

The resilience of many postcolonial states, quite ironically, derives from the persistence of this ambiguity, not its clarification. Those in power understand that their preeminence hinges on being able to maintain social control as state leaders *and* as leaders in their respective social networks. The failure of one side will mean the weakening of the other, leading ultimately to the diffusion of all power. Thus, in order to be effective, state actors must be representatives of society and vice versa. This absence of distinction personalizes governance but also ensures an adaptability which makes the state resilient. Further, the tenacious character of these states can be seen positively to rely on the survival of strong men. As the representatives of society who stand to lose the most from disorder and instability, strong men accept as intrinsic their responsibility to keep government running. As long as strong men keep up their end of the deal, and as long as leaders of the state accept the fusion of roles as part of the natural order of things at the local level, postcolonial states, though run-down, continue to run.

Finally, we should consider the relationship between states and popular revolutionary oppositions and the question of why certain states actually do break down. Skocpol and Goodwin attribute the decline of social order in part to a profound weakening of state control over a tumultuous society. The center tends to lose control of its localities and peripheries; the structural edifice cracks as social opposition mounts. Based on my elaboration of the strong society-weak state argument, there is another way of understanding social upheavals and the deterioration of states. I will show that weak states can degenerate or even collapse when the power of the strong man/state is challenged seriously from above.

A policy shift in the central state aimed at taking seriously its function as a centralized state, including the acceleration of reform and modernization of society, has been shown to cause massive social dislocation. While dislocation disproportionately affects the poor and the marginalized, the sweeping character of the change also affects those in power at the local level who can lose their control over material and human resources.[3] And, paradoxically, when authorities in the capital do away with the services of strong men and expand—most likely with coercion—their direct control of localities, the resulting destabilization of strong men initially weakens the state as well. During the interval between strong man-centered authority and state centralization, spaces are created that allow for rivals of strong men—including revolutionary movements—to defy all authority. In states like the Philippines and republican China, where power is concentrated at the local level, attempts by the national state to centralize seriously erode state authority and open it up to revolutionary challenge. The central state breaks down the strong man's amalgam of local power and state authority; an ironic result is the subversion of the state itself.

In conclusion, this reformulation of the strong society-weak state argument is a valuable guide to understanding weak states like the Philippines. It is also a constructive tool in discerning the nature of state-society relations as they unfold in peripheral regions like Mindanao. By proposing that states be disaggregated and that scholars shift their focus from the center to the peripheries of states, this argument provides pathways by which one can understand Mindanao's fragmented political landscape and the role of the state in it. But we also need to ask whether localities outside the center are actually "arenas of domination and opposition," or in fact realms of governance and accommodation. By revising the meaning of strong man and the notion of state accommodation, and by reminding ourselves that the line between state and society in most postcolonial countries is ambiguous, we can understand better why some weak states are more resilient than their stronger counterparts. Amending the strong society-weak state perspective gives us an analytical instrument to understand the unusual manner in which the state in Mindanao has been able to keep itself afloat despite serious social resistance. I will show in this study that the state's resilience is partly the result of blurry state-society distinctions, overlaid by such real or (re)constructed identities as language, class, communal identity, and religion. The rebellions of the 1970s erupted in part because that ambiguity was dissolved under the pressures of a centralizing authoritarian regime and the emergence of ideological revolutionary movements that tried to compete with old strong men.

## An Historical-Institutionalist Approach at the Local Level

The themes and issues discussed in the previous sections indicate how this study will proceed. I employ an historically grounded approach to analyze the structures and processes of state formation at the periphery of a nation-state. I focus my study on the situation of the southern half of Mindanao from 1900 to 1972, comparing the adjoining provinces of Davao and Cotabato.

From 1913, when they succeeded the Moro Province, to 1962, when they were subdivided, Davao and Cotabato were the two largest provinces of the Philippines. They were also, and remain to the present, two of the principal destinations for domestic migration. Cotabato was once a predominantly Muslim province. The Magindanaos, i.e., the Muslims who populate the province, began to lose their majority status when floods of settlers from the central and northern Philippines arrived after World War II. Davao did not have a large indigenous population and has essentially been, since the turn of the century, a shifting settler society dominated by plantation-type agriculture. These two provinces figured prominently in the separatist and communist rebellions. Cotabato became a major battlefield of the MNLF's war on Manila. And when the separatist group began to unravel, Magindanaos were among the first to break with the MNLF over "tribal" differences. Davao was known as the main laboratory for the CPP, and the party's forces experienced their fastest growth in that province. This was also where its power first collapsed after the ouster of Marcos. Scholars advancing cultural and economic explanations have sought substantive empirical proof in these two provinces. Through reexamination of the same evidence as well as through original research, I will offer an analysis that sees communal identity and economic change as derivative of a single process—the pattern of state construction and transformation.

The study falls into two major sections. The first covers colonial state formation in southern Mindanao, while the second focuses on the postwar period. The periodic divide is aimed at tracing longitudinally the process of state formation from one phase, with its specific features, to another. Chapter 2 examines how the colonial state was built in Cotabato and Davao, from the initial decade of United States army rule of the Moro Province through the subsequent transfer of power to a civilian, Filipino-dominated state based in Manila. Chapters 3 and 4 discuss state-society relations: in Cotabato, the changing political world of the Magindanaos, and in Davao, the relations of two settler societies with the colonial state. Chapters 5 and 6 tell the story of spiraling demographic change in the postwar period, the emergence of a "weak state," and the sources of political stability in a frontier zone. Chapter 7 examines in some detail the careers of two strong men—Salipada Pendatun of Cotabato and Alejandro Almendras of Davao. Chapter 8 traces how the efforts of Ferdinand Marcos to centralize the state undermined political stability and the strength of these local strong men. The study closes with some reflections on southern Mindanao's contribution to the question of state formation and state capacities in the postcolonial world and a reconsideration of primordial identities as the basis of understanding politics on the frontier.

The study ends on the eve of martial law for two reasons. While scholars have argued that the dictatorship did not fundamentally alter the character of Philippine politics, the change in state form and its consequences—a much stronger presidency, the emergence of the military as a major political player, a vigorous promotion of national development, and the rise of a potent antistate opposition—suggests that some break did occur in Philippine political development. Second, martial law affected southern Mindanao significantly, as a result of the state's war against the MNLF and the CPP. This alteration in the area's landscape calls for separate treatment, as well as a thorough investigation of the origins and development of the MNLF and the CPP, something beyond the parameters of this study. Therefore, 1972 is an appropriate time to pause to evaluate the process of state formation. My ultimate goal is to broaden understanding of the singular nature of Mindanao's political landscape, the underlying causes of the two rebellions, and the larger issue of the resilience of weak states like the Philippines.

CHAPTER 2

# Variation in Colonial State-Building

In 1909, Governor Tasker Bliss justified continued military rule in the Moro Province, arguing that "a purely civil government is quite impossible and at the present time would carry with it untold misery and suffering, for outside the provincial officials, employees, and the army, there are not enough qualified inhabitants to form any kind of government, or who have the remotest idea of our form of representative government or institutions" (Bliss 1909, 4). In 1912, Manuel L. Quezon (1912, 9) countered that despite their religious differences, Muslims and Filipinos shared "the common tie of kinship" and therefore should be united under one civilian regime. He hastened to add that since the Muslims had no experience in politics, they would be apprentices to the Filipinos. These disparate views of how to govern southern Mindanao reflect the perceptions of the two power blocs which vied for control of state-building there early in the twentieth century.

The first was the United States army, which ruled the Moro Province from 1900 to 1913. The second were the Filipino politicians who, led by Quezon, would displace Americans in most agencies and offices of the colonial state thereafter. The army had been given initial responsibility for governing southern Mindanao because the region's "savage" populations purportedly needed a ruler with a firm hand. The singular characteristic of the Moro Province was the autonomy its administrators sought to maintain from Manila on the basis of Muslim difference. In this attempt, army officials were for a time successful. Constabulary officer Cornelius Smith, for example, could recall the province as "practically independent of the Governor General in Manila" (Smith 1977, 93; *RPC* 1906, 375). However, the singular paradox of the province was that the more successful it was in its main goals of pacifying and "civilizing the Moros," the weaker its justification for a separate existence became. This was a case of ethnoreligious difference being used to hinder the integration of Muslim Mindanao into the Philippines.

Quezon sought to accomplish the opposite. He and other Filipino leaders wanted the full administrative integration of southern Mindanao into the colonial body politic. While they privately shared with Americans the notion of "Moro backwardness," they used the perception of difference to facilitate integration, combining some centralist features of army rule with the political and administrative practices they developed in the regular provinces. Renamed the Department of Mindanao and Sulu, the area came under direct Filipino control, and Muslim elites who accepted Filipino hegemony apprenticed in the art of patronage politics as representatives of the Moros. Centrifugal processes nurtured under army rule and local suspicion of the Filipinos did not disappear, but were subsumed into a colonial politics that rewarded integration with the recognition of cultural difference. On the eve of the Commonwealth, Quezon and the Filipinos had integrated most of southern Mindanao and the Muslims to the colonial state, though this was, of course, not the end of the process.

This chapter tells the story of these two phases of colonial state-building. It also introduces the way relations between local regimes and the colonial center(s) influenced the course of state-building in southern Mindanao. The interplay between local and center often set the parameters of what the local regime did, or what it tried to do. This was clearly true of the army's relations with Manila. In the case of a semiautonomous colonial periphery like Mindanao, moreover, there was also the possibility of engagement with the metropolitan center. While the intervention of Washington might not have been direct, the repercussions of politics there were at times decisive in shifting the direction of local state formation.

Broadly, then, this chapter critiques the prevailing notion among scholars of a singular, if decentralized, process of colonial state-building in the Philippines. While not a comprehensive account, it also seeks to fill gaps in southern Mindanao's colonial history. The period 1914–1941 in particular remains understudied, with no coherent explanation of how colonial rule continued after the army left. I will try to fill this gap, aware that there is still much to be written.

## The Moro Province as a Regime within a Regime

The Americans' foremost concern when it came to governing southern Mindanao was the Muslim communities, their history of independence and warfare against the Spanish, and their hostility toward the Filipinos.[1] From information provided to them by the Spanish, research on the British and Dutch colonial administrations in Malaya and the Dutch East Indies, and their own field reports, the Americans conjured up an image of Muslims as an unruly lot, little different from native Americans they had recently subdued (Gowing 1980, 125–49; *RPC*, 30 June 1904, 12). The army aimed to establish its authority over the large, inaccessible territory of Mindanao largely in order to control and administer these "tribes," believed to be unsullied by "any civilizing influence" (Davis 10 Apr. 1900, 2122–129). After resolving initial disagreements and concluding that no credible, local "body of laws" was a worthy guide to governing the Muslims, army authorities reached the consensus that southern Mindanao needed an entirely new legal and administrative system (*RPC*, vol. 12, part 2, 30 June 1904, 577). The backwardness of their "wards" dictated that this system be centralized, and where they deemed proper to give a role to Muslim leaders (the datus), it would be so under tight supervision. "Civilizing the Moros," the Americans surmised, was a long process, possibly extending beyond one generation; the best way to start was to conciliate the datus and work slowly down to the "ordinary Moros" through such devices as public education.

Gowing has written extensively about the Moro Province; I will highlight two significant features that he and others have not emphasized.[2] First was the size of the territory. The Moro Province was four times larger than any other Philippine province, and its districts dwarfed many regular provinces in the north.[3] Combined with the Cordillera region, which was also populated by non-Christians, the total area under army control was over half the territory of the Philippines. During the first decade of colonial rule, a large chunk of Philippine territory was thus insulated from the evolving colonial politics of the center. This expanse, however, was sparsely populated. The 1903 census reported that the Moro Province had a population of 395,000 (40,000 Christians, 275,000 Muslims, and 80,000 other non-Christian tribes) spread over 38,888 square miles, a ratio of ten people per square mile.[4]

The challenge for the army was to effectively govern this huge area with its widely dispersed and potentially hostile population. What it accomplished in a decade was notable. A network of roads, telegraph lines, military outposts, and naval patrols was set up to "pacify the Moros" and bring the technology and "reach of the [modern] state" to southern Mindanao.[5] The infrastructure facilitated brutal military campaigns against resistant Moros, a limited campaign of disarmament against others, and the judicious use of "divide-and-rule" tactics among the disunified Muslim communities generally.[6] Alliances with friendly datus helped destroy those who were implacably opposed to the new order and stabilized the army's presence in the region; these allies were then allowed to keep their weapons. As a result, for the first time in centuries, an external power effectively established its rule over Muslim Mindanao (*ARWD* 1908, 416–17). Lanao was declared peaceful in 1906, with Americans noting that Lanao datus had shifted "from war to agriculture." A year later, Governor Leonard Wood announced that "there need be no apprehension of a general Moro uprising or of concerted action among them" (*RPC* 1907, 351). Cotabato was proclaimed pacified in 1908, and in 1909, all of Mindanao was certified free of Muslim hostilities (*RGMP* 1906, 348; *MH,* 21 Sept. 1907).

The significance of the pacification campaigns lay not only in their swiftness but also in their implementation. The combination of suppression and accommodation, especially the limited disarmament of the Muslims, suggests a kind of indirect rule comparable to the U.S. army's treatment of native Americans. In the Indian campaigns, collaborators were allowed to take part in the policing of their communities as well as of the larger territories and were also permitted to keep their arms (Gowing 1980, 146–48). Moreover, the army envisioned the "civilizing process" of Moros as one of long duration, and this limited the objectives of pacification to the elimination of outright opposition. The army had no immediate plans to integrate datus into the colonial state machinery, beyond appointing allies as tribal ward leaders to collect taxes and police their own domains.

The second notable feature of the Moro Province was its early success in building economic self-sufficiency, a process that was integral to both the civilizing process and the quest for administrative autonomy. The same infrastructure that made suppression campaigns possible fostered a dynamic internal trade. So-called "Moro Exchanges," tightly supervised special markets that bypassed Chinese and Filipino middlemen, were set up to encourage non-Christian participation in that trade and provide an alternative to warfare.[7] Unprecedented earnings in regional trade and agriculture supplemented the internal trade. In order not to be dependent solely on commerce with Manila, Cebu, and Iloilo, provincial authorities revived shipping connections with Borneo, Singapore, and even Australia, increasing customs revenues in port towns like Zamboanga and Cotabato (*MH,* 15 Sept. 1906; *ARWD* 1907, 83; 1915, part 3, 381–82). In 1906, trade in Zamboanga alone had increased so dramatically that it was the top port town in the colony in terms of customs collection.[8] In the case of Cotabato, the district experienced "pyramiding" growth in exports, rising from 21,246.50 pesos ($10,623.25) in 1908 to 311,043.17 pesos ($155,521.58) in 1911 (*MT,* 7 Dec. 1912). One official described it as "little short of marvelous" (Forbes 1928, vol. 2, 28, n.1).

The growth in exports was fed by settler-based agriculture. In Davao, former American soldiers joined Spanish pioneers to transform this backwater into a nascent center for hemp agriculture. From virtually nothing in 1900, the industry grew to forty-two plantations by 1911, covering 16,410 hectares (*MH,* 3 Mar. 1907). Hemp production rose from 308 tons (1902) to 8,592 tons (1910) to become the province's top export (Gleeck 1974; Hayase 1984; Garchitorena 1938). Rubber and timber industries were also introduced in Cotabato, though with less success.[9] Together with timber, pearls, and coconuts, these commodities became the province's principal exports, generating earnings of 3,410,712 pesos in 1910, which almost doubled (6,468,587 pesos) in 1913 (Gowing 1983, 221–22). While the growth of these industries was hampered by production and marketing constraints, their embryonic presence sustained interest in the province's potential.

As a result of economic growth, authorities confidently noted in 1906 that the cost of administering the province was "only 72 percent of the average annual expenditure… in all the other provinces of the Philippines" (Gowing 1983, 210–11; *MH,* 2 June 1906). And by 1913, the province was "completely dependent upon its own revenues" (*RPC* 1906, part 3, 186–87). In short, from the perspective of revenue generation, which is a major feature of state-building, the Moro Province was off to an excellent start. With the exception of 1909, 1910, and 1912, when expenses surpassed income due to budget constraints and Manila's assertion of its fiscal prerogatives, the province's books were kept well in the black. Tight fiscal management supplemented by innovative promotion of trade and investment furthered this revenue-generating capacity (*RGMP* 1906, 349; 1904, 319–20). Constantly reminded of provincial financial dependence on Manila, especially its support for infrastructure, army officers prided themselves on their ability to self-fund projects (*MH,* 15 June 1907).

Administrative success kept Manila Filipinos off the province's back, allowing for "a considerable de facto autonomy for Mindanao and Sulu" (Mastura 1984, 71). When Manila did poke its nose into provincial affairs, the army conjured up the image of Mindanao as a vast frontier, peopled by savages who were once the scourge of the northern communities, to limit Manila's interference. Even as reports enthusiastically proclaimed successful pacification of non-Christian groups, the message was tempered by warnings of the potential for instability because of the "Moro problem." Officials insisted that the Muslims remained a threat, while American mistrust of Filipinos aided efforts to keep them out of Moro Mindanao (*RPC* 1907, 342–43, 355–56; *RGMP* 1914, 124). Officers believed that the forced Filipinization of Mindanao was motivated by self-interest and threatened provincial integrity. Filipinos were regarded as incompetent, a racist opinion which was reinforced by reports of corruption in certain Filipino-controlled municipalities. And as agitation for independence spread in the Christian-dominated municipalities of the province, talk of the "Moro problem" was laced with apprehension about Filipino inability to preserve American accomplishments. It was stressed that "civilizing the Moros" demanded an interminable period of time and that only the army was respected for its "prowess" by "warlike" Muslims. It was thus vital that the policy of noninterference by Manila and by Filipinos be continued. Argued one officer:

> We have not yet built up a state nor reached the mass of the people in any general uplifting movement… The mailed fist is the first law of the land—peace would be impossible without the actual presence of the troops—for this country is neither ready nor has it ever known any other form of government. The civil-military government—in which the Governor controls the armed forces—is indispensable now and will be for generations to come (*RGMP* 1909, 3–4).

Army officers became quite invested in the idea that southern Mindanao was different. While some accepted that the area was formally part of the colonial territory, others believed its history warranted separation or autonomy. The sentiment got official imprimatur when acting Governor Ralph Hoyt officially proposed that Mindanao, Sulu, and Palawan be disengaged from the rest of the Philippines and governed as a new territory called the "Mindanao Plantations." Hoyt recognized that there were Filipinos in the province. He argued, however, that the province was "essentially Moro, 90 percent of the total population being Moro and non-Christian, and any Filipino coming within its borders or residing therein should recognize that he must abide by the laws of the province and rest content to live within its territorial jurisdiction rather by sufferance than by right of heritage" (*MH,* 12 Aug. 1905; *RGMP* 1910, 21). Hoyt was not alone. The populist William Jennings Bryan gave credence to separatism when he claimed that the Philippines could be granted independence, except for Mindanao, where "the conditions existing… are so different from those existing in the northern islands that the two groups must be dealt with separately" (*MH,* 8 Aug. 1906). Finally, the American-owned *Manila Bulletin* (27 Oct. 1906) argued that the Filipinos had no business in Mindanao since they "never had any control over the Moro people and never had any sort of relations with Mindanao as being in the same class with other islands. If the Moros want to annex themselves to the United States, or to Borneo, or to the moon, why, what of it?"

The Filipinos were not oblivious to these separatist sentiments. In 1905, Philippine Commission Attorney-General Gregorio Araneta questioned the power of the province's legislative council to "modify, amend or repeal Acts of the Philippine Commission in their application to the Moro Province." Provincial authorities responded by citing ambiguities in the law enacted by the U.S. Congress, reminding the commission of that higher body and weakening its presumptive stance as a superior authority in the province. Wood, Bliss, and their subordinates could also count on allies in the Philippine Commission, the governor general's office, Washington, and most of all in the boisterous American community of Manila. This support was vital when Filipinos singled out the army's excessive use of force. When the media and his Filipino enemies criticized Wood for the massacre of rebelling Muslims at Bud Dajo, his defenders included Manila Americans and President Roosevelt himself, fellow Rough Rider and friend (Thompson 1975, 89; *MT*, 5 May 1906; *MH,* 17 Mar. 1906). When Filipino politicians questioned the autonomy given to the army, American officials used the "Moro problem" to deflect their critics (Thompson 1975, 139–40).

As Filipinos escalated their demands for the integration of Mindanao, army authorities looked to political figures in Washington to defend their cause (*M-A,* 12 Aug. 1906). They tapped the Washington media and were successful in getting former U.S. president and governor-general of the Philippines Howard Taft to warn of the inability of "the Filipino educated classes [to show] their capacity for just government as in the treatment of the Moros and non-Christian tribes" (Gleeck 1974, 157).

## The End of Martial Law

Between 1900 and 1913, therefore, the U.S. army successfully established an authority whose features were different from the rest of the colonial body politic (Gleeck 1984, 139). It was a regime-within-a-regime, which operated under different policy assumptions and had the capacity to raise its own revenues. Further, it had successfully pacified the population under its control. All this had spurred army officers to entertain the notion of strengthening the Moro Province's autonomy from Manila by completely separating Mindanao from the Philippines and transforming it into a "territorial possession" like Guam or Hawaii. Yet by 1914, the army had withdrawn from southern Mindanao and had conceded power to the Filipinos and Manila. Why this abrupt reversal, given the apparent success of the army's state-building process?

One key answer can be found in the problem of personnel. Benedict Anderson (1990, 95) describes the state as an institution that "ingests and excretes personnel in a continuous, steady process often over long periods of time." This requirement became the bane of the Moro Province: the more stable and successful the regime became, the more pressing was the need for personnel with appropriate skills serving sufficient time to manage an expanded administration. Yet a systemic feature of the army's structure made this need impossible to fulfill. The American army at the turn of the century was "the worst kind of patchwork," its national structure constrained by promilitia and antiprofessional forces in Congress (Skowronek 1982, 116–17). The pressures of the Progressive movement in the United States had started the ball rolling on a series of reforms designed to counteract congressional control and make the military a more efficient organization. One such measure was the rotation and reassignment of personnel, practices that benefited military cohesion and morale by exposing officers and men to different areas and experiences. When set against the personnel needs of the Moro Province, however, they proved disastrous in their disruption of administrative continuity. The turnover rate in Cotabato showed that governors of the district changed at the rate of almost 1.5 times a year.[10] Gowing (Gowing 1983, 184) noted that between 1906 and 1909, "the District of Lanao had no less than seven district governors and four different secretaries, while Cotabato had five governors and four secretaries in the same period. This continual flow of personnel naturally worked against efficient government because it meant that key officials hardly had time to learn their duties and get to know the people they governed before they were transferred."

The effects of this practice were felt less at the top of the hierarchy than at the bottom. Officers who replaced each other as provincial governor, engineer, or treasurer possessed comparable skills. As military men in bureaucratic positions, they had had previous administrative experience, as well as a chance to work together before being sent to the Moro Province. Moreover, since high-level administration consisted largely of long-term planning and general coordination, personnel transfers did not seriously disrupt work. At the lower rungs of the hierarchy, however, governing was gravely affected by the constant personnel rotation. Younger and lower-rank officers lacked the background, training, and experience of their superiors, the Moro Province often being their first assignment. Moreover, the organizational needs of the province were increasingly different from those of a fighting army; officers needed to be judges, secretaries, linguists, public works officials, and mediators. Even if a lieutenant appointed as district governor had the appropriate skills and found the bureaucratic skeleton of his command intact (offices, personnel records, reports, etc.), he still had to learn new languages, become familiar with a new milieu, establish ties with indigenous groups, and pick up where the previous administrator had left off. And he did this knowing that he would not be in the district for long. Administrative work became a constant and unstable learning process fostering instability in the otherwise steady provincial structure.

Making matters worse, provincial authorities had little say in directing the movement of personnel. Rotations and reassignments remained in the hands of superiors in Washington and Manila. Provincial officials could only make recommendations in their annual reports. In his last year in office, Wood warned that "officers are constantly undergoing a change of personnel, and if there is anything which should be avoided under conditions such as that existing in the Philippine Islands, it is this constant change of officials" (*RGMP* 1906, 365). Governor-General Cameron Forbes similarly complained that the "continuing change of [army] personnel in all these important positions... has militated against efficient administration" (*RPC* 1909, 67).

There were attempts to mitigate the impact of these routines and enhance administrative continuity. Through bureaucratic foot-dragging, provincial governors Wood, Bliss, and Pershing extended the tenure of service of officers and slowed reassignments. They fought to keep some of their subordinates in provincial posts and borrowed extensively from other agencies, like the Philippine Constabulary, to fill vacated posts (Gowing 1983, 249–50; Thomas 1971, 45–46). However, they were unable to prevent the administrative hemorrhage. Neither could sufficient non- or ex-military personnel be found. The possibilities were three: pro-American Filipinos, Americans in Manila, and Americans already in Mindanao.[11] For reasons previously described, Filipinos were promptly rejected. The military continued to believe that they were administratively incompetent, that they were inclined to exploit non-Christians, and that there was endemic hostility between them and the Muslims

(*RGMP* 1 July 1905–16 Apr. 1906, 423). Army officers were initially more hopeful that they could attract Americans to Mindanao. Wood appealed to an American sense of mission, declaring, "Young Americans of the best class are much needed in all branches of the government, especially as representatives of the government in remote districts among the half-civilized peoples… It is from the Americans in the islands that the people are forming their ideas of the American nation, and it is important that our representatives should be the best obtainable" (*RGMP* 1 Sept. 1904, 590). Such boosterish rhetoric, however, failed to interest Americans in Manila. Many remained reluctant to go to Mindanao, fearing the "Moro problem" — the very "bugaboo" the province had used to maintain its autonomy (Kalaw 1931). By engaging in double-talk regarding provincial stability, the army unintentionally frightened away the very Americans it wanted to attract (*MH,* 29 Feb. 1908).

The last, and best, possibility were Americans in Mindanao, who were regarded as the most qualified because of their familiarity with the area. Yet they, too, failed to respond to the call. Those in the settlement areas were usually ex-military men who wanted to own their own homesteads or become traders in one of the district capitals. They had ended their formal ties with the colonial bureaucracy in order to pursue private gain, and there was no reason for them to return to colonial service while the returns were higher in the private sector (*MH*, 22 June and 3 Aug. 1907). A comparison of the annual compensation of a military officer-*cum*-district administrator with the potential gross earnings of a homestead or plantation is illustrative. A captain appointed as district treasurer earned $1,900 a year; as provincial treasurer he earned $4,000. A 100-hectare hemp farm could gross up to 60,000 pesos (roughly $30,000) if the harvest was good (Official Register of Officers 1904, 89; *MH,* 24 Oct. 1908). The prospects of agricultural success thus made an administrative career less appealing. It was even difficult to convince those in active service to complete or extend their tour of duty in Mindanao. Many officers saw more chances of military advancement in the United States, nearer to the seat of power (*RPC* 1907, 340). The exodus began with the army, but later included Americans who had joined constabulary units. Col. Peter E. Traub, for example, spent over two years in Mindanao, rising through the ranks to become the island's Chief of Constabulary. In early 1917, however, he took leave and returned to the U.S., joining the United States cavalry with the rank of colonel. Traub not only retained his constabulary rank, a title conferred within the Philippines, but found new avenues for advancement in the United States (*PFP,* 10 Mar., 12 and 19 May 1917; *MH,* 15 June 1907).

Personnel problems peaked in 1912, when the U.S. Congress, mistrustful of military reformers, prohibited the assignment of military personnel to nonmilitary positions, even on a temporary basis (Forbes 1928, 190). The U.S. army was thereby prevented from solving, within its own territory, a problem that was also jeopardizing the larger Philippine civil service: what Onofre Corpuz (1957, 177–81) calls "the instability of the American personnel of the insular administration" arising from, among other things, lack of benefits, low salaries, and the greater proximity of Puerto Rico. These problems did not escape the attention of Americans living in Mindanao. If Manila itself was unable to "maintain a corps of permanent American administrators," what could be expected of a periphery famous for its volatile nature? An exasperated John Pershing, nearing the end of his term of office, finally admitted that the only viable solution was to increase native (i.e., Filipino) involvement in provincial administration (Elliot 1917, 94). In admitting this, the army, in effect, threw in the towel.

What sealed the fate of the Moro Province was American domestic politics. Political battles in the U.S. Congress, and between Congress, the presidency, and the War Department, had a profound impact on the army in Mindanao. While army reformers were able to institute some new measures designed to transform the federal army into a cohesive national military, they were unable to win battles against Congress on other fronts. Congress wanted a federal army based essentially on the contributions of state militia and the state-based national guards and, accordingly, cut military strength and blocked the institution of a standing force (Skowronek 1982, 223–28, 235–41). In Washington, supporters of army rule in Mindanao—especially Leonard Wood—became caught up in these bureaucratic and political wars; it meant they had less time to devote to the interests of a small distant territory of the American empire (Pohl 1967).

Beneath the political battles, moreover, was an underlying unanimity on the issue of empire. Debates over imperialism notwithstanding, both progressive reformers and machine politicians believed that imperialism should play a secondary role to domestic political battles. When imperialism abroad imperiled domestic politics, both sides acted to protect American society from the potentially detrimental effects of colonial policy (Leuchtenburg 1952, 483–504). Even while they argued over the benefits or drawbacks of imperialism, the belligerents agreed that imperial agencies directing colonial administration should draw only minimal resources away from domestic needs (Skowronek 1982, 218–34).

Politics in the metropolitan center, therefore, while not directly disallowing the army's ambition in Mindanao, effectively precluded the resolution of its most pressing problem. Further, Washington moved to strengthen the hand of Filipino politicians in the colonial center through its policy of Filipinization, the last factor in the unraveling of army rule (see further on). The United States was unique in Southeast Asia for having brought "natives" into the colonial state within the early years of its domination (Pomeroy 1947, xiii, 49–50,97). What further distinguished the Americans from the Dutch, British, and French was that opening the colonial state to Filipinos involved limited suffrage and representative politics.[12] The resulting emergence of the Philippines' future national elite was soon felt in the Moro Province as Filipino agitation for the administrative integration of Mindanao to the rest of the colony and criticism of American separatist sentiments became more boisterous (Gowing 1983, 205–6, 252–54). As the new decade began, Filipino members of the Philippine Commission began asserting their opinions on the Moro Province during deliberations; they blocked recommendations to enhance the powers of army administrators and got the American-dominated commission to clip some of the army's autonomy.[13] In the assembly, delegates from the Filipino-dominated areas of Mindanao pushed to accelerate the integration process and used their powers over the budget to weaken the financial capability of the army (Gowing 1983, 252). Their efforts were reinforced by pressures at the local level where municipal officials took up the cudgels of "nationalist agitations" (*RGMP* 1909, 31; 1910, 21).

Despite the province's impressive fiscal achievements, the army's position was further eroded when Manila centralized all revenue collection.[14] By 1912, the Philippine Assembly had absolute fiscal control over the Moro Province. Policy debates and turf battles in Manila also affected provincial fortunes. The debate and consequent impasse over foreigners' right to own land, for example, sent contradictory signals to potential investors who were waiting for a clear land policy to be enacted. This, in turn, affected provincial economic performance, prompting both officials and local entrepreneurs to continually demand clarification from Manila (*C-A,* 15 Aug. 1905; *MB,* 27 Oct. 1906; *MH,* 15 June 1905). Meanwhile, debates between the assembly and the commission over the qualification of land surveyors seriously decreased the availability of public lands for settlers in Mindanao (Stanley 1974, 169).

Lost battles in Washington exacerbated this erosion of standing in Manila; in both centers, the army ceased to be a major player. With "Moro Mindanao" already pacified and much of the Philippines under the rule of Filipinos and civilians, the existence of a military regime governing a special province had become an anomaly in the overall colonial design. Manila came to the conclusion that the province was ready for civilian control and that its fiercely independent legislative council and other bodies would be divested of their powers and transformed into advisory appendages of the Philippine Commission and the governor general (Thompson 1975, 190–91).

General Pershing, the province's last governor, recognized the approaching end of military rule and created measures to ease the transfer of power, especially by anticipating potential Muslim opposition (Casambre 1975, 54). Reversing the army's own policy of limited Muslim participation in colonial governance, Pershing recommended that Manila appoint Muslims and non-Christians to positions like deputy district governor "to show the Moros that loyal and efficient service is rewarded" and "to determine whether it is possible to develop sufficient native talent among the tribesmen to fill minor government offices in the future" (Gowing 1983, 245–46). Pershing also belatedly sought to ensure that the Muslims were completely disarmed. A weapons confiscation campaign in early 1913 led to the fiercest Muslim resistance in Jolo since Bud Dajo and the deaths of over 500 Muslims (*PFP,* 1 Feb. 1913; Smythe 1973, 166–73). As the "last large-scale action fought by Americans in the Moro country until their final withdrawal from the Philippines," Bud Bagsak was an ironic last act for the departing army (*RGMP* 1912, 14–15). It signaled the army's return to purely military objectives and ultimately unraveled whatever was left of its stature as the first effective colonial authority in southern Mindanao. Manila and Washington censured Pershing for brutality; unlike Wood, who had deflected similar criticism in 1906, Pershing had no effective answer.

On 20 December 1913, the Philippine Commission passed Act 2408 creating the Department of Mindanao and Sulu to replace the Moro Province. The commission saw the department as "a test of whether the non-Christian inhabitants of Mindanao and Sulu could be successfully brought *within the shortest time possible* under a democratically organized government such as the rest of the country's population are enjoying" (JRH Box 29–5). It was placed directly under the commission and the office of the governor general (Harrison 1929, 106–7). Shortly thereafter, Congress abolished the army's Department of Mindanao, and Philippine Scouts and Constabulary gradually replaced army troops. The withdrawal of the U.S. army and the failure of the movement to continue military rule set the stage for a Filipino-dominated colonial center to recast the nature of colonial authority in southern Mindanao. This time Manila intended to remove whatever distinction was left between southern Mindanao and the rest of the Philippines by integrating it into the larger body politic. Aware that opposition to the end of army rule was never consequential, Filipino leaders in Manila nevertheless remained sensitive to pervading anticenter sentiments among southern Mindanao's communities. They saw as their task the construction of a new politico-administrative apparatus recognizing such sentiments, with the goal of transforming them into an attitude favoring integration.

## The Department of Mindanao and Sulu

Filipino opinion on "Moro Mindanao" had became open and strident once the Philippine Assembly was created in 1907. The assembly became the forum for "nationalist views" demanding that southern Mindanao be fully incorporated into the Philippines and be granted its own representatives. The intensification of integrationist rhetoric reached a peak by the end of the first decade of colonial rule after Quezon and Osmeña consolidated their positions and created a formidable patronage party machine that dominated colonial politics (Cullinane 1989). From their new positions of power, these leaders focused their attention on Mindanao. Deciding to meet head-on American criticism of Filipino capacity to replace the American military, Quezon wrote an essay in 1912 attacking American claims that Filipinos would be undemocratic toward non-Christians. He pointed out that Americans could ill afford a moral stance, given that their government was guilty of just such treatment of native Americans (Quezon 1912, 4). To show that Filipino leaders would be more just, he pledged that upon assuming control of the Moro Province, Filipinos would grant non-Christians the right to vote. This was a powerful critique of the American position since suffrage was something the U.S. military refused to bestow on non-Christians during its rule. The Filipinos, Quezon argued, would not wait for the Muslims and other groups to overcome fully their backwardness. Suffrage would hasten civilization. Quezon (1912, 4–5) then attacked the perennial cliché of "Moros-as-savages," arguing that the Muslims had been misinterpreted:

> The assertion that the Moros are uncivilized or savage is not accurate, if it is meant that they have no civilization of any kind, but that they are living in a very primitive condition. It is only true in the sense that they are not under the influence of occidental civilization, unlike the Christian Filipinos. The Moros are Mohammedans and their ideas of right and wrong are, of course, accordingly based on the principles of

> Mohammedanism. They farm and trade; some of them, a small percentage of course, read and write, and some others are well versed in the doctrines of a war-like people. They are brave and they fight to the end when mistreated. The Spaniards have never exercised an absolute control over these people, except through their own chiefs.

He disputed the contention that there was no Muslim opposition to American rule, warning that continued army rule would become rougher and perhaps lead to more bloodshed. Under Filipino control, he argued, these conflicts were not likely to happen. Quezon maintained that Filipinos shared something with Muslims that Americans never would: "the common tie of kinship." Strengthening this bond was the common history of the Philippine revolution and, subsequently, cooperation between Muslims and Filipinos in making American rule a success. There was, therefore, no reason why Filipinos could not take over Mindanao. By way of insurance, Quezon proposed that "the Philippine independent government could support a standing army of at least 30,000 men and could place in Mindanao one-third of this force to keep order among the Moros." He noted, however, that "the Filipinos believe that their government of the Moros will meet with more sympathy on the part of the Moros and that they will have less trouble with them than the American government" (ibid., 5).

Quezon did not have to fight hard for his position because he had the ear of friendly American officials in Washington and Manila. The victory of Democratic presidential aspirant Woodrow Wilson in 1912 meant a new colonial administration sympathetic to self-rule for the colony. In October 1913, Wilson appointed as governor general of the Philippines Francis Burton Harrison, who early on proclaimed his full support for accelerating the move to self-rule (Grunder and Livezy 1951, 148). He promised to expand Filipino participation in government and granted those in office considerable autonomy in running their affairs (*PFP,* 31 May 1913). He also committed himself to Mindanao's integration despite his ignorance of politics there. He was critical of the Moro Province, charging that "men who had just come through many a hard-fought skirmish with and surprise attack from the Moros could hardly be expected to believe them fit for civil government" (Harrison 1922, 105). Among Harrison's first orders was to inform military leaders of his plan to reduce the army's presence in Mindanao and to ensure that units of the Philippine Scouts and Constabulary left there were kept under tight civilian control (Onorato 1975, 8). It was an order well received by Manila Filipinos but which caused considerable apprehension among Americans in Manila and Mindanao (*PFP,* 25 July 1914).

Responsibility for executing the "Moro reorganization plan" fell on the department's governor, Frank W. Carpenter, who was regarded as the best person for the job because of his strong sense of mission and impeccable credentials as a colonial official (Gleeck 1991, 71). Carpenter was also deemed the proper intermediary between the non-Christian communities and Manila leaders. He was said to be fluent in Spanish and Tagalog and had intimate rapport with Filipino politicians, especially Quezon. Like Harrison, Carpenter was a strong advocate of Filipinization (Harrison 1922, 112; Stanley 1974, 203). He shared Harrison's dislike of the army, called its policy of maintaining ethnic divisions in Mindanao a major error, and criticized Leonard Wood for keeping the Muslims and Filipinos apart (Gowing 1983, 312).

Carpenter (1916, 401) argued that "the Christian Filipino [must] seriously amalgamate the relatively small Mohammedan and pagan minorities in the population of the Archipelago" towards a "homogeneity of the entire mass of native population of the island" (Carpenter 1916, 401). For him, "the long term interests of these minorities lay in adapting themselves to what he saw as their inevitable absorption by the Filipinos (Gleeck 1989, 46–47)." If Quezon agreed with the language of homogeneity and absorption, he was careful not to say so publicly. Practically speaking, however, there was little difference in their views and Quezon could not have found a more reliable ally.

With this consensus in place, integration commenced in earnest. The new department's prime responsibility was to "prepare the way as rapidly as possible for the same system of government in the department of Mindanao and Sulu as prevails generally in the archipelago, thus making [it] more an integral part of the central government and putting it on the same basis as the rest of the islands" (*PFP,* 25 July 1914). The former districts of the Moro Province became seven new provinces. Those with Filipino majorities were classified as regular provinces and immediately enjoyed the same privileges as provinces in central and northern Philippines. Those with Muslim majorities remained special provinces and were subject to close supervision by department officials. A legislative council patterned after that of the Moro Province was created for the department and for each province. At the provincial level, the council consisted of a provincial governor and secretary-treasurer, both appointed by the department governor, and an elected third member (*RPC* 1914, 520–21). Similar councils were created at the municipal and municipal district levels. Municipalities "represented an advanced form of community organization" while municipal districts were a "rudimentary form of government... designed to meet the needs of those areas where the majority of the inhabitants had not developed a sufficient degree of political sophistication desired by the Government" (Gowing 1983, 263). The lowest administrative unit was the barrio (village), with councilors appointed by the provincial governor.

Although similar in structure to the Moro Province, the department had distinct features. Each provincial council was represented in Manila by a delegate to the Philippine Assembly, and the provinces' engineers, health officers, and superintendents of schools were under the jurisdiction of their respective Manila bureaus and departments (Carpenter 1917, 25). Most importantly, the department lacked the autonomy that the Moro Province for a time enjoyed. The Philippine Assembly made sure that the Philippine Commission gave the department neither power to enact its own laws nor exemption from general Philippine laws, despite the special status of some of its provinces. The commission allowed the use of special judicial procedures in consideration of the needs and practices of non-Christian groups, but these were regarded as temporary measures that would be removed once these groups became familiar with colonial laws (Philippine Commission Act 2520, 1915). Moreover, the department's legislative council was redefined as an advisory body with powers "limited practically to appropriation of funds under the control of the department government" (Carpenter 1916, 337). Even this prerogative was constrained; the department's ability to disburse funds was under the control of the commission (Carpenter 1915, 327–34; Guingona 1919, 58). The only area where the department was allowed some power was, ironically, the military sphere. The commission placed the constabulary under departmental control, concerned that disorder be addressed swiftly. Yet, this power, which the U.S. army had exercised freely in the first decade, was inconsequential in the absence of major uprisings and the lack of other measures of autonomy (*PFP,* 26 Sept. 1914).

The basic principle behind these regulations and the functions of the various offices was clear: the establishment of Manila's sovereignty over southern Mindanao. Quezon had bitter memories of army autonomy and insisted that Manila now exercise effective authority (Thompson 1975, 198–99). The first way to ensure this was to lay sole claim to legislative and fiscal power. And when it came to funding, the assembly was no Scrooge. Conscious that their claim to rightful governance rested on their ability to introduce progress, Filipino leaders—with support from Carpenter and other sympathetic

Americans—poured money into the department (*MB,* 23, 25, 26 and 29 Oct. 1915). They allocated one million pesos for the expansion of public education in Mindanao and Sulu (*MB,* 26 Jan. and 11 May 1915). They appropriated over 200,000 pesos for agricultural settler colonies to be set up in Lanao and Cotabato. Another 1.5 million pesos was allotted for agricultural and industrial development of the areas surrounding these colonies, as well as for export crop production. In all this, however, it was clear who held the purse (Gowing 1983, 292; *RF,* Nov. 1916).

Finally, legislative fiat and fiscal regulation required adequate personnel to implement laws and regulations. This is where Carpenter's support for Filipinization proved vital to Filipino leaders. Without much prodding, Carpenter set in motion the Filipinization of the entire department. He did this not only because he agreed with the policy, but also because he was desperate for people to fill positions for which Americans were now less likely to apply. He complained after two years in office that the department had difficulty obtaining "competent men… for appointment in the public service here" and attributed this to the hardship of the posting, fear of Muslims and other non-Christians, inadequate financial support from the Insular government, and low salaries. He warned that with incompetent officials "it will be impossible to accomplish the economic and political purposes of government here, and the contribution which thus by far the richest one-third of the archipelago may and should make to the national wealth and homogeneity will definitely be delayed and indeed endangered" (Carpenter 1917, 84).

The result was an almost frantic effort to implement Filipinization. The number of Americans in the administration decreased from twenty-six in 1914 (the first year of the department) to only five the following year. The number of Filipinos employed by the department increased from seventeen to thirty-seven during the same period (Department of Mindanao and Sulu Reports, 1915–20).

The department delegate was always a Filipino, and Carpenter also saw to it that the local military was Filipinized gradually (Pier 1971, 91–92). By 1918, when Carpenter left the department to become head of the Bureau of Non-Christian Tribes, he himself had turned over day-to-day departmental responsibilities to his Filipino assistant Teofisto Guingona. Guingona (1919, 49) saw to it that by the end of Carpenter's term, "the rank and file of the provincial and national [sic] governments in Mindanao and Sulu were… almost entirely Christian Filipinos" (Guingona 1919, 49).

Beyond the numbers lay the important issue of which Filipinos were to advance in the department's bureaucracy. Quezon and other leaders were interested not only in expanding Manila's formal control over the southern periphery; their concern was also to extend their political influence by putting their own people in the new local offices. Those appointed to the position of governor in Zamboanga, Bukidnon, and Agusan were Nacionalistas (*PFP,* 16 Oct. 1916). Those appointed to lower positions in municipalities and municipal districts were induced to join the party because they were seen as new leaders who could be the "transmission belts" of party politics (Carpenter 1915, 387). On this issue, the Filipinos encountered no obstacles from Carpenter and Harrison. Fiscal and legislative/party control as well as the numerical domination of Filipinos thus guaranteed that the department would be structurally embedded in the larger colonial framework and closely supervised by central state agencies. These two processes likewise secured for the increasingly influential Filipino leadership a foothold in a territory once kept out of their reach. This was only half the battle, though. Equally significant was the question of how to deal with the communities of southern Mindanao, most of whom remained hostile to Manila and the Filipinos.

Quezon and his American allies started with the assumption that the non-Christian communities were still relatively backward. There were signs of progress, to be sure, notably the emergence of non-Christian leaders willing to support the Filipinization process (see chapter 3). However, non-Christians clearly attached great significance to their religious differences from the northerners, and the new regime saw little choice but to accept the endurance of these sentiments. This was the very notion on which the army had based its rule, using religiocultural distinctions as a shield to fend off Manila's interference as well as Moro participation in government. Quezon, Carpenter, and Harrison, however, utilized them for quite the opposite purpose: to facilitate non-Christian participation in department and party politics (Quezon 1916, 11–21). Religiocultural identity was harnessed so that the Muslims were "essentially recreated to make them an integral governing part of the republican government reuniting them with Filipinos" (Elliot 1917, 95). This was done by introducing limited suffrage and by appointing supportive non-Christian leaders to offices opened up by the new regime.

There were two kinds of voting under the department. In provinces where Filipinos were in the majority, suffrage was granted to those who were male, propertied, and literate (as in the regular provinces). They voted for provincial council third members and municipal vice-presidents. In provinces with a Muslim majority, municipal and municipal district officials were appointed, and only these officials were entitled to participate in provincial council elections. These carefully chosen non-Christian officials, given a vote and some responsibility for village and small town administration, were the manifestation of Quezon's Filipino-Muslim brotherhood (Carpenter 1915, 395). Party politicians often reminded them of how important their offices were to the colonial state. Guingona (1919, 53), Carpenter's successor as department governor and top Nacionalista in Mindanao, declared that municipal districts replaced the "primitive organization of our people under the leadership of the headman" and would soon be responsible for the "moral and material welfare [of their constituents] and their habits and customs" (Guingona 1919, 53).

By granting these officials suffrage and administrative responsibility—no matter how limited—the department advanced integration in a number of ways. First, suffrage was considered the basic component of colonial governance, and the eventual transformation of special provinces into regular provinces would entail "full" suffrage. Second, the new voter/administrators would become indispensable in forming local networks and alliances under Quezon and Carpenter, keeping southern Mindanao as governable as it had become under the Moro Province (Thomas 1971, 48–49). Finally, a new kind of fellowship was fostered among Muslim leaders supporting the new regime, bringing opportunities to expand their local power through links with Manila.

Filipino politicians were offering Muslim leaders a mutually beneficial association. For Manila, Muslim voting blocs were potential additions to the expanding networks of the insular parties, providing the foundation for local chapters of the Nacionalistas or their weaker rivals. Therefore, Osmeña and Quezon "courted" Muslim elites, warmly receiving delegations of datus that accompanied Carpenter to Manila and visiting Mindanao to discuss budget appropriations and Philippine independence (*MB,* 5 Dec. 1914, 11 May, 22 June and 29 Oct. 1915; *PFP,* 29 Apr. 1916). Viewed from the other side, the Nacionalista-controlled Philippine Assembly appeared to be practically synonymous with the state. Therefore, the Nacionalistas had resources and connections unavailable to local officials within their narrow jurisdictions. For those with political aspirations, the benefits deriving from these connections could help immensely in the realization of their ambitions (Carpenter 1915, 387, 397).

The power of governors to appoint the majority of the department's officials also functioned in this manner. Through political appointments, a provincial governor could virtually create a power base to his liking, answering only to the department governor.[15] Muslims were never appointed to positions as high as provincial governor which remained in the hands of Filipinos and Americans. The enduring notion of Muslim "backwardness" evidently played a major role in this exclusion (Carpenter 1917, 34). Their marginalization annoyed Muslim leaders, and they soon demanded a greater role in provincial affairs (Gowing 1983, 328; *MB,* 11 May 1916). Yet, there was a positive aspect to the non-Muslim monopoly of high positions, one that further tied Muslim interests to the expansion of party politics. As the top officials were most often Nacionalistas, many municipal officials were able to strengthen their blocs and secure appointments outside their localities. Muslim leaders took advantage of such connections with provincial governors for the benefits they brought to themselves and their communities (*MB,* 22 June 1915; Harrison 1922, 119–20).

Finally, Filipino provincial governors, unfamiliar with their jurisdictions, invariably relied on subalterns to reach "constituents" and maintain the department's governability. Having allies below ensured implementation of projects and made governing non-Christian provinces less difficult. The alternative was an excessive exercise of authority that could cause many problems: projects blocked, "peace and order" destabilized, and governing obstructed through the election of antagonistic third members. Thus, while provincial governors had the authority to be despots, it was far more appropriate and practical to govern through a line of supportive subordinates. In Cotabato, Sulu, and Zamboanga, the development of such relationships lessened tension between provincial officials and local leaders, and between ethnic groups as well.[16]

Soon new positions were created for which Muslims were eligible. In 1916, the American congress passed the Jones Law, which provided for "a More Autonomous Government for Those Islands." It abolished the Philippine Commission and created a new bicameral legislature consisting of a senate and a house of representatives. The Jones Law reinforced ties between southern Mindanao and Manila, giving full legislative power over Mindanao and Sulu to the new assembly. The majority of the legislature was to be elected, with the exception of representatives from the non-Christian regions, who were to be appointed by the governor-general. The department was allowed five appointed delegates to the lower house and one to the senate, the latter to be chosen regardless of residence (Kalaw 1919, 111; Elliot 1917, 512). Harrison appointed Hadji Butu of Sulu to the senate, and Datu Piang of Cotabato and Datu Benito of Lanao to the lower house; in doing so he fulfilled an official pledge to give non-Christians representation. He thereby contributed to a larger effort to broaden the datus' exposure to Philippine colonial politics. Considerable publicity attended the formal assumption of power by these representatives, especially their swearing of the oath of office on the Koran. Carpenter lauded this act as exemplifying not only the success of integration, but also the prevalence of "an attitude of religious tolerance and respect on the part of the Christian Filipinos" (Kalaw 1919, 126).

Limited suffrage, party affiliation, and appointive office were thus offered to Muslim leaders. In a way these reinforced their status by the adding more titles to those they already held (datu, sultan, etc.). Unlike the earlier ranks, however, "municipal councilor" or "provincial board member" carried advantage specific to the realm of "the Philippines." Together with limited suffrage, these positions also encouraged horizontal linkages between different communities. All this took some time to blend with the social environment. Voting interfered with seasonal activities like planting, while municipal officers had a hard time traveling to voting centers because of bad or nonexistent roads.[17] But there were also signs of acceptance by Muslim officials as they became familiar with politics. During elections they issued statements of support for their favored candidates, and in their frequent interaction with Manila leaders, the datus quickly learned the techniques of negotiation and compromise.[18] By 1919, Guingona (1919, 95) noted "a certain tendency on the part of the leaders of some localities to strive for the highest political privileges, as in the election of municipal [vice] presidents" (Guingona 1919, 95). A Mindanao politician likewise reported, "The Moros ... are taking to politics… many of the candidates there being actively engaged in making political speeches about their elections" (*PFP*, 24 May 1919). The Filipinized colonial state had thus given Muslim leaders a chance to stake their claim in the new order. After accepting the reality of southern Mindanao's integration, many did (*PFP*, 1 Aug. 1914 and 29 Apr. 1916; *MB*, 1 May 1916). Gowing (1983, 119) described the department as having laid "the foundations upon which could be erected an enduring edifice of economic, political and social solidarity, integral with Luzon and the Visayas."

The ease with which the Department of Mindanao and Sulu was installed, however, was not matched by competent administration. Inadequate procedures, incompetent personnel, and petty quarrels plagued local offices of insular agencies (*PH,* 8 Jan. 1927). Land registration agencies (crucial insular offices set up during the first year of the department) became local fiefdoms of unscrupulous officials who took advantage of a still rudimentary system of oversight to accumulate "great powers." Coordination among different offices suffered from jurisdictional disputes between insular and provincial officials. The Bureau of Labor, the Bureau of Non-Christian Tribes, and the provincial governments of Lanao, Zamboanga, Sulu, and Cotabato quarreled with each other about who had ultimate authority over agricultural settler colonies (Thomas 1971, 91–92; Gowing 1983, 67). The bickering considerably affected the early stages of the government's colonization program, causing confusion among the first volunteer Filipino families and hampering their settlement (*PFP,* 7 and 21 June 1913). Even the constabulary had problems. Officers appointed as deputy governors clashed with local civilian leaders over the chain of command—whether to follow orders from the civilian provincial governor or the constabulary commander (*MB,* 5 June 1919).

The use of public education as an instrument of central state control appeared to have been the only colonial policy implemented with relative success in southern Mindanao.[19] A closer look at its projects, however, reveals problems. Carpenter discovered after three years as governor that Davao province had "not even one respectable school building" because the local elites felt "no particular need for the public schools" (*PFP,* 19 Oct. 1918). Personnel problems dogged the school system, as very few Filipino teachers were attracted to Mindanao and qualified Muslim teachers were even fewer. Where teachers were available, formal qualifications and the continuing bias against Muslims diminished the pool further. Low Muslim participation was pervasive, as Filipinos still dominated at the provincial and municipal levels (Carpenter 1917, 34).

In the constabulary's Filipinization program, only five Muslims attained officer rank (Thomas 1971, 93–94). When he wrote his final report, Guingona bluntly reminded everyone, including Muslim leaders, that Filipinization at the local level meant transferring to competent local authorities responsibility for governing "their respective territorial jurisdictions." Given the relative "backwardness" of most Muslims, those deemed competent were mainly Filipinos. This increasing "minoritization" of the Muslims was reflected up to the highest positions to which their leaders were appointed: they did not constitute a majority even among senate and house representatives of the special provinces.

Despite these flaws, Americans and Filipinos felt that implementing the new order in southern Mindanao was a success (Guingona 1919, 52–55).

Their optimism was bolstered by the lack of opposition from constituents of the new department, especially those expected to be loyal to the old regime. This confidence was the basis for Harrison's proposal for the abolition of "special provinces" and "the elimination of the present separation of a large section of the general commonwealth of the Filipino people, and the gradual complete equalization of its inhabitants with others in more favored parts of the Philippines" (*MT,* 16 Jan. 1920). On 5 February 1920, the Philippine legislature did abolish the Department of Mindanao and Sulu, but retained the category special province for Cotabato, Lanao, Sulu, and Zamboanga. It transferred jurisdiction over these provinces to the Bureau of Non-Christian Tribes within the Department of Interior. The new edict also implemented provisions of Act 2309 and the Jones law calling for the election of previously appointed provincial governors (*MT,* 5 Feb. 1920). An amendment to the bill gave the legislature full control over the appointment of the provinces' top executive and judicial officers (*MT,* 2 Feb. 1920). A few months later, Carpenter announced his retirement. Guingona, who now reported to the Secretary of Interior, replaced him. The transition was orderly because the actors were familiar with each other and had worked together to bring about the change (Thomas 1971, 87).

## The Restorationist Challenge

The Quezon-Carpenter plan for southern Mindanao hinged on adept control of the personnel and leaders of the department. Disorder or disunity at the center could disrupt the flow of authority, allow the reemergence of centrifugal tendencies, and weaken the center's hold on the periphery. This is precisely what occurred from 1921, and the catalyst was the return of Leonard Wood to the Philippines. The victory of the Republican party in the 1920 United States presidential election changed the regime once again in Manila as the Republicans, less receptive to Philippine independence, replaced Harrison with Wood as governor general. Wood was critical of what he regarded as the evils of the Harrison period: an inefficient bureaucracy plagued by corruption, a sluggish economy, and the persistence of cacique rule. He was disdainful of most Filipino leaders, notably Quezon, and thought that Filipinization was out of control (Tan 1993, 15).

Wood's appointment caused reverberations throughout the Filipinized colonial state, but this architect of the Moro Province took a special interest in reversing the policy of integrating southern Mindanao (Hagedorn 1931, 392). Wood was convinced that his former "Moro wards" shared his sentiments. More importantly, he believed that the Muslims were staunch opponents of Philippine independence (Tan 1993, 74). His first major decision on the Muslim provinces was to dismantle parts of the edifice Carpenter and his allies had built. Wood pushed for changes in the Bureau of Non-Christian Tribes jurisdiction and intervened in provincial affairs to challenge Filipino control over the Muslims. He proposed that the bureau be transferred to the American-controlled Department of Public Instruction. He also summarily replaced the Filipino governor of Lanao with an American on the pretext that datus were increasingly opposed to the Filipino (Thomas 1971, 137–38; Gowing 1983, 313).

Wood kept himself closely informed about Muslim affairs. He took two trips a year to Mindanao and received Muslim leaders who visited Manila. All the while, he assured the Muslims that Philippine independence was not in the offing and that the United States was not contemplating withdrawal from the colony (Cable, 14 Nov. 1923, BIA File 4865–150). Wood's actions immediately aroused Filipino concern, which heightened to anxiety when other Americans made similar policy recommendations. An investigator sent by Washington, for example, supported the idea of replacing Filipinos with Americans and Muslims in Cotabato, Lanao, and Sulu and advocated the restoration of some autonomy for Mindanao (U.S. Senate Document 180, 1926, 7; Mayo 1925, 298–99). A more serious threat issued from the United States senate in 1926 when New York senator Robert Bacon introduced a bill to separate Mindanao from the Philippines and restore the "Moro Province," this time to be governed by officials directly appointed by the American president with senate concurrence (Fry 1978, 267).

All this elicited a bellicose response from Filipino leaders, who correctly saw Wood as a threat to their role in colonial politics in general, and to their control over Mindanao in particular. Filipino leaders were most anxious about the impact of Wood's restorationism on Manila's ability to show a united front vis-à-vis southern Mindanao, as his attacks had led to rifts among the Nacionalistas and emboldened the oppositionist Democrata party to support Mindanao separatism. The years-long senate debate over the Bacon bill forced Quezon and his allies to fight more zealously (Tan 1993, 21–22; *PH,* 8 Jan. 1927; *PH,* 1 Aug. 1925). The result was a nasty battle between the two most important institutions in the colonial state: the American-held governor-general's office and the Filipino-controlled legislature. The Nacionalistas sought to block Wood's reforms and attacked his policies in every public venue they controlled. Wood, in turn, encouraged his allies to harass Quezon and Osmeña. The conflict permeated the entire colony and extended even to the United States, where Quezon clashed with Wood supporters for congressional and executive support (Churchill 1983, 187, 348–49).

While Quezon and Osmeña were able to fend off oppositionist attacks and maintain Nacionalista unity, their battle with Wood was seen in southern Mindanao as a sign of weakness at the center. This, in turn, precipitated acts of disloyalty from below (Thomas 1971, 85). As a substantive discussion of the Muslim response to Filipinization will be presented in the next chapter, here I simply note the salience of this response to the problem of local state-building. The swift revival of anti-Manila sentiments among Muslims indicated the fragility of integration, despite the degree of local empowerment built into the Quezon-Carpenter formula of central control. Clearly, Muslim political fidelity had yet to be fully secured, and the presence of a rival power center (Wood) easily caused desertion to the other side. This is an obvious point. If we place these "acts of betrayal" within the context of the full Muslim experience under colonial rule, however, we see that the assumption behind the colonial Muslim political identity was different between Muslims and Filipinos; this was paralleled by the autonomy the army sought from Manila. Muslims showed their customary political flexibility when the center asserted itself with Filipinization, but the disturbance at the center occasioned by Wood's return created the opportunity for datus to try to regain some autonomy. The only way for Filipinization to be restored was to reestablish unity in the center and secure the victory of procenter elites in the periphery.

Skirmishing continued well into 1927. Wood's battles with Quezon revealed that Filipinos had the advantage in Manila, but his supporters in Washington, notably Bacon, made the battle for Mindanao an open question. Then the fight abruptly ended when Wood died during surgery. His successor, Henry Stimson, chose to restore Filipino-American cooperation and steered clear of the political conflicts his predecessor had provoked. Without Wood, the United States senate began to lose interest in the Bacon bill and in the issue of retaining the Philippines as a colony. Quezon and Osmeña had a clear path to Philippine independence and the renewal of Mindanao's integration into the Philippines.

The Commonwealth of the Philippines was established on 15 November

1935, with Manuel L. Quezon as its first president. For Quezon and his allies, this transition to eventual independence marked the apex of their struggle to gain control over the colonial state. Henceforth, with only counsel and occasional pressure from an American resident commissioner, Filipinos were left to govern the Commonwealth. The Commonwealth period was also a time of considerable state centralization. Quezon was not content to achieve full Filipino control of the government; he was also bent on dominating colonial politics through a calculating use of his powers as paramount leader of the Nacionalista party and president of the new regime.

Joseph Ralston Hayden described the Commonwealth as developing "a natural impulse towards 'totalitarianism'" of which Quezon was the embodiment (McCoy 1989, 118). Hayden (1942, 58–59) further observed that the early years of the Commonwealth were "marked by the continuation of the trend towards a one party, one man political system and the appearance of a substantial, although not well organized minority of discontented, economically depressed people who were outside of the system and strongly opposed it."

Quezon's attitude toward the Muslim provinces reflected this trend. He used the power of appointment to place trusted lieutenants in provincial and municipal positions and reorganized Manila's administration of the Moro provinces.[20] Upon the recommendation of Teofisto Guingona, Quezon abolished the Bureau of Non-Christian Tribes and replaced it with a cabinet-level Commission for Mindanao and Sulu that would oversee the economic development of Mindanao and the civilianization of provincial and local personnel.[21] At first glance, this reduction of the state apparatus governing the Muslims might suggest a waning interest in southern Mindanao. After all, the "Moro problem" was all but resolved, as datus who were known allies of the Americans appeared to be growing comfortable with Filipino-dominated colonial politics in the legislature and the party system. Yet, in the context of Hayden's description of Quezon's ruling style, the opposite was true. The commission was an agency meant to keep Muslims under close executive supervision and further advance the Filipinization process. The Commonwealth president continued to be suspicious of the datus, never forgiving them for being turncoats when Leonard Wood returned (Forbes 1928, 294).

Now at the height of his power, Quezon gave them only one choice: abide by the commission's policies and play the political game as dictated by him or be marginalized by the state. On the eve of World War II, the Filipinos' domination of southern Mindanao was complete.

## Conclusion

This chapter has argued that colonial state-building in southern Mindanao was not a uniform process but was characterized by differences in regime forms. The Moro Province was run tightly and surprisingly well by the U.S. army. It was one of the fastest growing areas of the Philippines and its success placed the army leadership, suspicious of the designs of Filipinos, in a position to keep the province autonomous from the colonial center. But the Moro Province did not last long due to the army's inherent weakness as administrator, lost battles in the metropolitan center, and broader changes in American colonial policy.

Its successor, the Department of Mindanao and Sulu, had a shorter life span and did not have the same cohesiveness nor the skilled personnel of its military predecessor. Still, the department also achieved some success. Through limited suffrage, the use of appointments, and the exposure of Muslims to party politics, colonial officials offered Mindanao leaders a chance to participate in colonial government. As Filipino-style politics spread through Muslim communities, it was hoped that traditional affiliations would eventually be replaced by party-centered solidarity and allegiance to the colonial state. By utilizing, instead of opposing, religiocultural identities, the department was able to alleviate anxiety that the north would destroy Muslim culture through Christianization and to deflect lingering opposition to the colonial state engendered by precolonial histories as well as army separatism. What colonial officials feared would persist in the Muslim provinces was turned into something good by policies and processes introduced through Filipinization.

As successful as the department was in remaking the state in southern Mindanao, the Muslim response to the restorationist challenge of the 1920s indicates the fragility of the process of integration. The communities of southern Mindanao had been introduced to a colonial politics that could be beneficial to them, but which was clearly dominated by Filipinos. This domination became manifest when Quezon reduced southern Mindanao governance to one executive agency, the Commission for Mindanao and Sulu. The commission represented Quezon's confidence in his power over the weakened Muslims as well as his warning that any signs of insubordination would be dealt with directly and swiftly by him. How the Muslims and other communities of southern Mindanao responded to these changes will be addressed in the next two chapters.

## CHAPTER 3

# Making Muslim Filipinos

Writing about the Moro Province, the political tourist Vic Hurley (1936, 154–56) describes an incident during the 1898 negotiation of the Bates Treaty: the Sultan of Sulu insisted that the Americans allow him "to hoist the American flag together with his own" when he traveled around and beyond his domain. Though the Americans refused, the sultan's demand reflected a pragmatic willingness to identify with American power and use it to enhance his own position in Southeast Asia. In 1933, Abdullah Piang, Cotabato's representative to the Philippine Assembly, displayed a very different political orientation. Rising as a matter of privilege during legislative debate, Piang (1933) warned that if the Bacon bill became law and separated Mindanao from the Philippines, he would "reside during the rest of my life in Manila because I do not want to separate from you. Look at my skin. The blood that runs in my veins is not different from that of you Christian Filipinos."

The temporal proximity of these two episodes (roughly thirty years) indicates a rapid shift in the position of Muslim elites vis-à-vis powerful outside actors like the Americans and the Filipinos. In light of subsequent history, it also suggests questions of motivation and identity: What was signified by a willingness to accommodate American rule? How did Mindanao's Muslims acquire a Filipino identity so quickly and how sincere was that identification? Scholars have generally interpreted these responses to the changing colonial state along a nationalist/collaborationist axis, attempting to fit Mindanao politics into a Filipino nationalist framework. This framework imagines Muslim resistance against the Spanish and later against the Americans as an organic part of Filipino nationalism. First articulated by Quezon as part of his attack on army rule in Mindanao (see chapter 2), this view became popular after the war as scholars sought evidence of widespread resistance to colonialism. With the radicalization of nationalist scholarship in the 1970s, the purported nationalism of the Muslims reached the status of a near-orthodoxy.

If rebellion epitomized nationalism, then accommodating or supporting colonial rule was a betrayal of the nationalist cause (Majul 1985, 20; Tan 1977, 95–105; and Tan 1982, 62–69). Datus who collaborated were as duplicitous as the Filipino oligarchs who became pawns of the Americans. Revealing the common shortcoming of these two elites strengthened the framework's premise that there was only one nation. But while one might argue that these instances of elite opportunism make the oligarchs and datus somewhat fraternal, overall, the nationalist framework obscures rather than clarifies the nature of the Muslim response. Rather than read nationalism and failures of nationalism into Mindanao's past, I suggest two interpretive strategies: first, read the meaning of datu accommodation with the Americans and the Filipinos from a Southeast Asian perspective; and second, trace how the meaning of accommodation changed from one period to the next.

In the beginning of colonial rule, Muslim datus regarded the Americans as yet another outside power, like the Spanish, indeed, like the Filipinos. The datus attempted to deal with this power the way other Southeast Asian "men of prowess" (orang besar) dealt with outside forces: make an alliance to enhance one's own status. Thus the Sultan of Sulu's proposal. Unfortunately for the sultan, and for the datus generally, the Americans were concerned with the colonial map and with making real the imagined border separating American territory from the territories of other colonial powers. This boundary clashed with the sultan's idea of his domain and international standing, but the more powerful Americans prevailed and compelled him to narrow his vista to conform to the colonial map. The sultan of Sulu's acquiescence prefigured similar accommodations by other datus. And as the colonial state form changed, so did the character of datu accommodation with the increasingly powerful overlord. In time, the datus accepted the contracted world of colonial Philippines. They no longer sought a role in an expansive maritime world, but aspired to positions within the colonial state. The culmination was Abdullah Piang's symbolic assertion of being one in blood with his Christian Filipino brethren.

This chapter is an overview of this change from maritime Southeast Asian to Philippine framework among the Magindanaos of Cotabato. Through the story of Cotabato's Datu Piang (Abdullah's father), I will illustrate the transformation of power from that of a Malay orang besar to that of a nascent colonial politico. I will show that accommodation with the Americans enhanced a datu's power locally—Piang became chief of the Magindanaos—but narrowed the reach of that power. I will examine the difficulty faced by this first generation of pro-American datus in dealing with the rise to power of the Filipinos, and describe the appearance of a second generation of Muslim leaders, a group whose identification with the Filipinized colonial state was more or less complete. Finally I will explain why, despite their familiarity with colonial politics, the Muslim leaders remained minor players in the game.

## Magindanao as a Southeast Asian Society

Communities of southern Mindanao, including those in the Cotabato region, were prominently involved in precolonial trading in maritime Southeast Asia.[1] Several scholars have documented extensive trading activities in the area.[2] This involvement was propitious for the Magindanaos as it facilitated the unification of two kingdoms that were constantly at war with each other over control of forest and other products. Under the seventeenth-century sultan Kachil Kudrat, the divided Magindanao communities—those belonging to *sa-ilud* (lower valley and coastal area), of which Cotabato town was the known capital, and those in *sa-raya* (upper valley), of which Dulawan was the capital—were unified, leading to the establishment of the first centralized Magindanao sultanate (Laarhoven 1990, 164–68). Under Kudrat, Magindanao's trade expanded considerably, sending wax, slaves, gold, tobacco, cinnamon, and rice to Ternate, Manila, and Melaka. When the Dutch appeared on the scene, Magindanaos traded slaves, cinnamon, and wax with them. The English soon followed to compete with the Dutch. European rivalry proved useful to a neutral sultanate, and Magindanaos benefited from the competition between these powers (Ibid., 175–79).

Magindanaos displayed close affinity with other maritime Southeast Asian communities in how their communities were organized ("upstream" versus "downstream") and how they did business with each other (trading in forest products and slaves). They acted like the Southeast Asian "men of prowess" that O.W. Wolters writes of: strong men whose power lay not in a span of territory, but in their ability to project armed power to gain control of slave labor and monopolies on tradable products (Andaya 1993, 91–95). As orang besar, they sought constantly to enrich their followers and engaged in wary interaction with fellow datus, for theirs was a precarious position that was always subject to challenge. Cognatic kinship bonds with other datus were strengthened by marriage alliances, and they also accumulated what Wolters (1982, 6, 8–9,17–19) calls "political intelligence" about their rivals and were involved in diplomatic negotiations with forces stronger than they. When they felt their power base stable enough, they engaged in war with each other or against other powers in pursuit of slaves and products.

The sultanate's ties with the region nurtured an "internationalist" outlook that Wolters (1982, 3) describes as "likely to have looked outward to what is the Vietnamese coast today or to southern China for the more distant worlds that mattered to them." Sultan Kudrat himself was a polyglot who "engage[d] foreign visitors in conversation whenever he would find time. He liked to discuss world affairs with them and was avidly curious about European life and governance. He also asked about the habits and customs of other nations. He always put many questions to his guests and made efforts to learn their language from them."[3] The Spaniards, therefore, were not confronted by an isolated society, but by a port-state with a sophisticated organization led by people who were quite aware of their place in a regional trading network and the world beyond it. By the time the Americans arrived, the Magindanaos already had a tradition of dealing with the Dutch, the Spanish, and the English. When they cooperated with or fought against the Americans, their actions were informed by this Southeast Asian experience, not by a Filipino nationalist agenda.

Yet there was something Magindanao-specific to these encounters and this had to do with the steadily diminishing fortunes of the sultanate that began soon after Kudrat's death. The rise of Sulu as the new entrepot, the defeat of the Magindanaos by this new rival, and increasing Spanish manipulation of the treaty system caused the general decline of the Magindanaos. In the late nineteenth century, Datu Uto of Buayan attempted to resurrect the glories of old, but by the 1880s, the Spanish were successfully fueling divisions among the Magindanaos, and Uto's was the last attempt to reverse the process.[4] The Americans, therefore, confronted a society considerably weakened by local and colonial rivalries and by increasing internal division. The Magindanao datus continued to display an orang besar mentality, but their weakened condition gave them fewer options in dealing with the Americans.[5] It is within this context that we should situate Datu Piang's response to the American colonial presence.

## From Orang Besar to Colonial Politico

Datu Piang, at first glance, fits the paradigm imagined by nationalist scholars of the Muslim collaborator and, in fact, has been portrayed as such (Glang 1969, 47). A reconsideration of his life story using the argument laid down above, however, immediately reveals a coastal Malay disposition. Piang's power base was located at a strategic "choke point" of the Pulangi river: Cotabato, the river-mouth and coastal town where products from outside Magindanao flowed to the inland communities and inland products entered the trading network. Piang was lord of the sa-ilud (*hilir*), a position akin to strong men noted by Andaya (1993) in the Malay peninsula.

Piang's rise to power strengthens the resemblance. He was a parvenu datu who rose to prominence under the patronage of Datu Uto and ascended the hierarchy by means of displays of prowess (Ileto 1971, 8). His rise both reconfirms the relative openness of positions of authority in the region's polities and shows how nominal adherence to Islam was as a criterion for the selection of leaders (Kathirithamby-Wells 1993, 132; Sawyer 1900, 375). He was a mestizo, the youngest of six children, whose father was one Tan Toy from Amoy, China and whose mother, Tico, was a "Mora" from Sillik Cotabato. Piang's father rose from Chinese trader to Minister of Lands and economic adviser to Datu Uto. His marriage to Tico, the daughter of Uto's ally Ayunan, further cemented his links with the stronger datus of Magindanao society (Box 28–24, Piang biography). Piang thus grew up with economic and political opportunities awaiting him. His father's side gave him a line to the Cotabato Chinese, who controlled much of the local economy, and also ingratiated him with the Spanish, who wrongly thought he could be used to deter further Chinese economic expansion in Magindanao. He would, in turn, transform his cooperation with the Spaniards into another business arrangement (Cabañero-Mapanao 1985, 21).

On the eve of American rule, Piang and an ally, Datu Ali of Kudarangan, broke with their old patron Uto and gave their support to the Spaniards (Ileto 1971, 63). They used their wealth to win the old man's supporters over to their side and cemented their own alliance with a marriage between Ali and Piang's daughter Minka, another practice common in Southeast Asian port-states.[6] While they appeared to subordinate their interests to the Spanish, even allowing the establishment of forts at strategic points on the Pulangi River, there was no question that Piang and Ali also profited from this arrangement. They used Spanish help to eclipse Uto, expropriated his land and work force, and then invested in the economic opportunities provided by the Spanish presence. When the Spanish withdrew, Piang and Ali received weapons from them, ostensibly to help oversee a peaceful transition. Both would use their new firepower to brutally crush a third rival, the Filipinos who wanted to attach Cotabato to the nationalist revolutionary government in Luzon (Gowing 1983, 23). By the time the Americans arrived, Piang and Ali had become the major powers of Magindanao. Their joint power reunified the sa-ilud and sa-raya communities of Cotabato, a unification last achieved in the seventeenth century under Kudrat. Piang's influence, in particular, spread. Designating himself "chief of the central district of Cotabato," he expanded his sphere of influence to towns previously controlled by Uto, making their datus pay tribute to him (Ileto 1971, 38–39).

Once the Americans started to enact and enforce laws governing the Magindanaos under the new order, however, the Piang-Ali alliance unraveled. Piang decided to work with the new order, while Ali opposed it (a position strengthened when the Americans banned slavery, a profitable enterprise for Magindanao datus). By accommodating, Piang signaled the emergence of a different kind of Muslim leader who, while still articulating pre-American norms, also sought advantage in the colonial state. By rebelling, Ali represented an orang besar's last stand: the attempted preservation of southern Mindanao-Southeast Asian political and economic moorings. Ali symbolized the old order, while Piang became a prelude to a new type of Muslim datu. Ali's end came when the Americans—aided by Piang—surprised him in his Davao hideout (*MH,* 12 March, 1 May, 28 May, 25 June, and 20 October 1904). With Ali's death, Piang became the undisputed leader of the Magindanaos and his metamorphosis from a southern Mindanao orang besar into a colonial politico had begun.[7]

That he opted to work with the Americans rather than heed Uto's advice to resist the new colonizer indicated how sensitive Piang was to changed conditions. Instead of regarding the Americans as colonizers, he saw a powerful ally who would help him consolidate his position over rival datus in the northern periphery of his domain and protect his business interests, which included close ties with Chinese merchants (Gowing 1983, 83–84; Elarth 1949, 110–11). American protection particularly helped expand his wealth, allowing him to monopolize the harvest and trade of gutta percha and rubber, to lend money, and to oversee the trade on Cotabato's river systems (*RGMP* 1904, 573; Taft 1914, 174–75; Hagedorn 1931, 19;

Ileto 1971, 63–64; Mastura 1984, 78–79). Additionally, he "personally organized the collection of forest products, and maintained a virtual monopoly through his connections with the Chinese merchants. He also extended his interest into rice milling and lumber" (Beckett 1982, 401).

The Americans recognized Piang's preeminence, impressed by his influence in Cotabato, but were also sympathetic to his "humble" nonroyal origins and rags-to-riches life story. It was clear that army officers saw in Piang a chief to whom they could relate. This opinion of Piang was widely shared by Americans:

> He is very shrewd, has brains and is self-made, being now quite wealthy and a power in the valley, as he controls all of Dato Ali's influence over the tribes and adds to this his own brain. He is the only prominent Moro who seems to appreciate what the American invasion means and the business opportunities it brings with it. The Chinese blood in him makes him a shrewd businessman, and he has accumulated quite a fortune and is daily adding to it. He practically controls all the business of Cotabato, especially exports, through his Chinese agents in that place; has complete control of the Moro productions, and working with the Chinese merchants makes it practically impossible for a white firm to enter into business in the Rio Grande, even with much capital behind them (*ARWD* 1902, 528, as quoted in Beckett 1982, 401).

Army officers made sure that their relationship with Piang was tight, and the datu obliged by working actively for the Americans, helping to suppress recalcitrant datus and becoming personally involved in keeping the new district stable. In exchange, the Americans allowed him to keep and expand his wealth and ignored "indiscretions" like the occasional abuse of power and influence (Williams 1913, 199–200; Beckett 1982, 401). The American presence also made certain administrative positions available to Piang, purportedly to facilitate the colonial civilizing process. Piang became a tribal ward leader, a position that he used to bring his entourage under American protection. With American blessings, he recruited into the wardship system his own allies (including Ali's half brother who had betrayed him), and even the weakened heir to the Magindanao sultanate, the powerless but still symbolically valuable Dato Mastula.[8] The most important privilege Piang derived from his accommodation, however, was the opportunity and the power to reinvent himself. Piang had himself declared the Sultan of

Mindanao, despite questions of his Chinese mestizo lineage and nonroyal standing. With his power secured by the colonial presence and propped up by Chinese wealth, Piang was in a position to create his own myth, one that was rumored to run closely to the bloodline of an admired idol, the seventeenth century great man Kachil Kudrat (Ileto 1971, 63). With Piang's active support, Cotabato was declared the most peaceful district of the Moro Province.

This sketch of Piang's ascension makes it easy to see why he is often likened to Filipino politicians: he "collaborated," gained a niche in the colonial state, created a patronage network, and reinvented his standing in society (*ARWD* 1900, 260). To accept the similarity, however, is misleading, because describing Piang as a Filipino politician is like putting the cart before the horse. He did indeed become a powerful politico, but his integration into the colonial state was driven by his experience as a Southeast Asian datu. Wolters' description of Muslim polities allying with certain European country traders to "thwart the monopolistic plans of other Europeans" could easily apply to Piang (Wolters 1982, 25). It was also normal for orang besar to seek the assistance of more powerful foreign forces to alter the internal balance of power in their favor (Laarhoven 1990, 165). Perak's Raja Abdullah, for example, accepted British protection because "the British would make him Sultan" and force his rivals to recognize him as such.[9] And like Abu Bakar of Johor, with whom he shared royal pretensions, Piang projected himself as a link to the colonizers, a go-between who could translate the strange ways of the foreign power (Amoroso 1996, 39). To the Americans, he promoted himself as a crucial stabilizer who would preserve Magindanao loyalty to the Moro Province. The hoped-for result was, of course, the reinforcing of his own power, an obvious motive that sometimes made the Americans uncomfortable (*MH*, 19 May 1906).

There was no doubt, therefore, that Piang's decision to "collaborate" was taken in a Southeast Asian context. Yet, at the same time, he was starting to shift his mindset, recognizing that the powerful Americans were committed to narrowing his world to fit the colonial map. Colonial administrative reclassification, beginning with the creation of districts with explicit boundaries, circumscribed the Magindanaos to a new territory called the Cotabato district. Once a locality in a trading world in which yesterday's backwater could become tomorrow's center, Cotabato was now administratively fixed as a subordinate district in a larger colonial body politic. No longer part of Southeast Asia, Cotabato belonged to the Moro

Province. With this reclassification, earlier Southeast Asian notions of domain faded, upstream and downstream giving way to district, municipality, and village. Trade, too, was affected as Magindanao was cut off from the indigenous Southeast Asian trading network. The colonial state now determined the parameters of trade (no slaves), and customs officials took over the regulation of that trade from the orang besar.

This sealing off of Magindanao society from the region was not as thorough as the Americans wanted it to be, and there were those who continued to operate under the old system (*MH*, 13 Apr. 1907). But the new administrative boundary rendered them illegal traders who were subject to prosecution. Magindanaos had either to operate under the new perimeter rules (and submit to its extractions, i.e., customs and revenue taxes), or be relentlessly pursued as "smugglers" (*RGGPI* 1917, 90). Moreover, the slave system, long a crucial basis of orang besar power, was destroyed by the Americans, who regarded it as a prime symbol of Muslim backwardness (Mastura 1984, 83). With the slave trade over, Piang shifted from the supervision and control of people to the ownership and management of agricultural commodities (Mastura 1984, 84; Beckett 1982, 401–2). Accordingly, land became a new source of wealth, aided by the American's declared intent to open up and exploit the resources of Mindanao.

The shift in importance from people to territory was reflected in the changing nature of Piang's power. The new colonial reality meant that Piang could no longer manipulate Southeast Asian-style alliances with fellow datus or with outsiders. The old notion of prowess was also fading away, displaced by a pedigree associated with American rule. This pedigree gave Piang the opportunity to expand his influence using powers associated with his office, but they were powers that were local in character, tied to the administratively defined district of Cotabato. Unchallenged within Cotabato, his influence beyond this realm was now slight. The new limits to Piang's power thus mirrored the diminishment of the territory itself. Piang's full domination of the Magindanaos therefore signaled the end of the era of the orang besar in southern Mindanao. The period of the Muslim politico had commenced, just in time to meet renewed Filipino demands for southern Mindanao's integration.

When the Muslims recognized the reality of American rule, their acceptance was based on the inaccurate premise that Mindanao would be kept separate from the Philippines. They believed American assurances that they would be protected from their "traditional enemies" and that as long as the Americans were present, "they will never be under Filipino rule" (Horn 194, 155; Elarth 1991, 4–6; Thomas 1971, 100). Politically astute datus therefore saw fit to establish long-term associations with Americans in the hope of gaining political benefit; none sought political associations in Manila. Accepting the new local reality, they worked in their districts confident of the American umbrella that protected them.

It was therefore natural for the datus to be apprehensive when Filipinos and Americans began to clash over the fate of "Moro Mindanao." When nationalist agitation reached southern Mindanao, certain datus attempted to project a unified opposition to integration (Gowing 1983, 250–51, 254; Saleeby 1913, 15). This effort unraveled when the Filipinos were able to produce their own datu supporters (*MH*, 18 Aug., 15 and 22 Sept. 1906; *PFP,* 31 Aug. 1907). More significant than Muslim disunity, however, was the absence of Muslim participation in the debate between American separatists and Filipino nationalists. For while both sides actively solicited Muslim support, it was clear that the outcome of the debate was to be determined by the two major contestants. Both regarded the Muslims as backward and differed only on the preferred path towards their "civilization" (*PFP*, 17 Aug. 1907). Americans wanted to "civilize" under army rule and without Manila's interference; Filipinos demanded integration and close supervision from Manila because of shared (Malay?) identity (*RGMP* 1909, 3–4; Saleeby 1913, 14–15; Quezon 1912, 4–5; *PFP*, 9 Nov. 1907; Gowing 1983, 254). Neither side regarded the Muslims as participants in the debate in their own right.

This inability to influence the debate over their future revealed to many datus the stark reality of their circumscribed territory, power, and status within the larger colonial body politic. Moreover, as Filipinos emerged victors, the datus faced the prospect of being mere provincial politicians in an arena defined by Filipino rules. Piang, who was eventually appointed to the national assembly as "representative of the Moros," accepted this new reality with deep ambivalence. In 1926, reflecting on integration and asked by Joseph Ralston Hayden what he thought was "best for my country," Piang struggled with contradictory feelings. On the one hand, there was relative appreciation for American colonial control. There was also the hope that Americans sympathetic to the separation of Mindanao from the Philippines might succeed and that the Muslims would eventually be given the "independence" promised them after the completion of the "civilizing process." Stated Piang (1926, JRH Box 28–24):

> My sons have told [me of] one of the bills presented to Congress by Mr. Bacon of New York. They tell me that this is to separate Mindanao, Sulu and Palawan from the rest of the Philippines. That would be better. Perhaps not the best solution but better than present conditions. Our hearts are heavy just now. [If Bacon's] bill becomes a law then more capital would come to Mindanao. That would be good. Then we would have those roads and telegraphs... We can raise many things in the Moro country that they cannot grow in America... My own province can raise enough rice to feed all of these islands... We want schools, so the younger Moros will be better educated than their fathers are. But we do not want to be taught religion. We already have our own religion... Then—some time, after we have learned enough and are prosperous enough, and everything is peaceful in the Far East, then liberty and independence for ourselves, for everyone loves to be free.

On the other hand, there was a growing and cheerless realization that this would not happen, as Filipinos increasingly assumed the leading positions in the colonial state:

> The American Army officers who governed us then were good men and just. They gave us assurance that they would protect us and not turn us over to those whom we do not trust. Whether those officers had the power to make those promises we do not know. But we trusted them.... But year after year, slowly, they have given the Christian Filipinos more power over us.

Piang lived seven more years, dying on 23 August 1933 at the age of 87. He lived long enough to see his son Abdullah appointed to the Philippine assembly. This was his legacy—ensuring that his progeny mastered the art of Manila's politics.

## Filipinization and the Further Contraction of the Muslim World

After the army withdrew and Manila extended its powers to Mindanao, some datus continued to oppose Filipinization.[10] But given their loss of firepower and their dependent leadership, reports of "Muslim resistance" were more noise than substance; actual battles against Filipino or American forces were insignificant (*PFP*, 17 Nov. 1917; *Mtr*, 2 Dec. 1937; Tan 1933, 44–46). Warnings of an impending breakdown of order once Filipinos took over were empty rhetoric, aimed at changing the American decision to hand over "Moro Mindanao" to the Filipinos (Forbes 1928, 293–94; Glang 1969, 16–17). Whether the Filipinos took the threat seriously was incidental. The Muslims knew that Americans had the final say; if they could successfully revive the myth of Muslim ungovernability (the "Moro problem"), southern Mindanao might remain free of Filipino control (Tan 1993, 47–48). Resistance, ineffectual though it proved, should be understood not as Muslim resistance *against* American rule, but as an appeal *to* American rule. The more strident these "warnings" became, the more apparent it was that resistance had no potency.

If "Moro opposition" made an impact on Philippine politics, it was in how it redefined the notion of a "Moro problem" and provided a launch pad for a group of datus who opted to participate in the politics of Filipinization. These leaders declared themselves the moderate alternative to the more rebellious types and volunteered to mediate between suspicious Moros and Filipinos. Who were these Muslim moderates and why did they choose to work within the new Filipino-dominated system? A 1917 listing of those who publicly expressed their support for Filipinization, Muslim representation in the colonial legislature, and the eventual granting of Philippine independence were described as men of distinction in their communities (Carpenter 1917, 295). Most had already worked with the Americans as advisers or tribal ward leaders and were familiar with aspects of colonial practice. In fact, many had been among the first to accept the transformation of their "traditional political system" and to take advantage of the new, narrower opportunities offered by American rule.

These leaders now concluded that their fortunes would be better served by changing patrons. They included Hadji Butu, who was appointed to the Senate, and Hadji Gulamu Rasul, who became Carpenter's aide-de-camp and a supporter of government settlement programs in Mindanao (*PFP*, 1 Sept. 1914, 29 Apr. and 9 Dec. 1916, 10 and 17 Nov. 1917). In Zamboanga, former rebel Awkara Sampang, his Lanao counterpart, Amai Manabilang, and the German-Jolo mestizo Julius Schuck became champions of Filipinization and were all elected to the provincial board (*MB*, 6 May and 15 Oct. 1915; *PFP,* 24 Apr. and 5 June 1915; Tan 1993, 75–76). Others tried to overcome their enfeebled status. The Sultan of Sulu supported Filipinization hoping that Quezon would reinstate him as leader of the Sulu archipelago (*PFP*, 5 Dec. 1914; Gowing 1983, 172). Yet others became pro-Filipinization because they were impressed by the "progress" colonial rule had brought to the rest of the colony and they hoped similar improvements could reach Mindanao. Datus who shared this view were lured by the promise of universal primary public education and the creation of a development plan for Mindanao (*PFP,* 4 and 22 Mar. 1916, 21 Oct. 1933). Finally, certain datus were simply awed by Manila's glitter. Governor-General Harrison (1922, 108) described the transformation of Datu Alamada, who had defied Spanish and American authorities for twenty years before surrendering in 1914 to Carpenter, after the datu visited the colonial capital:

> He seemed to me like a wild bird, poised for instant flight, and supremely uncomfortable among the large crowd of officials at Malacanang Palace; his hand was cold from suppressed nervousness and embarrassment. He had agreed to come to Manila upon the assurance that he could carry his *kris*... at all times, and that he would not be obliged to wear "Christian" clothing. Before the end of his first day in Manila, he had discarded his *kris* and surreptitiously procured an American suit of clothes. Upon his return to Cotabato, he became insistent in his demands for schools.

Nevertheless, partisans of Filipinization were not what they seemed. Even those who were appointed to the legislative assembly remained mistrustful of Filipinos and secretly hoped for American intervention. Leonard Wood's appointment suggested this possibility and Muslim leaders quickly spoke up when Wood and Cameron Forbes visited Mindanao in 1921 (Forbes 1928, 47). Those considered dedicated to integration were the first to support Wood and criticize what they called the excesses of Filipinization (Gowing 1988, 102). Hadji Butu, who had voted for Philippine independence, switched sides to advocate the retention of American rule in Mindanao even if the Philippines became independent (Fry 1978, 260, 267). Other datus followed suit: the rivals Mandi and Hadji Abdulla Nuno reconciled and declared themselves firmly in support of continued American rule (Forbes 1928, 44–45). Gumbay and Ugalingan Piang joined the chorus championing the Bacon bill (Thomas 1971, 132; Fry 1978, 267).

The separatist spirit was embodied in a circulating manifesto addressed to President Coolidge. This "Declaration of Rights and Purpose" demanded the creation of an "independent constitutional sultanate," eventually to be termed "the Moro nation" (Tan 1993, 47–48). The spirit was not unanimous. In Lanao, datus were split between the "proindependence" and "pro-American" factions, raising fears of renewed violence in what had always been regarded as the most volatile of the Muslim provinces (Tan 1993, 75–76; *MB*, 22 Aug. 1926). But in Zamboanga, the Muslim volte-face reinvigorated American separatists who now invoked Bacon's assessment of Mindanao's economic potential as a reason for detaching the island from the Philippines (Fry 1878, 226; Smith 1990, 37; Forbes 1928, 47). It is also notable that the datus used new methods of political action: petitions, letters of protest, speeches, and even discussed sending "missions" to the United States to argue their case.[11] With the loss of firepower, these actions were clearly the only ones available. Yet, they were also significant because they show that the Muslim datus had learned a new way of doing politics. In fact, the entreaties, requests, lobbying, and threats of "bloodshed and disorder" were tactics first used by Manuel Quezon when negotiating with the Americans (*The Philippine Policy* 1939, 8). In picking up the political tactics of their opponents, datus showed the extent to which they were—perhaps unconsciously—being drawn into the world of Filipino-dominated colonial politics.

The datus were thus feeling their way through a process whose outcome remained unclear until the 1930s. As noted above, Hadji Butu at different times was to be found on different sides of the separatist debate. And Hadji Gulamu Rasul, another high-ranking integrationist, was always intensely pro-Filipino and proindependence when in Manila. When he and his father addressed their fellow Muslims, however, "they spoke of continued American protection in the face of Christian Filipino domination" (Thomas 1971, 76–77). Both Maximo Kalaw, the first Filipino political scientist and an advisor to Quezon, and Cameron Forbes, with his opposing view of Mindanao, noted datu deception. Forbes observed that even as Muslim representatives voted consistently with Quezon's Nacionalista party in the assembly, in "talking with Americans and disinterested parties, they frequently express the desire for separation from the rest of the archipelago and a continuance of American rule in case independence is granted" (Forbes 1928, 33; Fry 1978, 260; Thomas 1971, 132). Kalaw (1931, 73–74), on the other hand, cited an incident that convinced him that datus "secretly" favored Filipinization:

> I am reminded of a story about the Moros told me by Director Hidrosollo himself. The Director accompanied some Americans to Mindanao and on one occasion, the Moro chieftains in their usual oratorical fashion told the Americans that they did not want the Christian Filipino to rule them, and that they wanted the Americans to remain there. Later on when one of those Moro chiefs realized that Director Hidrosollo was there, he invited the Director to a private corner. When they were out of hearing of the Americans, the Moro datu said, "Well, Director, don't mind what we said in our speeches. They are for American consumption. The real thing is that we are brothers. Christian Filipinos and Moros are of the same blood and race. So don't believe what I told them." The Moros are unfortunately forced by circumstances to play that kind of politics.

Datu Piang also talked out of both sides of his mouth. He opposed Filipinization with Americans he trusted and supported the separatist plots of his eldest son. However, he also made sure that one foot was in the other camp by accepting nomination to the Philippine assembly (*RGMP* 1916, 77). And, despite his sons' anti-Filipino sentiments, he sent Ugalingan and Gumbay to schools which would prepare them for employment in the colonial state. Piang might have agonized over the pressure, but he was astute enough to realize the political value of supporting both sides, if not for his personal benefit then at least for the future of his political clan (Piang, JRH Box 28–33; Mastura 1984, 84; Hagedorn 1969, 392).

These various acts of cooperation and duplicity were not immutable positions based on unchanging motivations. Only a few datus were staunchly pro-Filipino or pro-American. Instead we see in these overlapping and contradictory responses an effort by Muslim elites to negotiate their way through political change. The switching of sides, the discrepancy between public declarations and private assurances, and the attempt to play Americans off against Filipinos were less the actions of slick operators or small-time conspirators than of a local elite unsure of its fate (Piang, JRH Box 28–24). In its eyes, the Americans appeared to give way to the Filipinos, but this was not definite, as the return of Leonard Wood seemed to portend (Piang, 26 Aug. 1927, JRH Box 28–33). It was only when Filipinization consolidated itself in Mindanao following Wood's death that these political ambiguities were clarified. Anti-Filipino and separatist sentiments steadily diminished in rhetoric and influence as more datus accepted Filipino rule (Kalaw 1931, 74).

As the ranks of integrationists grew, a number of them began to stand out for the way they identified with the Philippines. These datus recognized the consolidation of the new order and realized the potential of "working within the system." They saw political opportunities in appointment to official position, from the insular assembly down to municipal councils, in membership in the expanding "national" parties, and in the forging of political and social ties with both Americans and Filipinos (*MB*, 22 Aug. 1926 and 4 July 1931; *PH*, 4 Aug. 1931). This cabal included old hands like Datu Piang and Hadji Butu. It also included, however, fresh faces like Datu Sinsuat, the nationalist sultans of Lanao, and educated leaders like Gulamu Rasul, Tarhata Kiram, and the brothers Menandang and Ugalingan Piang.[12] From these younger datus rose the first generation of Muslim leaders who accepted that Mindanao was inextricably linked to the larger political framework centered in Manila. It was this group that became known as the first "Muslim-Filipinos."

## The "Muslim-Filipinos"

While there was some overlap between the "old" Muslim leaders and their successors, a generational and political shift unfolded as Filipinization moved forward. Younger datus set themselves apart from their predecessors, many of whom found working in Manila difficult, by embracing the inevitability of southern Mindanao's integration. Recognizing the new reality, they also embraced the rules of the game, including the new requirements for being representatives of the "Moro people." One way of appreciating these changes among the younger datus is to look at their educational and political "pilgrimages."[13] While many began with pedigreed origins and thus had substantial resources and power behind them, the next steps in their political and administrative journeys were closely linked to the colonial state. Schooling, the opportunity for higher education, in particular, was vital in the emergence of what Majul (1976, 91) calls a "group of young professionals who were generally co-opted by the powers that be."

The case of Ugalingan Piang, the second son of Cotabato's Datu Piang, is illustrative. Ugalingan was sent to public schools in Cotabato and Zamboanga and then to the Central Luzon Agricultural School in Manila where he earned a teacher's degree and showed "signs of leadership" (*PFP*, 6 Jan. 1917). He returned to Cotabato to become the principal of the Dulawan Elementary School, then became the head cashier of Settlement

Colony 2. He was appointed deputy provincial treasurer of Cotabato and auxiliary justice of the peace for the province. From there Ugalingan was sent back to Dulawan and was appointed municipal president. This demotion was more than made up for by his appointment to the lower house of the Philippine legislature. After his term, he was appointed mayor of Dulawan and then elected third member of the provincial board. In 1938, Ugalingan won election to the Philippine legislature and held that position until World War II. He was reported to have been involved in separatist schemes during the 1920s, but once elected to a state position, it was clear where his intentions lay (Bautista 1939, 32–33).

Ugalingan Piang thus signified the appearance of a new kind of Muslim leader, fully devoted to the colonial state and valuing official position as much as other Filipino politicians. Continuing to use the traditional titles of "datu" and "sultan," the new leaders also relished being "representative," "senator," "deputy governor," "municipal president," "captain," and "director," and openly expressed their support for Quezon and the Filipino leadership (Mastura 1984, 46; Horn 1941, 162; Murphy 1937). "Such a leader holding a dual role," according to Magindanao scholar Mamitua Saber (1974, 300–1), "bridge[d] the relationship between the traditional community and the modern government."

The formal "national" debut of these leaders in the colonial arena appropriately came during the convention to formulate a constitution for the new Commonwealth. Several Muslim leaders were elected to the convention, led prominently by old supporters of Quezon, but also included new faces like Cotabato's Menandang Piang and Blah Sinsuat, and Lanao's Aluya Alonto.[14] In his first speech before the convention, Alonto implored his fellow delegates to stop referring to Muslims as "Moros":

> We do not like to be called "Moros" because when we are called "Moros" we feel that we are not considered as part of the Filipino people. You also know that the name "Moro" was given to us by the Spaniards because Morocco had been under the rule of Spain like Mindanao and Sulu. So that I would like to request the members of this Convention that we prefer to be called "Mohammedan Filipinos" and not "moros," because if we are called Moros we will be considered as enemies, for the name "Moro" was given to us by the Spaniards because they failed to penetrate into the Island of Mindanao (*Philippine Constitutional Convention* 1935, 420).

Alonto then proposed that a "permanent and final solution" to the "Moro problem" would come only by giving Mindanao its appropriate share of economic and infrastructural aid and by granting "Mohammedan Filipinos" equal status with Filipinos under the constitution, beginning with the right to full suffrage. Manila officials received his speech with approval. Maximo Kalaw (1931, 66–67) proclaimed that with the recognition given by Alonto and his colleagues to the convention and their acceptance of their roles, Mindanao's integration was only a matter of time.

In demanding that they be referred to as "Mohammedan Filipinos" (later "Muslim-Filipinos"), Alonto and others also conveyed the message that the special character of southern Mindanao communities must continue to underpin their participation. Simply making Muslims politicians or citizens would not eliminate the "Moro problem"; it was necessary to acknowledge a "Muslim voice" within colonial politics (Heffington, JRH Box 27–31). This was how leaders would make their pitch for a measure of "autonomy" in the Muslim-dominated provinces. The vice-president of the "Sulu Mohammedan Students Association" joined Datu Balabaran Sinsuat in proposing that given the "political background," the "peculiar makeup," and the "long independent existence" of Muslim groups, Cotabato, Sulu, Lanao, and Zamboanga should be granted some form of autonomy to ensure Muslim "advancement in the social and political fields" (*Mtr*, 12 Jan. 1936; *PFP,* 30 Nov. 1935).

In short, Muslims expressed their willingness to participate in the Filipinization process if they were allowed to retain the identity of "Muslim" alongside that of "Filipino." While none of these leaders cared to elaborate on the meaning of being Muslim, it was clear that religion itself was not foremost in their minds. Alonto and Sinsuat regarded religious identity as a means of making their mark in colonial politics. Islam had become a vehicle to unite constituents and give leaders credentials as representatives of a specific sector involved in the governing process. Instead of evoking difference to defy the center, Islam was now a tool to get more concessions through participation in the center's politics.

This recasting of Islam from a symbol of Moro opposition into a tool of colonial politics in part reflected the success of two earlier projects of the American regime. The first was to colonize and control the Muslims, but not to convert them, as the Spanish had tried to do. This was a policy that the U.S. army closely adhered to and which the Department of Mindanao and Sulu continued (Malcolm 1936, 45). Secondly, the Americans had refused to allow religion to be handled by Islamic clerics, but instead secured it as the responsibility of datus as "titular head[s] of the Mohammedan Church" (Thompson 1983, 240–41; Gowing 1983, 286). This move precluded the possibility of an alternative center of power emerging through an independent (and potentially radical) clergy. It also channeled Islamic sentiment away from the path of resistance by delegating the guardianship of spiritual needs to Muslim leaders who had already made their peace with the colonial state.

With the emergence of a new generation of Muslim leaders who embraced their religious identity within politics, Islam's value became tied to political aspirations closely identified with the Filipinized colonial state and an identifying mark distinguishing one set of politicians from another. I would suggest that it functioned for Muslims as other markers functioned for Filipino politicians who represented "regional blocs" (northern Luzon or western Visayas), "language groups" (the Cebuano alliance or the Ilocano bloc), or "economic sectors" (farmers or labor). In constitutional or assembly deliberations and debates, Alonto and his colleagues were representatives of an "interest group" that happened to be Muslim. And following Alonto's declaration of fealty, local politics in the Muslim provinces began to resemble politics in other areas of the Philippines. There were conflicts over spoils of office that often hampered administration (*MB*, 31 Oct. 1934). Embryonic clan-based political battles took place in Muslim provinces as families fought for control over local offices, especially during, but not limited to, election seasons. Even armed showdowns between rival groups, which first appeared in Cotabato in the 1940s, became regular fare in local politics (*MB*, 10 Jan. 1940).

In Sulu, for example, the election victory of Ombra Amilbangsa over his rival Gulamu Rasul in the 1935 legislative elections was offset by Rasul's gaining the support of Manila leaders who installed him as special adviser to the provincial government. Ombra then protested that Rasul was removing his "political and personal friends and supporters" from their local positions through "threats and coercion" (Ombra 1936, JRH Box 27–2). He warned Quezon, Rasul's patron, that a breakdown of peace and order would likely ensue, forcing Quezon to accommodate the new leader while maintaining his ties with Rasul (Ombra 1936, JRH Box 27–2). In Cotabato, the Piangs fought patronage battles with appointed officials as well. Menandang Piang wrote a letter to Quezon accusing the provincial governor, Dionisio Gutierrez, and two members of the provincial board, of supporting the candidacy of Piang's opponent, Datu Sinsuat. Piang specifically denounced Gutierrez, who was a military man, for using soldiers as election inspectors to ensure Sinsuat's victory. The first of several factional battles with the Sinsuat family had commenced (*MTr*, 6 Aug. 1935; *PH*, 16, 17 and 21 Aug. 1935; Beckett 1977, 60–61).

These "Muslim Filipinos" showed that they were learning the ropes of colonial politics. They joined the Manila-based political parties and formed youth associations that articulated the "Muslim voice" in Mindanao and Manila. The Anak Sug (Sons of Jolo) was established "to enlighten the Moro youths along moral and religious lines, to lift the Moro youth from their ignorance, and to cooperate with the government in the maintenance of peace and order not only in the Sulu islands, but in the entire Mohammedan province of Mindanao." Its real purpose was to be the vehicle for the "political ambitions [of certain Sulu leaders] for the coming general elections" after "the people of Sulu were... granted the right to elect the third member of the provincial board and the president of the city of Jolo" (*PFP*, 15 Feb. 1930). Its counterpart in Cotabato, the Association of Muslims, was likewise created "to act as the unofficial representative of our people at home, in order to protect their rights and interests, to help them realize the value of education, to inculcate in them the merits of cooperating with the leaders of Christian Filipinos in working for the common welfare of the country" (Association petition, 4 Aug. 1935, JRH Box 27–32; Gopinath 1989, 98).

The effectiveness of this new "Muslim voice," however, depended on how the colonial government received it. While Quezon had opened a path for datu participation, he also ensured that Mindanao's governance stayed under his direct supervision through the Commission for Mindanao and Sulu. Quezon's continuing distrust of the Muslims can be seen as an unintended outcome of the way the integration process itself predicated on the maintenance of "difference." Muslim politicians had eagerly embraced this formula as the basis of their participation in colonial politics, and though now utilized for integration, difference could still evoke separatism, as seen during Wood's tenure. This easily awakened nostalgia for the autonomy of the Moro Province put the Muslims in the position of a mistrusted minority, not simply another interest group.

Muslim difference was politically signified in the 1930s not in religious practice, but in the social tags of datu and sultan. Dual leadership had made the integration of Mindanao possible, but by existing in part outside the conceptualization of Philippine politics, the Muslim-Filipino could also be seen as a "double agent of two kinds of authority systems" (Saber 1974, 300–1). Quezon was not inclined to accept authority drawing legitimacy from outside his domain so he declared that one of the Commission's responsibilities was to work for the "removal from all datos and local Mohammedan officials all official recognition" under the Commonwealth (*MB*, 20 May 1937; *MTr*, 21 and 27 May, 13 June and 8 July 1937; *PH,* 22 Sept. 1937). He explained his hostility:

> [There is a] weakness in the policy heretofore adopted by the government... in dealing with the Mohammedan Filipinos or Moros in Mindanao and the Sulu Archipelago to give some sort of recognition to the datus so that they have become in practice ex-officio officials of the government... This policy must be stopped and changed radically. It gives the impression that there is a dual government for the Moros—one exercised by the appointed or elected officials of the government, and the other by the datus and sultans. It perpetuates the overlordship exercised throughout the ages by these datus and sultans over their *sacup*, who continue to be, in fact, slaves of their sultans and datus as they were under the Spanish regime (Memorandum to the Secretary of Interior, 30 Sept. 1937, JRH Box 27–27).

He reiterated his disapproval of dual authority among Muslims in 1938 when he reminded Muslim representatives that only duly elected or appointed officers, not sultans or datus, were recognized as legitimate leaders of municipalities. He added that he "recognized the title sultan that the people before him have, but added that such a title was only expressive of a social distinction and not in any way representing official authority." He allowed, however, that "there [was] no reason why [the Muslims] need not be governed as Christian Filipinos are governed."[15]

Thus while Quezon promised to open more offices and expand "non-Christian" rights, he also made sure that Filipinos became the new political majority in the Muslim provinces. Filipinization "at the expense of Moro aspirations" continued, with provincial and municipal seats still given to Filipinos over Muslims (Pelzer 1945, 102). And Quezon let Muslim-Filipinos know they were token representatives of a "non-Christian group" with little to offer the political parties; this continued to be true as the "special provinces" were never granted full suffrage under the Commonwealth (*PFP*,

23 Oct. 1916; 27 Oct. and 10 Nov. 1917). All this prompted Muslims to complain that Filipinization should become synonymous with "Moroization" (*MTr*, 22 Sept. 1936). But these complainants had no leverage in Manila.

Finally, Muslim leaders as a group were hindered by their own limitations. As colonial politics progressed, it became clear that Muslim participation in convention or assembly deliberations required not only rhetorical prowess, but also an analytical sophistication associated with formal education. The Alontos and Sinsuats notwithstanding, the new generation of leaders drew from a very small pool. Public education in the Muslim provinces was largely confined to the primary school level (Bentley 1989, 78–80). In 1935, the majority of the thirty-seven government-supported scholars were high school or vocational students. Of the tertiary-level students, only five were studying liberal arts, the discipline in which most ambitious youth were first exposed to politics. Of those who finished college, only two decided to go to law school, an important stepping stone to a political career (Bureau of Non-Christian Tribes Scholarship Fund Report, 1935, JRH, Box 29–24). This group hardly represented what Carpenter wanted for the leaders of the Muslim provinces, "the men constituting the controlling factor for or against peace and order under whatever may then be the constituted government" (Carpenter 1917, 85; *PFP,* 19 Apr. and 27 Apr. 1919).

Nevertheless, Aluya Alonto's and Ugalingan Piang's generation laid the foundation for future Muslim participation in Philippine politics. World War II halted Quezon's centralizing streak and presented an opportunity for these Muslim-Filipinos to reinvigorate their local power. In the postwar period, they would again aspire for "national" stature.

## Conclusion

The essential error in most studies of Muslim relations to American colonialism is in accepting the Philippine contextual framework as a "given" at the beginning of colonial rule in Mindanao. The nationalist imagination that underpins most such scholarship is based on this orientation. Yet, standing on a hill in Cotabato with one's back to Manila is to face the world that was maritime Southeast Asia, a world in which the colonial Philippines was a minor player. It was this wider world that initially framed the way Muslims related to the American colonial state.

The transformation of Muslim datus from Malay men of prowess into provincial politicians characterized the wider evolution of Muslim support for the Moro Province. Yet, it would still be erroneous to liken these reconfigured strong men to Filipino caciques. I have suggested that the datus were in what amounted to a transitional stage in the process of becoming Muslim counterparts to the northern caciques. They remained fiercely loyal only to the Americans in the province and not to the larger American colonial system; they retained their suspicion and dislike of Filipinos; and they still—with American sympathy and backing—refused to regard themselves as Filipinos.

Moreover, as nascent colonial politicians, the datus were not as privileged as their cacique counterparts, who enjoyed the right and opportunity to use their positions as stepping stones for advancement through the state hierarchy. The datus became territorially limited as American paternalism worked against their political and administrative pilgrimages through the colonial state. As long as they could not go beyond the district level, their political import was negligible. The Moro Province, then, had a kind of colonial legitimacy which was founded on a firm but fatally restricted social base. As long as the province was left to itself, Muslim support was more than adequate to maintain colonial stability. Once the fate of the province was debated in Manila, however, Muslim consent and support were insufficient to maintain the status quo. By the middle of the first decade, the transformed Muslim leadership had already outlived its usefulness as a support for the Moro Province.

While the army had contained Muslims to the narrow horizons of a provincial boundary, cutting them off from maritime Southeast Asian connections, the Department of Mindanao and Sulu integrated them into the larger Philippine administrative grid. The Muslim response to Filipinization remains an understudied episode in state formation and local power in southern Mindanao because scholars continue to regard the resistance-collaboration dichotomy as unproblematic. This simple (and often simplistic) explanation obscures a more complex situation. Much like their reactions to the Moro Province, Muslim responses to Filipinization were diverse and often overlapping. Instead of collaboration as sheer opportunism and resistance as proof of a multifaceted "nationalist struggle," I view these responses as efforts to cope with a power transition in which datus had little room to maneuver. Having accepted the restricted horizons of American colonialism and facing integration on Manila's terms, the datus' vulnerability was compounded by the army's assault on their capacities.

Consequently, some datus acknowledged the new order, while others resisted it. Some adjusted to it while attempting to preserve a semblance of autonomy. Still others attempted to postpone the inevitable by playing Filipinos and Americans off against each other. In the end, weakened by army occupation, but also divided by their responses to changes in the colonial center, most leaders made peace with the new order and chose to integrate. In doing so, they once more redefined the relationship between the various Muslim groups and the colonial state. During this period, today's prosaic term "Muslim-Filipino" appeared, articulated consciously by those datus who had come to accept as their political arena the agencies, institutions, and offices opened to them by the Filipino authorities.

CHAPTER 4

# Davao and the Dynamics of a Settler Zone

Davao was the most isolated district of the Moro Province and one of the farthest from Manila. Davao was also sparsely populated, its indigenous communities scattered throughout a huge area. Unlike Cotabato which was dominated by the Magindanaos, no group dominated Davao, and the "natives" there were said to be at a "low level of existence" (Rodil 1961, 41). Davao thus constituted the colonial frontier and was approached as such by those who sought to determine its place in southern Mindanao's development. For the Americans, the issue was not just how to construct a state, but how to achieve a critical mass of people for the state to govern. For the Filipinos, the goal was to maintain Davao's economic development after the Americans left, while incorporating it into the Filipino-dominated state. For both regimes, therefore, the settling of Davao was a priority.

Two groups made Davao their destination during this period—Americans under the Moro Province and the Japanese under Filipinization. Both groups, whose presence overlapped, were involved in the production of abaca (hemp) and were responsible for making Davao an economic growth zone. They were also vital to the construction of colonial authority in the area, as both were quite autonomous from the regimes that administered them. Moro Province officials were confident that their fellow Americans had the economic and political wherewithal to transform Davao, while the Filipinos, then expanding their power in Manila, were content to make political alliances with the commercially successful Japanese.

The similarities, however, end there. The American settlers failed to recreate the American western frontier, while the Japanese transformed Davao into one of the fastest-growing provinces of the Philippines. In this chapter, I will argue that to understand the divergent outcomes one must consider the relationship each community had with the colonial state. While both groups enjoyed autonomy from central authority, the effects were strikingly different. The Moro Province's loose supervision of Davao offered no help to American settlers who lacked experience, labor and capital, and marketing skills. Their economic decline in turn undermined the image of an effective administration that provincial officials had wanted to project.

Neither did the Japanese receive any help from the colonial state. But a creative labor organization and links with Japanese trading companies, coordinated by the Japanese state, ensured that their hemp was effectively produced and marketed abroad. Their economic success thus bolstered their unusually favorable relationship with the colonial state. Powerful politicians like Manuel Quezon protected Japanese investments in exchange for the latter's full support for Filipinization. Allowed a powerful say in local politics, the Japanese were crucial to the success of Quezon's Nacionalista party in Davao.

For both groups, however, Manila's control of land law was a major source of frustration for it limited the accumulation of large tracts of land. This impediment to plantation agriculture is a recurring theme in the story of Davao's prewar settlement. And the way the local regime and settlers dealt with it illuminates not only their relationship with Manila, but also their ultimate success or failure.

## The Moro Province as the "Last Western Frontier"

In 1901, the population of the Moro Province was estimated at between 4,000 and 6,000 (*C-A* 13 July 1901). To its first colonial rulers, civilizing the province was not merely a matter of subduing its "wild tribes" and establishing colonial authority. It also entailed peopling a huge unexplored area and exploiting its untapped wealth. Thus, even before military operations had ended, the army was engaged in an aggressive campaign to attract settlers (*MH*, 29 July 1905; *RGMP* 1904, 22). Its efforts were supported by the American-dominated private sector based in Zamboanga and spearheaded by the *Mindanao Herald,* which publicized positive impressions of Mindanao by visiting Americans.[1] Mindanao was advertised as changing from a territory of "savage tribes" battling American troops into a Mecca awaiting the daring Anglo-Saxon settler (*MH,* 23 Dec. 1905; *RGMP* 1905, 2).

Army officials and their businessmen allies were open about their preference for white American or other Western settlers. One 1908 advertisement stated: "To make it easy and attractive for [settlers] is the only hope for the rapid progress of the Province. The majority of men who are

attracted to the Province are men of small means; young men lik
'took up claims' in Kansas and Nebraska, and who are now the le
of their states. One of the most successful planters of Davao, a ma
made a plantation worth 60,000 pesos began on 600 pesos. He is t
thousands of men who will eventually settle here to establish centers of employment for the native and to contribute to the educational and social advancement of the Province" (*MH*, 24 Oct. 1908).

White settlers were expected to confer certain benefits, including uncomplicated relations with provincial authorities and favorable treatment from Manila (*MH*, 4 Nov. 1905). Officials saw them as potential allies in lobbying for a bigger share of the colonial budget. White American settlement was also regarded as a possible solution to the "Moro Problem," an alternative to the conciliation of friendly datus and the slow introduction of American ideals. By simply overwhelming indigenes with settlers, a new majority would emerge which would accelerate the "civilization" of the native population. An army officer made the comparison with the American West explicit, if not the likely outcome for the indigenes themselves: "If the Anglo-Saxons, Irish, Italians, Germans, Danes and Swedes could be induced to emigrate to the Moro country in tens and hundreds of thousands and take up and possess the earth as these people have done in the United States, Canada, New Zealand and the Argentine Republic, the Moro problem would soon be solved" (as quoted by Tan 1977; Corcino 1981-82, 101-2).

But there were problems. Public land laws had not yet been extended to the Moro Province and the delay was hampering settlement. Officials argued for their speedy enactment as the only way the province could attract homesteaders and businesses. The Philippine Commission, however, was reluctant to extend the land law quickly to the Moro Province. It was still grappling with the corruption of the previous Spanish titling system and the absence of a land survey and was having difficulty implementing the land laws in the regular provinces. Further, the Commission did not share the province's enthusiasm for accelerated settlement. Noting the existence of "some 200,000 to 400,000 'squatters'" throughout the Philippines, it feared an uncontrolled rush to Mindanao (Corpuz 1997, 272). It therefore warned that settlers in any part of the Philippines who did not hold titles to their land would be considered illegal occupants and subject to litigation. This measure probably reflects an effort on the part of Americans on the Commission to stop the spread of caciquism throughout the colony (Golay 1997, 122).

Seeing Manila's policy as a hindrance to southern Mindanao's economic development, provincial officials continued to press their demands. They expressed their disappointment in the "squatter" rule and in the land law's acquisition limits of sixteen hectares for individuals and 1,024 hectares for corporations. Leonard Wood, asserting that 10,000 acres (roughly 4,000 hectares) was the minimum parcel of land necessary for a modern sugar mill, complained that "the present land law, restricting as it does the ownership of land in any considerable quantity by a single individual or corporation effectively prohibits the development of the sugar industry and to a very [great] extent also the development of hemp and cocoanut culture on a large scale" (*RGMP* 1904, 22-23; Lunaria 1975, 67). In its first session, therefore, the provincial legislative resolved to petition Manila that Philippine general land laws be extended to southern Mindanao with modification to exempt the Moro Province from acquisition limits on ownership and leasing.[2] Zamboanga's American community echoed official sentiments that land law changes would go a long way toward populating Mindanao with able and skilled hands (*MH*, 29 July 1905; *MH,* 24 Oct. 1908).

Manila eventually responded and in 1905 the Philippine Commission extended the privileges outlined by the general land laws of the Philippines to the Moro Province, granting free patents to settlers who met occupancy and cultivation requirements.[3] It was unwilling, however, to exempt Mindanao from the land acquisition limits, due to "a very powerful lobby maintained in Washington by the beet sugar interests, who looked with alarm upon possible Philippine competition" (Cameron Forbes, as quoted by Corpuz 1997, 273). Nevertheless, the response to the new law was a flurry of applications for individual land titles, mostly by Muslims and Filipinos in Zamboanga. Americans concentrated on obtaining corporate leases for plantation agriculture rather than individual homesteads, leases, or ownership (*MH*, 24 Mar. 1906). Most of these plantation applications were aimed at developing marketable agricultural commodities in two of the targeted settlement districts of the province, Cotabato and Davao.

Early on these two districts were trumpeted as the pacesetters of the colonization plan. Cotabato, dubbed the "Valley of the Nile," was said to offer "the best opportunities for the cultivation of rice and sugar." It was portrayed as a fertile paradise whose "mountains abound in gutta percha trees and wild rubber, coffee, cocoa and hemp" (*MH,* 17 Mar. 1906). Davao was described as a "field of promise" which settlers were encouraged to turn into the "nucleus of a great industry in Mindanao" (*MH*, 15, 22, 29 Apr. 1905; 16 Dec. 1905; 17 Feb. 1906). Official reports underscored the fact that engaging in agriculture in Davao was an inexpensive venture—"$50 per month to live properly"—and that all a settler needed was "to be energetic, [have a] good constitution, and [be] of good character" (*RGMP* 1905, 34).

Advertisements initially failed to draw the desired number of American settlers. Most who eventually came played it safe and stayed in Zamboanga for economic and security reasons. Davao would also become a popular destination because it was perceived as safe. Despite the support given to colonization by the Cotabato datus and the assurances of security from the army and constabulary, most settlers remained wary of the Muslims, especially in areas where they constituted the majority among indigenous groups (Hancock 1912, 49-50). In Davao, Muslim communities were smaller and regarded as less warlike than their counterparts in Jolo, Cotabato, and Lanao. Indigenous groups (whom the Americans erroneously lumped together and called "Bagobos") were seen as even less of a menace than the Muslims (Cole 1913, 149-52; Sawyer 1900, 335).

## The Davao Settlement

Davao was called Nueva Guipuzcoa by the Spanish and classified as a politico-military province after it was "occupied" by the adventurer Jose Cruz Oyanguren in 1858 (Corcino 1969; Dabbay 1987, 23). It was largely unexplored for another thirty years despite the presence of an army unit and a Jesuit mission in the Banganga-Cateel area in 1894 (Arcilla 1989-1990, 49; Rodil 1961, 41). In 1899, when the Spanish withdrew, the area was engulfed in internal conflict among a small group of Filipino settlers. A self-appointed local government left by the Spaniards to await the American arrival was overthrown by a rebel faction, which was in turn toppled by another rebel group (*RGMP* 1913, 65-66; Corcino c1968, 41). Order came only when the Americans arrived on 20 December 1899. The leading faction, recognizing American military superiority, welcomed the new colonizers, accepted viva voce the announcement of a military government, and received appointment to municipal president positions (Suazo 1961, 6).

In 1905, provincial officials declared Davao ready for settlement. Five municipalities had been created (Davao, Mati, Caraga, Banganga, and Cateel), as well as four tribal wards covering all forty-eight villages (twelve of which were newly founded in July 1904). The army likewise reported progress in organizing the "many wild tribes" of the district into tribal wards and in encouraging the "Moros, Bagobos, Tagacaolos, Mandayas, Atas, and

Guiangas" to become involved in agricultural production (*RGMP* 1906, 419-20; 484-46; *MH*, 23 Apr. 1904, 24 Apr. 1905). By 1906, these communities had a stable tribal ward organization overlaying their preexisting affiliations. They also had intermediaries who could protect them from efforts by "the comparatively civilized people on the sea coast to peon the uncivilized people of the interior (*RGMP* 1904, 20-21; *RGMP* 1906, 419-20)." Only two incidents bothered the serene establishment: the killing of the district governor, Lt. Edward Bolton, in 1906 and a short-lived mutiny by Filipino constabulary soldiers protesting their officers' abuses in 1909 (*RGMP* 1906, 419-20; *PFP,* 10 July 1909). These episodes rekindled an image of Davao as similar to the rest of "savage" Mindanao. Their swift resolution, however, assured the curious that Davao was more stable than other districts of the Moro Province (*MH*, 16 June 1905; *MH,* 21 July and 25 Aug. 1906).

With assurances from authorities that land laws would be amended in their favor and that their land rights would be protected, American settlers began to arrive, joining the small groups of Spaniards and Filipino mestizos who preceded them. Between 1906 and 1909, a continuous trickle of settlers arrived in Davao, the first batch consisting mainly of discharged military men from units assigned to the Moro Province. Those who followed came from as far as Manila, inspired by survey reports that Davao had potential (Corcino 1981-82, 104; *MH*, 25 May and 6 June 1907; 22 Feb. 1908). There were also civilians: teachers, entrepreneurs, contractors wanting to do business with the army, and agents of American and other trading companies sent to investigate Davao's resources (*MH,* 1962, 10-11; Corcino 1981-82, 102). By 1908, various agricultural tracts were being cultivated, mostly in the coastal plains of the district. Optimism for growth was strong (*MH*, 3 Mar. 1907; *PFP*, 3 Feb. 1907; Phin-keong 1977).

The most popular product was hemp, which was used to make rope. Hemp was first farmed by the Spanish in small quantities, but when the American and British markets opened up to Philippine hemp, the new demand led to an almost overnight production boom. Within a year of the arrival of the first settlers, hemp cultivation covered "89,000 hills," yielding 3,018 piculs of abaca (from 1,500 in 1906). By 1909, there were forty plantations in Davao, "their areas ranging from 100 hectares to 1,024 hectares... [with] plantings at that time aggregated to 2,670,000 hills of hemp." Abaca export revenues reached 625,246 pesos, rising to 871,053 pesos in 1910 (Corcino 1981-82, 105; *RGMP* 1910, 4).

As hemp production rose, so did the population: by 1909 over 5,000 Americans had come to Davao, attracted by the potential profitability of abaca (Hayase 1984, 71). The transformation of this provincial backwater into a viable commercial area appeared to be under way under the management of the American settlers (Gleeck 1974, 221).

Herein lay the distinctiveness of this evolving settler society as compared to the Magindanao and other Muslim communities. While the latter were tightly supervised by the colonial state, the American settlers were largely left alone. Given the army's severe personnel shortage, these settlers were the province's ideal population, considered self-governing and reliable. They were, in the words of Leonard Wood, not only "a suitable class [who brought] with them some knowledge of modern agricultural methods, enterprise and some capital," but people who were the "better medium through which to inculcate American ideals and to set up American standards among the Moros."[4] Thus in Davao, where the indigenous communities were small and scattered, the army saw no need for close supervision. Save for the Bolton episode, the "Bagobos" were never a threat. Because they were regarded as even less civilized than the Muslims, they also had to be "civilized." Who would oversee this "civilization" better than a "suitable class" of American settlers?

In Davao, the settlers were clearly the dominant group and the most reliable supporters of the Moro Province, while leaders of the indigenous communities, unlike the Cotabato datus, were very marginal. And the relative prosperity of Davao's settlers distinguished them from settlers in other districts, those in and around Lanao's military camps, for example, who continued to live precarious lives (Tan 1977, 74). Finally, unlike the cosmopolitan Zamboanga Americans, Davao settlers imagined themselves as latter-day frontiersmen rather than well-established businessmen taking advantage of the conveniences of a provincial center (Hartley 1983, 68). Yet these settlers were confident of their abilities, partly because of the military experience many had and partly because they fancied themselves pioneers prospering "with little or no aid from the government" (*MH*, 25 May 1907; 3 Feb. 1909). This bred a sense of unity and influence that was reflected in the Davao Planters Association.

The association was organized on 15 February 1905 by fifteen American and Spanish planters who regarded cooperation as crucial in making their district economically viable and giving their industry a voice within and outside the Moro Province (*MH*, 23 Feb. 1904 and 16 Dec. 1905; *MA*, 20 Mar. 1905; *MT*, 1910 anniversary issue). Its membership reached a peak of forty-eight Americans and twelve Spaniards in 1909. Its members controlled "1,001,000 hemp hills, 39,489 cocoanut trees, and 7,750 rubber trees" in 1906 alone (*RGMP* 1906, 419-20, 484-86). In 1907, plantations were "bearing over 100,000 hemps and other plants" and had become "profitable enough to finance a year's vacation for their owners" (Gleeck 1974, 107-8). The association was firmly committed to land law revision (pursued through lobbying in Zamboanga and Manila) and the establishment of commercial ties with shipping companies, manufacturers, and other sectors to gain better prices and profit margins (*MH*, 22 Sept. 1906; *PFP*, 8 May 1908).

The association aided authorities with infrastructure projects to strengthen Davao's links with the Asian and American trade and was active in trying to attract indigenous (i.e., "Bagobo") labor (*MH*, 23 Apr. 1904; *MH*, 3 Mar., 16 June, and 9 Nov. 1907; 19 Dec. 1908). The planters understood that without sufficient labor, hemp production would suffer; thus, they supported government efforts to economically integrate the communities (*RGMP* 1907, 65; *MH*, 9 Nov. 1907). In 1907, officials reported that "some 4,000 [natives are] living on American plantations [who] not only work for a daily wage but are [also] planting hemp on their own account and thus taking the first steps toward becoming a class of peasant proprietors" (*RGMP* 1907, 32). The association's efforts drew praise from many. American officials in Manila lauded the settlers for "doing more than any other agency in getting in touch with these people... teaching them the desirability of labor and guiding them along the first stretches of the road leading to a settled life" (*RPC* 1908, 387). The *Mindanao Herald* (24 Nov. 1906) described the planters' association as representing "the most thoroughly American community in the Philippine Islands" for the frontier spirit its members embodied.

Association members also nurtured a strong sense of regional identity. As Hartley observed, "The isolation and small population gave the expatriate community [in Davao] an identity and regional influence which exceeded that of their compatriots in both Zamboanga and Manila" (Hartley 1983, 66). This community believed in its dominance over the territory it had opened and the distinctiveness of its development from the rest of the Philippines. In particular, the Americans fought off Filipino attempts to set up plantations under the pretext of protecting the Muslims and other "wild tribes." Although individual settlers were tolerated, Filipino plantation owners were forced to pack up and go "to other sections of the country" (Lunaria 1975, 69-70). Thus the Americans imagined themselves belonging to a community answerable only to the Moro Province and, by extension, Washington. It was a sentiment paralleling that of the provincial leadership, a solidarity that is hardly surprising, given that many of the settlers were former soldiers. The prevalence of this sentiment and their early agricultural success determined the settlers' attitude toward Filipinization and Mindanao separatism.

When, by the mid-1900s, Filipino agitation for independence reached Mindanao, separatist Americans in Davao and Zamboanga increased the tempo of their campaign to gain support from fellow Americans in Manila and the United States. Many reiterated the familiar themes that "only the American [was capable of] carrying progress in Mindanao" and peace among the indigenous communities had only occurred "with the coming of the Americans" (*MH*, 26 Jan. 1907). Others challenged the right of Filipinos to rule Mindanao, denying that the Muslims and other indigenous communities regarded themselves as Filipino or that Mindanao had ever figured "into the Philippine political situation," as alleged by Filipino leaders. Americans emphasized the divergence of history, religion, and way of life to show that Mindanao was unsuited to be a "Filipino habitat." Since it was the Americans who had dominated the "wild tribes," settlers declared, "the Moro Province is a white man's country and will remain so" (*MH*, 27 Mar. 1905).

Moreover, American settlers argued that if the Filipinos desired independence, they should be allowed it, but should not be burdened "with a load they cannot carry by making them responsible for the good behavior of tribes they are powerless to control" (*SFC*, 16 Dec. 1907). If America remained "dubious of Filipino ability to initiate just laws governing themselves, how much more dubious should it be as to Filipino ability to initiate just laws for the government of others" (*MH*, 15 Sept. 1906). Declared the *Herald*:

> The future of the Moro country is menaced through no more serious offence on our part than being incorporated with the Philippine Islands. As a matter of fact, conditions here are such that one government for both the Moro and Filipino countries is as unreasonable as it would be to maintain the same local government over Hawaii and Puerto Rico. Remove the Moro country from the bane of revolutionary agitation (12 Aug. 1905).

Support from outside was actively sought. After visiting Mindanao, Howard W. Taft and presidential aspirant William Jennings Bryan gave statements favoring separation and these were given full publicity (*MH*, 16 June, 19 Aug. 1905). There was also support from the American-controlled Manila press (*MT*, 16 Aug. 1905; *MA*, 18 Aug. 1905; *C-A*, 14 Sept. 1909). Racist sentiments were stirred up by the *Herald* (18 Sept. 1909) which proclaimed Mindanao a prime example of "Anglo-Saxon statesmanship" menaced by the "prospect... of being turned over to the vagaries of a people a very small percentage of whom are far removed from the petty tribal headman." The campaign was strongest between 1905 and 1909 and was led mainly by Zamboanga merchants. Despite their distance, Davao planters were also active, spurred by "a personal pride in the Davao colony [in which] many of them have a financial interest" (*MH*, 20 June 1906; Hartley 1981-82, 105). Planters capitalized on official pronouncements that argued the uniqueness of the province when compared to the rest of the Philippines (*MH*, 29 July 1905). In 1909, when Acting Governor Hoyt recommended that Mindanao be separated from the Philippines, many planters welcomed this possibility of a "separatist" alliance between officials and settlers (*RGMP* 1909, 5). This was, in fact, the apex of the movement, however, which thereafter quickly lost steam.

## The End of a Frontier Dream

The structural weaknesses that undermined the province's ability to fight for autonomy, much less separation, from Manila (see chapter 2) were aggravated by the failure of its supporters to provide the "popular groundswell" needed to refute Filipino claims that separatism was an army fabrication. The American settlers, in particular, the province's most reliable supporters, failed to live up to official expectations. For while they were indeed enjoying a new status in Davao, underneath the veneer of success, a series of problems plagued them.

First was stalled population growth and capital investment. After the 1906-1909 "abaca boom" which attracted over 5,000 Americans, the population did not increase further because Davao was unable to compete with other locations for settlers and capital. Two factors seem to have been significant: the district's remoteness, which offset abaca's profitability, and the 1,024-hectare limit for corporations, which was deemed inadequate to achieve sufficient economies of scale (Wernstedt and Simkins 1965, 87). Potential investors, "fearful of Philippine restrictions, opted to invest instead in Hawaii and Cuba (Smith 1969, 20)." And within the Philippines, Zamboanga, the provincial capital, and Manila, the colonial capital, were more attractive areas for start-up businesses. Officials subsidized shipping links between Zamboanga and Davao in an attempt to facilitate intraprovincial trade in hemp. Most Zamboanga merchants, however, preferred to trade with Manila, Australia, or Hong Kong. Furthermore, hemp could be purchased in Bikol, where production would peak in 1915, rather than in Davao, which lacked a sizeable local market for goods from outside (Owen 1984, 79; *MH*, 6 July 1907, 12 June 1909).

Second, the settlers were unable to sustain the boom in the face of problems like pestilence and a sporadic labor supply, which ultimately spelled disaster for many hemp (and also coconut) plantations (Hartley 1983, 214; Boyce 1914, 364-65). The basic problem was that the supply of indigenous labor could not keep up with the increase in the number of plantations (*RGMP* 1904, 2 and 1907, 32; Hartley 1983, 75). The Americans also encountered resistance to the new work routine and complained that the "hill people... were timid and not used to disciplined hard work measured by the clock. They knew nothing about the value of time as money. Even when they had worked on a plantation for quite some time, the majority of them would occasionally take a week or a month off without prior notice to hunt in the mountains or trade with neighboring tribes" (Hayase 1984, 75-76). Inadequate wages (50 centavos a day), at a time of worsening labor shortage, led indigenous laborers to steadily abandon their new livelihoods and return to the hills (*RGMP* 1911, 11). Neither could the settlers attract enough labor from the Visayas. Low wages, competition from state road-building projects closer to home, fear of Muslims, planter racism, and the opposition of Visayan politicians to the loss of their constituents stymied these efforts (Hayase 1984, 76-78; *RGMP* 1912, 12-13; *PFP*, 17 Mar. 1907).

Third, while the Moro Province supervised Davao lightly, its few interventions into district affairs proved detrimental to settler needs. One example is the case of the tribal ward system. In an effort to gain control over indigenous labor, settlers had themselves appointed ward leaders, positions meant to be filled by "natives." Zamboanga, however, rejected this use of the ward system as a tool of labor management (*MH*, 29 Feb. 1908). In 1908, Governor Bliss censured the Davao district governor for permitting a situation that would lead to labor exploitation and reminded him that there "is no safety except in the absolute separation of the planters from any direct or indirect official connection with the Government" (as quoted in Hayase 1984, 95). Reports of abuses, however, continued. A 1910 court case involving the killing of an escaping Bilaan datu, allegedly by an American constabulary inspector, turned out to be a cover-up for the conduct of planters who "go to extreme lengths to secure the native tribesmen and compel them to work in the hemp plantation" (*PFP*, 7 May 1910). To stop the abuses, officials concerned eventually passed a provincial law ensuring fair treatment of labor

(*RGMP* 1913, 57). The policy of "native" protection as an aspect of the "civilizing" mission thus worked against the settlers' interests and added to growing settler frustration.

The "civil society" that both settlers and Moro Province officials thought would spring from Davao therefore fell short of expectations. The settlers brought about the initial economic growth of the provincial backwater, but were unable to sustain it. This, in turn, diminished the efficacy of their voice in the debate over the fate of the Moro Province. Provincial officials might declare them trailblazers on the last American frontier, but in reality they were simply rural counterparts of their more cosmopolitan countrymen in Manila and Zamboanga. As Americans, they were privileged in their district, but as country-brothers, their voice was the last to be considered in Manila.

In a peculiar way, therefore, the politically reliable American settlers were no more useful to the Moro Province than the less-trusted Magindanaos. Both were minor actors whose influence was restricted to their respective districts and whose fate was dependent on the actions of more powerful external actors. The defeat of the proautonomy forces within southern Mindanao and in Manila, and the approval by Washington of increased Filipino participation, spelled the end of the settlers' political dream. Whereas the Magindanaos, as "natives" of the integrated colonial body politic, could shift loyalties to Manila and start new political lives, the Davao settlers, being American, had only two unattractive options. They could accept Filipino hegemony, or leave.

At the same time, the limits to abaca production within the existing land, labor, and capital parameters were being reached and settler corporations were beginning to falter.[5] Then the price of hemp slumped, and attempts to control production and fix prices failed because of limited resources. As their condition worsened, planters began to react individually and the Davao Planters Association unraveled (*MH*, 20 June 1908; Hayase 1984, 63, 73, 207). By 1915, the second year into Filipinization and of the new Manila-run Department of Mindanao and Sulu, American planters had lost most of their money as well as their interest in hemp production (Gowing 1981-82, 19; Gowing 1983, 197). In the second decade of colonial rule, most of the farms were sold to the Japanese and the last western frontier faded into memory.

## Davao-kuo

The Japanese began arriving in the Philippines in small groups in 1903.[6]

Most were escaping a rural Japan that was "hard hit by the increase in land taxes following the Meiji Restoration of 1868... fluctuating rice prices, the influx of demobilized soldiers after the 1894-1895 Sino-Japanese war, and the 1898 crop failure" (Furiya 1993, 156). The first wave of immigrant workers were granted work permits by the Philippine colonial government and found employment as far north as the Benguet road construction project and as far south as the hemp plantations of Davao. In Davao, their numbers increased steadily during the first decade of American rule and their involvement in abaca production resembled that of the Americans: business ventures by small independent producers and their laborers (Hashiya 1993, 137). These first landowners were forced to abandon their farms after colonial laws made explicit the prohibition of land ownership by foreigners, but the next wave of immigrants was able to skirt the regulations and renew their involvement in hemp production.[7] They steadily caught up with American and Spanish abaca planters by duplicating and then improving on their technology, and by the second decade of colonial rule had replaced their rivals (Hashiya 1993; *MN*, Apr. 1938). The Japanese population declined in the first half of the 1920s but rebounded after the Great Depression, and by the eve of World War II reached 20,000. This pervasive Japanese presence earned the province the moniker "Davao-kuo" (Furiya 1993, 155; see, in particular, Furiya's table 1).

Several things distinguish the experience of the Japanese from the Americans in Davao and help us understand why the later migrants were so much more successful. While both regarded Davao as a potential source of wealth, the Americans saw themselves as settlers taking possession of the frontier, superior to all other residents and settlers in the Moro Province. This self-image narrowly channeled their efforts into the single ambition of becoming plantation owners. The Japanese came with the intention of amassing savings, returning home, and living improved lives; they were therefore willing to take advantage of any opportunity that presented itself, from land purchase to retail trade to work as hired plantation hands.

The Japanese also had the full support of their state. After its victory in the Russo-Japanese War of 1904-1905, the Japanese state expanded its presence in Southeast Asia. Japanese consulates established in the late 1890s and the early 1900s began to assert their authority over Japanese communities in Singapore, Manila, Batavia, and Surabaya. They oversaw the removal of Japanese prostitutes whose presence in the region contradicted the new Japanese image of "honorary Europeans" and assisted "associations" in their economic ventures and welfare programs for their communities. The consulates also facilitated migration from the Japanese prefectures to Davao. Very soon, the Japanese presence in the hemp, as well as in the smaller coconut industry, began to be conspicuous (Shiraishi and Shiraishi 1993, 8-9, 14-15).

The role of the Japanese state (a *fourth* state actor in addition to the provincial, colonial, and metropolitan states) underscores the importance of institutional support to those involved in opening frontier areas like Davao. Settlers might have enthusiasm and serious commitment to "taming the frontier," but these were not enough to sustain success. State support was particularly important in facilitating initial capital investment, maintaining a steady supply of labor, and creating marketing networks. State support for settlement was what Moro Province officials had ignored, blinded by their misplaced sense of American superiority. In conjunction with this crucial factor, Japanese production had three further interlocking features that help explain its success: superior corporate organization with adequate capital support; ingenious schemes of accumulating land to achieve both economies of scale and a well-organized labor pool; and a comfortable relationship with the Filipinized colonial state.

Remembering the forced abandonment of landownership by the first planters, the second wave of Japanese settlers devised a number of schemes to circumvent the prohibition on foreign ownership and leasing. At the heart of all these ventures was an agreement between a Filipino with land title or lease and a Japanese flagship corporation, formed to achieve economies of scale and coordinated production (Hayase 1984, 137-38). Two such Japanese corporations came to establish a commanding presence in Davao. The Ohta Development Corporation, set up by Ohta Kyosaburo, "father of Davao's development," was the pioneer in Davao abaca production (*PFP,* 10 Nov. 1917). Established on 3 May 1907, with very little capital, Ohta went through the birth pangs of the industry, at one time facing bankruptcy, before becoming successful. Ohta's biggest competitor, Furukawa Yoshizu's Furukawa Plantation Company, entered the industry almost a decade later with financial backing from a Japanese *zaibatsu*, Ito Shoten. This capitalization and the timing of his start-up allowed Furukawa to quickly gain control of failing American and Filipino plantations and farms (Hashiya 1993, 137; Corcino 1992, 13, 30; Hayase 1984, 158). After World War I, other large Japanese firms began investing in Mindanao, led by Mitsui Corporation, which established its own trading firms and timber sawmills. Their entry into Davao marked a considerable expansion of Japanese capital and they became a stabilizing presence in the province (*Commonwealth Advocate*, 18 July 1941).

Japanese corporate partnership with Filipino leaseholders and landowners took a variety of forms, the purpose of all of which was land accumulation. Some partnerships were characterized as "farm management contracts." The Filipino partners were settlers who had mortgaged their land or had difficulty paying their lease and found the Japanese offer of management in return for a fixed percentage of revenues quite attractive (*Commonwealth Advocate*, Dec. 1940; Yulo 1934). The "joint venture agreement" with local "companies" was an expanded version of the management contract and involved the Japanese providing capital to a Filipino (or American) partner to set up a local corporation. This local corporation then entered into joint abaca production with either Ohta or Furukawa, which lined up Japanese buyers. The links between manufacturer and market were strengthened by lines of credit from Japanese banks, present in Davao by the 1930s (Hartendorp 1961, 377).

Finally, a popular system of subleasing introduced by Ohta, called *pakyaw,* gained notoriety in the 1910s and 1920s (Hayase 1984, 251). Farolan (1935, 113) described the system this way:

> A [Japanese] fellow gathers a group of workers then enters into a contract with a [usually Filipino] lessor or landowner to work up the latter's landholding, the crop proceeds to be divided between the two parties in accordance with the nature of the work to be done. Where the land to be worked is still a virgin forest, the crop proceeds are so divided as to give the contractor 85 or 90 percent and the owner over 10 or 15 percent. Where the land has been partly cleared, the share of the owner may be more. Generally the contractors have insisted on a definite period in which they should develop and cultivate the land, 10 to 15 years, so as to be able to recover with a fair return the investment of capital and labor they have made.

Many Filipino lessors and landowners, lacking capital, labor, and government support to open up virgin forests, were happy to lease their lands to the Japanese. Not only was someone else clearing and cultivating the land, but they were also assured a percentage of production for ten to fifteen years (Farolan 1935, 11-12; Horn 1941, 271. Pakyaw became a source of tension between the Japanese and colonial officials who regarded it as a violation of land laws prohibiting subleasing and/or subcontracting to foreigners (Report of the Special Congressional Committee on Land Grants,

6 Nov. 1931, 5, 9). But as the American high commissioner admitted, the Japanese could easily argue that "the agreements were 'managerial contracts' and not subleases" (U.S. High Commissioner to the Philippines Sixth Annual Report 1943, 106).

Like pakyaw, the nature of Japanese and Japanese-sponsored corporations was ambiguous and controversial (Early 1930, 10). By presenting a Filipino board of directors, these corporations qualified as nonforeign and could acquire land for abaca production within the prescribed legal limit. Acquisition beyond the limit, necessary for sufficient economies of scale, led to the creation of more and more corporations. Legally "separate entities," these subsidiaries, joint ventures, and interlocking directorates of Ohta and Furukawa were "in reality... units in a large and general scheme of exploitation and colonization" (Hayase 1984, 159; *PFP*, 3 Nov. 1917; Furiya 1993, 157). The legal status of the "dummy" corporations was never resolved, partly because the Japanese were able to twist legal logic in their favor. And while there were protests by politicians and journalists in Manila, Japanese influence over local and colonial officials (see further on) ensured that both the pakyaw and the dummies were protected from policies that could eliminate them (Report of the Special Committee on Land Grants in Mindanao, 6 Nov. 1931, 7).

Labor supply proved less of a problem for the Japanese than the Americans because the Japanese state recruited at home, amply supplying Japanese plantations with workers from the rural prefectures. With supply assured, the corporations streamlined the organization of labor in two ways: through direct company employment and via growers' contracts with Japanese farmers. Under the first system, Ohta and Furukawa used their own laborers to work on farms under the pakyaw and "dummy" systems (*PFP*, 3 May 1919). Under the second, lands would be parceled out to Japanese farmers who signed contracts to undertake the work for the company and sell it the produce later (*MT*, 31 Oct. 1917). The farmer (*jieisha*) cleared the land, planted it with abaca, and administered it for ten to fifteen years, one life cycle of the abaca plant. He shouldered all expenses related to production, including payment of land taxes. He then sold his harvest to the company (owned by Furukawa or Ohta) and received 95 percent of the profit from the yield while the corporation retained 5 percent as land rent.[8] The jieisha often hired Filipinos to clear lands and plant abaca; otherwise they used family labor, which accrued substantial savings for themselves and the companies they worked for (Corcino 1993, 12; Hayase 1984, 186-87; Cody 1959, 174).

The number of jieisha reached 3,062 by 1935. They worked on over 18,933 hectares of non-Japanese lands and 7,818 hectares of Japanese land. Hayase (1984, 188) adds that "[2,064] of the 3,062 Japanese jieisha worked on non-Japanese plantations and among them 1,798 were situated in Filipino plantations. By 1935, out of a total of 34,689,340 abaca hills planted by the Japanese, 6,358,990 hills or 18 percent were cultivated directly by Japanese plantation companies; an additional 30 percent was done by the jieisha on Japanese plantations, while 52 percent was tended by the *jieisha* on non-Japanese plantations. In other words, 82 percent of all Japanese abaca plants were planted by Japanese jieisha." This system was profitable for both corporations and the jieisha who were remitting about 75,000 pesos home per week (Trinidad, 1935, 14). The Japanese association gave the jieisha support, taking "charge of depositing its members' savings in Tokyo banks" and functioning as a lending agency for the jieisha (Saniel 1966, 125-26). The Japanese state continued to play a role as well, with the consulate exercising "a large measure of control over emigrants [so that] the companies [had] no difficulty in the selection of competent assignees nor in exerting a comprehensive social and economic discipline over them" (United States High Commissioner 1943, 106).

As news of Japanese success spread beyond Davao, their plantations began to attract Filipino migrant labor. By the end of 1936, Filipinos had become the largest group in Davao (79,092), surpassing both the non-Christians (68,346) and the Japanese (12,244).[9] Filipinos were drawn to Japanese plantations (as they had not been to American plantations) because of decent treatment and adequate social welfare (Cody 1959, 182-83). There were occasional reports of Japanese labor abuse on the plantations, but these were the exception; in general, Filipinos appeared to have no problems working for the Japanese (*Roth,* 19 May 1935). While critical of them, Vice-Governor Joseph Hayden (23 Feb. 1935) conceded that the "Japanese have invested forty to fifty million pesos and given employment to about forty thousand Filipinos... At present 12,000 Filipinos [are] employed by the Japanese [and] three-fifths (3/5) of government revenues [of] Davao [come] from Japanese plantations and stores."

In 1917, Japanese control of plantation lands stood at 19,833 hectares, while American control had fallen to 4,543 hectares; Filipino, 7,294 hectares; Chinese, 1,314 hectares; and Arab, 960 hectares (*PFP*, 16 Feb. 1918). By the late 1920s the Japanese had full economic control of the abaca industry, from production to trading, from land control to labor supervision (De

Guzman, 8 Dec. 1930). In 1930, the Davao governor reported that the Japanese "control all the regions between the Davao and Hijo rivers, as well as Samal Island—that is their control covers the richest agricultural lands in the province" (Early 1930). The industry leveled off in the early 1930s, but boomed again in the middle of the decade when direct shipping links were established between Davao and Japan (Wernstedt 1957, 79). Through these connections, Japanese demand kept production rising and balanced out the low seasons with extended booms. In 1932, Japan become the second leading importer of Manila hemp and the following year surpassed the United States to become the top importer of that product, the Philippines' second most important export.[10] And in 1937, despite the Sino-Japanese war, Japan entrenched herself further as second to the United States as the Philippines' overall trade partner with an annual trade of 52 million pesos (Saniel 1966, 115-16). So important was the Philippines that, according to one author, the "trade map on the wall of the Japanese consul [in Davao] labeled the island of Mindanao, along with Korea and Formosa, as 'domestic'" (Friend 1965, 76).

By the Commonwealth period, Japanese control of abaca lands had achieved the American ambition of making Davao a thriving economic zone and abaca a major Philippine commodity (*ET*, 24 Mar. 1931; Hayase 1984, 208; *PFP*, 4 July 1931, and 11 Nov. 1933). The colonial state benefited immensely from this transformation, reaping unexpected revenue earnings from the province's tax payments which by 1932-33 exceeded those of Zamboanga, the erstwhile top tax contributor from Mindanao (table 1). Other evidence of its progress was an increased cost of living. Because abaca dominated agriculture (90 percent of exports), over half of Mindanao's imports were foodstuffs. According to Hayase (1984, 276), "from its inception Davao was importing only 1,200 piculs of rice a month. But by 1929, over 12 million kilos of rice were imported. The people of Davao had become totally dependent on a cash crop economy developed around abaca cultivation." As a result, in the 1930s cost of living was very high in Davao, being more expensive than Lingayen, Manila, and Zamboanga (ibid., 277-78). These changes in the local economy had detrimental effects on subsistence crops and consumer access to them. But it also signified the success that abaca production had brought to the province.

Table 1. Internal revenue collection, Mindanao, 1932-33 (in pesos)

| Province | 1932 | 1933 |
|---|---|---|
| Agusan | 80,466 | 69,267 |
| Bukidnon | 24,940 | 21,292 |
| Cotabato | 128,736 | 107,469 |
| Davao | 484,840 | 416,906 |
| Lanao | 107,856 | 101,422 |
| Misamis Occidental | 144,684 | 121,622 |
| Misamis Oriental | 155,639 | 134,713 |
| Sulu | 112,335 | 100,770 |
| Surigao | 117,581 | 95,679 |
| Zamboanga | 411,307 | 309,742 |

Source: *Philippine Statistical Review* 1, 2 (1934): 92.

## Local Power and Colonial Authority

Davao's contributions to colonial coffers made the province an economic asset to the Commonwealth and to Manuel Quezon. Yet, instead of extending his authoritarian grasp, Quezon did nothing to alter Japanese domination of Davao. On the contrary, he took steps to protect their de facto control. One obvious reason was that Quezon could use the enormous wealth of the Japanese to enhance his power more advantageously through ongoing political relations than through outright expropriation. In fact, as noted by Grant Goodman (1967, vii-viii), the relationship between the Japanese in Davao and the Philippine government was "basically good and in fact getting better as World War II began." Still, Goodman leaves unexplained the process by which the Japanese became the most important political force in the province. We need to know how this foreign minority group wielded power locally and beyond, while indigenous "minorities" in Mindanao were unable to do so. I suggest that an important clue is revealed by the territory's relationship with Manila during the two important phases of colonial state formation in southern Mindanao.

Populated mainly by small and diverse "Bagobo" tribes, Davao under the Moro Province did not warrant the same attention the U.S. army gave to the "unstable" districts of Sulu, Cotabato, and Lanao. The province encouraged American settlement, but its failure to prosper underscored the peripheral nature of the district. Under Filipinization, Davao became a regular province and had a provincial and municipal government structure controlled by the local Nacionalistas. Yet the province's distance meant that Filipino leaders gave little attention to the province. Not until the 1930s, when Manila-based journalists noticed the extent of Japanese control in Davao, did Manila politicians act. And when they did, they defended rather than criticized the Japanese.

This official indifference allowed the Japanese to establish themselves in Davao's abaca economy and to play an influential role in its emergent local politics. Corruption and administrative ineptitude facilitated Japanese ability to put these officials under their sway (Manrique, 18 June to 31 Dec. 1938). For a fee, local Filipino leaders assisted the Japanese in convincing, and if necessary forcing, indigenous communities to work on Japanese farms (Hayase 1984, 253; *MT*, 4 Jan. 1920; Jose 1992, 44-45). They protected the Japanese from the local "gangsters and racketeers" who thrived in Davao and helped them accumulate land (Hayase 1984, 169-70). Gov. Sebastian Generoso, who was actively involved in amassing lands for the Japanese, was known as a petty tyrant who used his official position for personal ends.[11] Generoso was in good company. Juan Sarenas was accused of the same charges, especially of using his office to employ family and friends (Early n.d.; *MT*, 18 July 1916). Romualdo Quimpo, a former justice of the peace and later Davao governor, not only filled staff positions with relatives and town mates, but also demanded "15.00 pesos to 20.00 pesos for every homestead application and for every final proof thereafter." He was known to "oversee" the disposition of Bagobo lands and to send policemen to intimidate those who refused to abide by his wishes (JRH Box 30-17). It is not far-fetched to suppose that the Japanese were prepared to capitalize on these transgressions to maintain their influence.

Low salaries and the displeasure of some insular officials with their assignments also provided motivation to work for the Japanese (Official Roster of Employees 1929, 172-73). Extra income was indispensable and much could be earned working as "dummies" or subcontracting land purchased with financial assistance from the Japanese (*PFP*, 26 Jan. 1918; *ABK*, 24 Oct. 1930). The Japanese paid well for the services of such officials. A Captain Valeriano, for example, was observed to be "notoriously friendly towards the Japanese and intolerant towards the Bagobos [and] was rumored [to have] received 6,000 pesos from the Japanese funds of Akamine and Furukawa" (Hayase 1984, 271, n. 89; *PFP*, 17 Feb. 1917). Similar complaints were raised with the Bureau of Non-Christian Tribes about its own agents filing land claims on behalf of the Bagobos, then subletting these lands to the Japanese (Early 1930, 11).

Personal interest was not the sole reason for seeking support from the Japanese. Local officials were also encouraged by political circumstances to do so. While the provincial capital had been designated a city by the Commonwealth and received the highest provincial allocation, its administrative infrastructure and financial management remained inadequate (*PFP*, 21 Oct. 1915). Davao's minor role in Manila's affairs often left it short of funds due to delayed disbursements. Gov. J.C. Early (n.d., 11) commented that the provincial government had only "built 50 kilometers [of roads] in 20 years" while the "larger planters in the same time have built 450 kilometers." To enable their offices to remain in operation, officials often turned to the Japanese for financial help (Elayda, 30 Oct. 1939). The Japanese were happy to oblige in order to strengthen their influence among provincial officials.

Intimate ties with leading Davao personalities were also vital. Many were placed on retainership and "wined-and-dined" by their benefactors (Goodman 1967, 46). The Japanese were particularly aware that these officials were allies of powerful politicians like Quezon. Legally trained as lawyers, many city and municipal officials were hired by the Japanese to take care of legal matters and present a unified stand against any effort to investigate Japanese companies (Farolan 1935, 7-8; 9-11; Goodman 1967, 34-35; Hayase 1984, 171-72). So powerful was the hold of the Japanese over the local legal profession that a special committee report to the Philippine Assembly admitted that "any practicing attorney and the Fiscal [involved] in the investigation of violations of the Public Land Laws would surely fail in his practice here in Davao" because "almost all [Davao lawyers] are dependent in their practice upon the alien residents whose disfavor may result in professional suicide" (Report of the Special Committee on Land Grants, 6 Nov. 1931, 2). That Davao's political leaders were engaged in partisan politics did not worry the Japanese. To ensure that they would not be caught in the middle of vicious disputes, the Japanese association and the local consulate supported both factions (*ABK*, 17 Oct. 1930; *PFP*, 4 Nov. 1933). While Filipino politicians traded charges of being in the pay of the Japanese, it was clear to all that these "accusations were only campaign propaganda and had no malicious intent against the Japanese" (Goodman 1967, 46). This influence over local politics guaranteed unhampered economic activity on the abaca farms and created a mantle of protection from questions from Manila about their control over the province.

A feature that further distinguished the Japanese from the other Mindanao "minorities" was their influence on politics at the center. Unlike the Muslims, the Japanese had influence at the highest levels of the colonial state, thanks to an energetic consulate that solicited allies in the constitutional convention and legislature and among Quezon and his allies.[12] All this became valuable once anti-Japanese political forces attacked the economic success of Davao.[13] With their allies' support, the Japanese were able to deflect criticism in the media and the efforts of unsympathetic government officials to undermine their control of the abaca industry. Legislators defended Japanese interests in the halls of congress, while political leaders were even reported to have exonerated the Japanese invasion of Manchuria (Horn 1941, 263-64). Jose P. Laurel, Pedro Sabido, and Bureau of Commerce Secretary Tomas Confesor lobbied on behalf of Japanese interests in the cabinet (*MH*, 14 May 1931; *Commonwealth Advocate*, 1 June 1936). Laurel, principal in a top Manila law firm, was particularly active in representing his Japanese clients against charges of illegal land arrangements (Gleeck 1984, 343). He fought hard to pressure officials in charge of public lands to exclude the Japanese from their investigations and appealed cases decided against them (Laurel, 25 Oct. 1933).

The Japanese knew that their economic interests could not be seriously threatened because they had sympathy in two important places: with Quezon and the Americans. In 1920, Quezon was instrumental in passing a senate act giving legal recognition to existing Japanese leases, thereby exempting them from the stipulations of the Public Land Act.[14] Quezon's close ties with American supporters of Filipinization, notably Harrison, also effectively neutralized potential opposition to the Japanese from the American side (Hayase 1984, 174). As Commonwealth president, Quezon was believed to be influenced strongly by the views of his pro-Japanese officials, notably Laurel. Yet it was also clear that he saw the advantages of a friendly Japan to the soon-to-be-independent Philippines (Friend 1965, 181). The Quezon-controlled *Manila Times* was a consistent defender of Japanese interests in Davao and led the propaganda counteroffensive in Manila against those demanding the termination of Japanese subleases and the pakyaw system (24 Oct. 1918). Quezon, according to Morokuma Yasaku, head of the Ohta Development Company, was a good friend (Goodman 1967, 13-14).

Despite occasional muckraking in American-owned newspapers,

American attitudes toward the Davao Japanese were mainly positive. Officials applauded the superiority of Japanese economic organization that played a big role in the economic development of Davao. Others even publicly denied that the Japanese had violated land laws (Goodman 1967, 8-10). By the late 1930s, pressure from Washington to keep American-Japanese relations harmonious dictated American local official actions. The American high commissioner Frank Murphy, for example, assured the Japanese consul general Uchiyama that United States-Japanese relations were of such importance that what was happening in the Philippines would not be allowed to cloud the "friendship." He also promised to "work for an equitable solution [to the 'Davao problem'] by conveying Uchiyama's views to Quezon the next time he talked with him" (Goodman 1967, 72).

That the Davao lands escaped expropriation under Quezon was evidence of the utility of maintaining influence in Manila. Apart from defending the Japanese from attack in congress and the media, this coterie of supporters helped the Japanese lobby for revisions in public land laws to prevent the confiscation of their lands (Jose 1992, 81, 87). They stymied efforts by crucial agencies like the Lands Office to implement directives detrimental to the Japanese (Annual Report of the Director of Lands 1939, 62, 77). The most important public statement of support came from Quezon who, after a Davao visit, declared that "there is nothing in the so-called Davao problem that should cause concern" in the Philippines.[15] He reiterated this official—and unchallenged—position in a speech at a Tokyo dinner given in his honor by the Philippine Society of Japan, where he informed his audience that "nothing more has been said in the newspaper about the so-called problem" (Quirino 1971, 81). These two assertions made by Quezon at the height of his power ended debate on the issue and the efforts by some of his officials to investigate and terminate the Japanese land leases (Goodman 1967, 25).

These allies also emboldened the Japanese. The Japanese Club of Davao issued a statement that it would defend "to the last drop of their blood" the lands under their control (Jose 1992, 155). There were also Japanese public protests in Davao against statements and actions by Filipino officials pursuing the investigation and confiscation of Japanese lands (*PM*, July 1938). While the consulate and leaders of the Japanese associations in Davao and Manila preferred to use the quiet and effective influence of Filipino and American leaders, they could not totally stop such public displays among their constituents. These began to be more prominent just as the Japanese state was perceived to be increasingly expansionist (Jose 1992, 88).

On the eve of World War II, the Japanese had reached the peak of their economic control of Davao. This was not power in the service of an expansionist state; its origins predated Japanese militarist expansionism. While there were those who did support militarism, the majority of the colonists were concerned with the original economic goals of the settlement (Jose 1992, 115-16). All this ended with the outbreak of World War II.

## Conclusion

As a settlement zone in the farthest periphery, Davao's role in colonial state formation was dependent on the deployment of people who would proceed to exploit its resources while assisting colonial officials in establishing a state presence. The better organized the deployment, the more successful were economic development and political administration. This was the crucial distinction between the Japanese and the American settlers. The superior organization of the Japanese was employed to bring in settlers and achieve maximum productivity from Japanese migrant labor. This efficient machine was particularly vital for a commodity like hemp which demands economies of scale in both the production and distribution phases. The Americans, spurred by the western frontier tradition, encouraged individual settlers to tame the Davao frontier, only to discover fatally that the rugged individual was not appropriate for a commodity that was extensively traded worldwide.

There was closer similarity between the two settler groups in facilitating colonial state formation in Davao. Both were effect agents of the two regimes (the army and the Filipinos) in helping the state set up structures and agencies, and, in the case of the American settlers, helping provide the necessary personnel for the state to start functioning. The settler groups were also pioneers of local power in the area by virtue of their close collaboration with the colonial state. The army usually deferred to the settlers in Davao, while Quezon and the Filipinos set up an arrangement with the Japanese that acknowledged their control of Davao (including power over local Filipino politicians) in exchange for monetary and other patronage support. But the superiority of the Japanese organizational machine made it more influential in defining local politics and in determining how Manila politicians treated Davao. In fact, the Japanese were the only "minority" group to achieve such power over colonial politics.

"Davao-kuo's" progress ended with World War II, after which the settlers were "relocated" back to Okinawa and the Japanese main islands. These settlers and their American predecessors, however, had laid an economic infrastructure that would define the future of Davao under the new republic. The origins of this plantation-based, settler- and corporation-managed infrastructure have been erroneously dated by more recent scholarship to Marcos' martial law regime. This brief historical review, however, shows that the "spread of capitalism" in southern Mindanao far predated 1972. Its lineage can be traced to the first decade of colonial rule when American settlers opened up their first hemp plantation. That lineage blossomed under the Japanese whose exceptional labor, production, and marketing organization boosted Davao into one of the Philippines'—not just southern Mindanao's—top export-producing regions. After World War II, this stature was temporarily lost, but the infrastructure remained. Under the Marcos dictatorship it would be revived.

CHAPTER 5

# Demographic Change and Social Stability on the Postwar Frontier

Like the Dutch in the Netherlands East Indies and the British in Malaya, the American colonial state in Mindanao collapsed abruptly during World War II (Baclagon 1988, 6–7). In its wake, scattered incidents of Muslim-Christian confrontation and other forms of "privatized" violence took place all over the island.[1] But numerous anti-Japanese guerrilla groups also materialized from among those Filipino and American troops who refused to surrender. These units were formally organized under one guerrilla command but remained mistrustful of each other. The lure of military largesse from Australia put a stop to the unrestrained violence that preceded their unification and kept them focused on the Japanese.[2]

Within two years, this guerrilla army controlled "about 95 percent of the total area of the island" and awaited the return of the Americans.[3] Guerrilla success, however, owed less to fighting ability than to Japanese indifference to Mindanao and the rest of the Philippines, which they saw mainly as a transit connection between Japan and the more strategic Netherlands East Indies.[4] In Mindanao, therefore, certain prewar processes survived because of the absence of war-induced social disruption. Some political leaders who had worked for the Americans became prominent collaborators under the Japanese. Those who became guerrillas essentially continued governing the areas they controlled in much the same manner as before the war, with provisions for Japanese attacks as the only new and complicating factor.[5]

The Americans returned to Mindanao in April 1945, just as the Japanese launched their only major offensive against guerrilla forces in the Bukidnon, Misamis, and Cotabato areas (Baclagon 1963, 292–94). The "liberation" of Mindanao—an unnecessary exercise given Mindanao's limited value to the Allied counteroffensive—took four months to complete but was relatively uncomplicated. No cities or towns were destroyed, no province was burned to the ground by either the retreating Japanese or the advancing Americans, and while over 36,000 Japanese were killed, Filipino and American casualties were light. Mindanao was thus spared the devastation American liberation wrought on the rest of the Philippines, and it was this condition that made the island an asset to the new Philippine Republic, whose problems after the war were abundant: the outbreak of a communist-led rebellion in the northern Philippines and a rapid downturn of the economy, exacerbated by elite plundering of rehabilitation funds. Relatively unscathed Mindanao appeared a likely safety valve, and attention quickly turned to its settlement and economic development.

This chapter examines the settlement of southern Mindanao, focusing on the spontaneous migration that dominated the process from 1946 to the early 1960s, and exploring the factors behind the surprising social stability of the frontier. Scholars have argued that the dramatic postwar demographic shift spawned a fragmented and volatile landscape that was itself partly responsible for the outbreak of secessionist war and communist insurgency in the 1970s and 1980s. This argument is accurate in a broad sense, although in stressing the eventual social breakdown, it is unable to explain the social stability that prevailed for roughly two decades—the period most characterized by destabilizing demographic change.

Migration did disturb the frontier, but it did not fully eliminate mechanisms of social cohesion operating within the communities in conflict. One reason for this was the absence of a feudalistic political economy: the majority of residents were owner-cultivators of small- to medium-sized properties. Both indigenous and settler groups who took possession of the available—and expanding—public lands aspired less toward increased accumulation than enhanced productivity. And while conflict did occur, these communities were less engaged in escalating confrontation than in exploiting their new lands. The other factor was the social solidarity that emerged out of these groups' proximity which had both communal (religious, linguistic) and community (place of origin) bases. Indigenous groups threatened by the deluge of migrants found that strengthening their "ethnic" and religious ties was an effective way to establish (or reestablish) a unified voice. Settlers found solidarity by preserving and reproducing in their new homes social ties from their provinces of origin. Language and kinship were especially important bonds, reinforced later by cultural animosity toward both indigenes and other settler groups. As tension between communities became more acute with the passing years, unity through these "identities" appears to have become stronger.

These were the two major reasons why social conflict was held in check from 1946 to the mid-1960s and Mindanao was not yet on the rapid downward spiral scholars have suggested. They were also the foundation upon which local power would be rejuvenated and reshaped.

## Demographic Transformation

If there is a single issue connecting the colonial and immediate postcolonial periods, it is the so-called land problem and its repercussions for the stability of the Philippine state (Sorongon 1955). An increasingly embittered peasantry became the concern of both American and Filipino leaders as revolts broke out intermittently in the late colonial period and then erupted on an unprecedented scale in the early years of the republic (Sturtevant 1976). Both the colonial and postcolonial states saw a solution to the land problem as crucial to order and economic progress for the Philippines. In attempting to resolve the issue, however, both states fell short of a radical breakup of landed estates and distribution of land to landless peasants. Such changes to the land tenure system would have destroyed the power of the landed elite, and opposition by their representatives in the colonial and postcolonial legislatures weakened any effort to effect this measure (Cushner 1976; Wurfel 1960; Connolly 1992). The preferred policy solution of state leaders was the improvement of existing land patterns without radical disturbance of landlord-tenant relations: limited land distribution, introduction of technology to increase productivity, and encouragement of migration to less developed areas where public lands could be distributed for homestead (Putzel 1992, 43–105).

Because 90 percent of its land was public, postwar Mindanao came to play a major part in this policy. In 1951, of the 29,740,972 hectares of the total Philippine land area, 61 percent (18,162,668 hectares) was classified as potential agricultural land, much of it located in "the southern underdeveloped regions of the archipelago" (Report of Special Committee on Land Settlement, mss, 1951). Mindanao's attraction was enhanced by its sparse population, having the lowest population density in the nation between 1939 and 1948. State leaders thus saw the chance to offer a discontented Filipino peasantry the opportunity to become owner-cultivators without changing existing tenancy arrangements. Migration to Mindanao was at once expected to accomplish peasant aspirations, dissipate the predilection to rebel, and ease population pressure in other parts of the Philippines.

During the colonial period, officials had also expected that migration from the civilized north would hasten the integration of non-Christian groups and improve the Filipinos themselves—making them quintessential owner-cultivators who would combine a desire for self-improvement with service to "the general welfare of the community" (Pelzer 1945, 129; Carpenter 1917, 375). The result of these early efforts, mainly directed toward Cotabato, was uneven. Peasant refusal to break ties with their home communities and reports of settlers' inability to cope with natural obstacles discouraged migration and led a number of settlements to close down (Pelzer 1945, 114; *PFP,* 11 Nov. 1933; Hartley 1983, 200–17). The Commonwealth government did a little better, especially after it became clear that "subsidized settlement was necessary for any successful major relocation to the island."[6] In 1939, the National Land Settlement Authority (NLSA) began the organized transfer of colonists to NLSA farms in Cotabato and Davao.[7] On the eve of World War II, Commonwealth planners were optimistic and intended to open more areas for colonization.[8]

Backed by memories of the NLSA's early success, postwar leaders promoting migration had a warm reception from would-be settlers (*Commerce* May 1949; *PR,* Feb. 1952, 13). Postwar economic difficulties, combined with shrinking man-to-land ratios in the northern provinces, encouraged many peasants to consider resettlement and overcome their fears of "the wild country" that was Mindanao. The result was the most massive movement of Filipinos in the history of the nation. From 1946 to about 1960, Mindanao's population grew from less than three million people to over five million, a 7.4 percent annual growth rate that was double the national rate (Oosterhout May-June 1983, 30). Net migration accounted for over half of this growth, while the rest was attributed to local births (Wernstedt and Simkins 1965, 83). There was also movement within Mindanao. Over 1.2 million people moved from densely populated to sparsely populated areas, following the opening of roads by either the government or timber companies (table 2) (Krinks 1974, ix).

In the first decade and a half after the war, newspapers reported that an average of 3,000 to 3,200 families were disembarking at major Mindanao ports every month (*MT,* 25 July 1953). The favored destinations were Cotabato and Davao, which absorbed over 60 percent of the migrants from the central and northern Philippines (Pernia 1983, 180). These provinces became the favorite terminus for migrants for a number of reasons. Cotabato had attracted settlers ever since it was targeted as the prime area for settlement in the late colonial period, and success stories from the NLSA farms were still vivid (Pelzer 1945,

Table 2. Destination of migrants to Mindanao, 1903-1909 and 1948-60, by province

| Province | Net Migration (1903–1909) | % of Total Migration | Net Migration (1948–1960) | % of Total Migration |
|---|---|---|---|---|
| Agusan | 3,014 | 4.7 | 92,971 | 7.4 |
| Bukidnon | 7,104 | 1.0 | 105,002 | 8.4 |
| Cotabato | 34,306 | 4.9 | 410,065 | 32.7 |
| Davao | 144,990 | 20.7 | 379,309 | 30.3 |
| Lanao | 163,209 | 23.3 | 164,694 | 13.2 |
| Misamis Occ. | 104,123 | 14.9 | -43,895 | -3.5 |
| Misamis Or. | 26,103 | 3.7 | -131,882 | -10.5 |
| Surigao | 43,963 | 6.3 | -13,055 | -1.0 |
| Zamboanga del Norte | 84,126 | 12.0 | 45,307 | 3.6 |
| Zamboanga del Sur | 58,163 | 8.3 | 243,633 | 19.5 |
| Total | 699,101 | 99.8 | 1,252,149 | 100.1 |

*Source:* Wernstedt and Simkins 1965, 92.

127–59; Pfanner 1958, 29–48). Cotabato in particular drew settlers from the western Visayan provinces who were compelled to move by the displacement of food crop farms by sugar plantations in Negros Occidental and Oriental and by poor land quality in Aklan, Antique, Capiz, and Panay. The desire to escape destitution coincided with the development of interisland shipping as some semblance of normalcy returned in the postwar period. Shipping companies found a mother lode in the settlers, while families were assured that there was regular passage between their old and new homes. The result of this mutual interest was the development of a western shipping route that connected the western Visayas to Cotabato. While it was not as profitable as the routes that developed in central Philippines, and was plied by ships which were slow and unsafe for perilous passages, this western route gave some regularity to the movement of people.[9] Enterprising individuals and groups enhanced this connection by organizing the recruitment and transportation of settlers to Cotabato (Resettlement in the Philippines, n.d., 148–53).

Davao's appeal came from its wide expanse of public land. In 1949, out of Davao's total area of 1,949,895 hectares, 373,383 hectares were "certified alienable" and 4,818 hectares were pending certification from the Bureau of Lands, "leaving thereby an area about 1,571,649 hectares of public forest lands, 87 to 90 percent of which are heavily forested" (Pacis 1930, 99). This land was available for settlement once timber companies had cleared their concessions (*MinT,* 30 Mar. 1951). Migrants from central and northern Philippines quickly seized this opportunity and arrived in substantial numbers.[10] There were also former Japanese abaca lands which had been reverted back to the Philippine government after the war (*MinT,* 13 Sept. 1952). These too were declared public lands available to homesteaders and agricultural corporations interested in reviving the once-flourishing abaca industry (*MT,* 25 Jan. 1948). The Japanese legacy in Davao was a sense of prosperity and a tradition of starting from scratch. If the Japanese could transform Davao into the most productive province of the country, Filipino migrants saw no reason why they could not duplicate the feat. The government encouraged this sentiment of inevitable progress with Mindanao's popular postwar description, "Land of Promise."

In the 1950s, migration to Mindanao further accelerated. The secretary of agriculture's report to the Cabinet illustrated the speed with which people applied for land in Mindanao. He reported late in 1950 that

> applications approved from 1949 to date totaled 29,756, covering an area of 222,474 hectares, against 9,737 applications covering 76,438 hectares during the preceding two years… [P]atents [i.e., land titles] approved during the period totaled 6,564 covering 70,872 hectares, against 1,245 in 1947–48, covering an area of 24,042 hectares (*MinT,* 14 Sept. 1950).

Within a decade and a half over 1.2 million Filipinos left their homes to move to the frontier (Wernstedt and Simkins 1965, 92). This postwar movement of people constitutes the most important social change in the Philippines in the postwar period. Studies of the 1950s, however, generally emphasize the communist rebellion in Luzon island and the regeneration of the Philippine polity with the installation of a "reformist" regime as the major events defining the decade. Scholars highlight these issues for good reason: the postwar state experienced a profound crisis during this period (Wurfel 1988, 13–17). But they generally overlook the remarkable role migration played in restoring state capacities. The demographic shift helped to undermine the communist movement by providing an alternative to rebellion for actual and potential supporters of the Partido Komunista ng Pilipinas. It alleviated land pressure in provinces with high population density. And most important of all, it allowed state leaders to address the land problem without resorting to radical measures like ending the onerous tenancy system or expropriating huge landed estates for distribution to the rural poor (*MinT*, 14 Sept. 1950).

These benefits accrued without the need for much state effort or expenditure, for postwar migration was dominated by spontaneous and unorganized movement of people. As the phenomenon acquired a self-sustaining momentum, government-sponsored settlement became a minor player in the process. Among those participating in government-sponsored migration, many found that the programs did not live up to their expectations. Most failed to achieve their goal of making independent owner-cultivators out of settlers and many of the colonies were described as economically unviable. Reasons for the failure of these planned colonization programs ranged from incompetence and corruption in the land settlement agencies to the failure of settlements to coalesce into productive associations (see chapter 6).

While the state thus had reason to laud voluntary resettlement, this type of population movement had its own problems (Cuthell 1952, 1–2). Because land title applications were approved only in Manila and only upon completion of an officially designated land survey, classification, and division, disputes over first rights to a given piece of public land were frequent. Those who duly applied in Manila were often confronted with rival claimants when they arrived at their homesteads. These claimants might have made application through a land survey branch office in Cebu or another regional center. Because both claims were valid and the underdeveloped judicial structure was unprepared for the flood of litigation, such disputes were not quickly or easily resolved. Other prior claimants might simply have proceeded directly to Mindanao, hoping to gain official titles after finding suitable land. If these spontaneous migrants arrived in unsurveyed areas, they found themselves unable to acquire official status (Employment Problems 1969, 107). Without titles, these settlers were classified as squatters and were liable to be expelled once the land was surveyed and someone else appeared with a title. Some without titles faced penury and at least temporarily resumed their old role of tenant, now working for another settler. Others drifted into government settlement projects, hoping to be granted land titles, but living under wretched conditions.[11] Problems linked to squatting were aggravated further by corporate and individual landgrabbing, as well as by land occupation rackets that pitted one group of squatters against another (*PFP*, 12 July 1952 and 6 June 1953).

Spontaneous migration, not surprisingly, affected relations between indigenous communities and the new arrivals. While historic enmity between Muslims and Filipinos was always available as a political issue, I have argued that social friction had not been the sole determinant of their relationship before the war. In fact, throughout most of the colonial period and even during World War II, these groups had adapted to each other's needs. There was wholehearted cooperation by Magindanao datus in ensuring the success of early agricultural colonies set up by the NLSA. During World War II, the largest guerrilla force operating on the island was a combination of both groups led by Magindanao and Filipino commanders. This accommodation began to show signs of strain after the war as the abrupt change in the demographic environment and the rush for land disrupted the relationship. Tensions heightened as Muslims clashed with Christian settlers over land ownership and the role of the government land survey (Davis 1957, 17). Relations further suffered as datus who once supported colonization programs began to utilize historic differences as a tool either to launch their political careers or to invoke their status as defenders of their constituents' right to own land (*MT,* 20 Mar. 1951).

The same conditions prevailed in non-Muslim areas. In Davao, the smaller Bagobo and Ata communities found themselves increasingly marginalized by settlers, squatters, corporations, and even government land agencies seeking to appropriate land for settlement. The expansion of these outsiders was hastened as timber firms cleared their concessions, opened up new lands, and pushed indigenous groups further into the interior (Magsalin 1948). By the 1950s, signs of indigene restlessness surfaced. Davao's inner municipalities, for example, had become targets of "marauding Bagobo outlaws" seeking retaliation against the interlopers. While constabulary forces easily suppressed these bands, they nevertheless signified the appearance of social tension engendered by massive demographic movement.

Yet all this social tension was insufficient to seriously undermine political and social conditions. In the first decade and a half of the postwar period, southern Mindanao was largely stable. The volatility popularly identified with the region had not yet emerged as settlers and indigenes preserved a tenuous peace while hostility within and between the groups remained intermittent and under control (Wernstedt and Simkins 1965, 94). To account for this unusual restraint in an otherwise precarious situation, we need to look at the sources of social cohesion that survived the spontaneous, massive migration.

## Stability and the Political Economy of Postwar Mindanao

Frederick Jackson Turner (1921) argued that the American frontier created a more democratic landscape because of the freedom it offered. The easy availability of large tracts of free land not only enhanced an egalitarian condition, but allowed varied communities to coexist without constant battles over resources. Critics of Turner have pointed to the debilitating impact of frontier expansion on indigenous communities, the destruction of the ecology, and the reemergence of inequalities that settlers were trying to escape in the first place (Limerick 1987). They see the frontier as unstable, a site of cultural, economic, and political conflict involving the state, ambitious landowners, indigenous communities, and migrants, all of whom were immersed in a local political economy tied to the larger regional, national, and world economies (White 1991). The debate between Turnerians and their critics has now gone beyond the "either-or" stage, and more recent works recognize that frontier processes can be complex, with social conflict often commingling with cooperation and negotiation (Turner 1994). This contemporary awareness of a more nuanced situation on the frontier strongly resonates with the experience of southern Mindanao.

Studies of Mindanao's political economy tend to overstate the argument that capitalist and state penetration precipitated social marginalization, antistate resistance, and ethnic conflict in southern Mindanao as far back as 1946 (Mercado 1984, 154). The evidence suggests otherwise. During the period 1946–1960, southern Mindanao remained largely undeveloped. Most of Davao and Cotabato were still heavily forested and poor infrastructure limited linkages between provinces and towns. With the exception of the timber industry and a moderately sized livestock industry, few capitalist enterprises were drawn to southern Mindanao (*CR* 1959, 8–9). In fact, until the 1960s, Mindanao's richest families were not landlords or industrial capitalists but lumbermen, "new rich" who amassed wealth from timber licenses covering huge areas of forested land in Davao. This business elite belonged to the Philippine Lumbermen's Association, included the province's top income tax payers from 1946 onwards, and had extensive ties with local politicians (*MT,* 29 Dec. 1950; 15 Feb. 1951).

It was not until the mid-1960s that corporate agriculture began to establish a presence (Spencer 1952, 202). Before this, corporations were mostly content to acquire undeveloped land for future exploitation. Some attempted to revive the abaca industry and to introduce cotton production, but these were minor efforts, making little impact on the overall island economy (*MinT*, 26 Jan., 29 May, 5 July 1952; and 13 Feb. 1954). Government tried to jump start economic interest by creating its own corporations and announcing big infrastructure development. But throughout the 1950s, most of these failed to go beyond the planning stage, while road-building projects and port facility improvement were painfully slow in coming (see chapter 6). With government unable to accomplish its economic programs and corporations showing little interest in investing, the underdeveloped condition of southern Mindanao persisted, and with it the dominance of the less powerful but numerous indigenes and settlers.

Turner's argument that a frontier's free land provides opportunity for freedom and progress thus finds partial application in Cotabato and Davao. While there was always news of land title battles and squatting, it would be a mistake to take this as the determining condition of the frontier. Claimants did fight each other, but with huge swaths of land available, many pursued a quicker path to ownership: they simply moved on, made a new claim, and faced the challenge of making the land productive, in effect favoring stability and economic advancement over incessant conflict which tended to produce the opposite. Moreover, while certain individuals, families, and corporations possessed lands of over 1,000 hectares (many of which remained uncultivated during this period), the majority of holdings in southern Mindanao were small- to medium-sized. The Hardie Report (1951, A2–A3), prepared by American officials surveying land tenure patterns in the Philippines in the immediate postwar period, showed that Cotabato and Davao ranked high in the number and proportion of residents owning farm lands of 24 hectares and over. These provinces also ranked high in farmers categorized as full owners of their land and had tenancy rates below the national average (table 3). There was thus a preponderance of owner-cultivators, the kind of people often identified as the ideal majority in a rural society because they are the most ambitious, least rebellious, and the strongest advocates of social peace and "fair play" (Monk 1990, 10; Hardie 1951, v-vi).

In 1953, a government listing of the top Philippine landholders further confirmed the small- and medium-sized nature of Cotabato and Davao landholdings (table 4). Cotabato had a total of 925 individuals, families, and corporations owning lands of 50 hectares or more, while Davao had 352. These landowners owned 134,552 hectares in Cotabato and 58,236 hectares in Davao. While these were fairly substantial landholdings, they were only a fraction of the total land (5.6 percent of Cotabato and 3 percent of Davao), attesting to the vastness of the yet-to-be-classified, categorized, and owned

Table 3. Frequency of farm tenure by category, 1951

| Region | No. of Farmers | Owners (%) | Part-owners (%) | Tenants (%) | Farm Managers (%) |
|---|---|---|---|---|---|
| Luzon | 832,203 | 45.47 | 21.75 | 35.48 | 0.11 |
| Visayas | 577,668 | 53.46 | 12.66 | 34.5 | 0.24 |
| Mindanao | 212,773 | 68.46 | 4.53 | 26.83 | 0.18 |
| Zamboanga | 32,877 | 71.8 | 2.4 | 25.7 | 0.1 |
| Surigao | 28,982 | 72.7 | 13.3 | 14.0 | 0.0 |
| Davao | 26,251 | 72.6 | 1.0 | 26.2 | 0.3 |
| Misamis Occ. | 25,650 | 46.3 | 11.5 | 42.3 | 0.0 |
| Cotabato | 25,018 | 75.4 | 1.2 | 23.3 | 0.0 |
| Lanao | 24,529 | 68.2 | 2.9 | 28.9 | 0.0 |
| Misamis Or. | 22,521 | 71.6 | 6.9 | 21.4 | 0.1 |
| Sulu | 20,384 | 73.0 | 0.5 | 26.4 | 0.0 |
| Bukidnon | 6,561 | 64.6 | 1.1 | 33.3 | 1.0 |
| Philippines | 1,634,716 | | | | |

*Source:* Hardie, "Philippine Land Tenure Reform," A2-A3.

public lands. Cotabato, before it was divided in 1967, had a total area of 2,393,447 hectares, making it the largest province of the country (Economic Development Foundation 1970, 1). Davao was nearly as large. Before it was divided into three smaller provinces in 1964, it had a total area of 1,949,895 hectares, with Davao City alone apportioned 244,000 hectares (Mariano 1953, 4–5). These frontier provinces were capable of accommodating far more people, either through natural population increase or through the continuous flow of migrants from the north.

Cotabato and Davao also ranked high in landowners residing in the provinces (table 5) and municipalities (table 6) where they owned land. Only sixteen Cotabato landowners lived outside of the province, while Davao did not even figure in the top ten provinces in this category (table 7). These figures translate into strong familiarity and even intimacy among landowners, maintained through kinship networks. More importantly, they indicate that a major source of rural hostilities, absentee landlordism, played no prominent role in southern Mindanao. In short, we do not find antagonism erupting

Table 4. Range of landownership, by hectare, Cotabato and Davao, 1953

| Range | Cotabato Landowners | Davao Landowners |
|---|---|---|
| 1,000 – above | 13 | 8 |
| 900 – 999 | 5 | 2 |
| 800 – 899 | 6 | 4 |
| 700 – 799 | 7 | 4 |
| 600 – 699 | 12 | 5 |
| 500 – 599 | 8 | 8 |
| 400 – 499 | 10 | 2 |
| 300 – 399 | 25 | 10 |
| 200 – 299 | 52 | 16 |
| 101 – 199 | 240 | 74 |
| 100 | 103 | 7 |
| 90 – 99 | 31 | 18 |
| 80 – 89 | 26 | 26 |
| 70 – 79 | 49 | 33 |
| 60 – 69 | 71 | 49 |
| 50 – 59 | 266 | 79 |
| 40 – 49 | 0 | 0 |
| 30 – 39 | 1 | 4 |
| 20 – 29 | 0 | 3 |
| Total | 925 | 352 |

*Source:* Department of Finance, "Farm Holdings of 50 Hectares or More," 31 December 1953.

between a large landlord and an agricultural proletariat because neither of these classes yet had a substantial presence in the area. Class division within the settlements remained incipient, social antagonisms were muted, and conflict was limited to small battles between migrants and indigenes and among migrants themselves (Scaff 1955, 84–89). Even as a rural elite was observed to be forming in the settlement zones in the mid-1960s, it took several more years before this stratification had an effect on social relationships at the village and municipal levels (Sandoval 1957, 503–4; Scaff 1954, 84).

I am not suggesting that a rural economy dominated by small- and

Table 5. Owners of farm lands of 24 hectares and above residing in province where land is located, 1951

| Province | Number of Owners | Area (hectares) |
|---|---|---|
| Masbate | 6,062 | 24,148 |
| Cotabato | 1,719 | 156,487 |
| Davao | 769 | 25,109 |
| Camarines Sur | 570 | 24,696 |
| Lanao | 502 | 23,401 |
| Zamboanga | 430 | 12,949 |
| Mindoro | 420 | 26,341 |
| Isabela | 405 | 17,407 |
| Negros Occidental | 396 | 41,086 |
| Quezon | 370 | 21,940 |
| Philippines | 15,390 | 599,599 |

*Source:* Hardie, "Philippine Land Tenure Reform," A2-A3.

Table 6. Owners of farm lands of 24 hectares and above residing in different barrios of the same municipality, 1951

| Province | Number of Owners | Area (hectares) |
|---|---|---|
| Negros Occidental | 678 | 75,028 |
| Davao | 499 | 31,982 |
| Zamboanga | 420 | 17,017 |
| Cotabato | 355 | 22,821 |
| Camarines Sur | 339 | 15,246 |
| Quezon | 302 | 13,154 |
| Bukidnon | 245 | 22,252 |
| Lanao | 216 | 9,909 |
| Samar | 185 | 7,189 |
| Albay | 175 | 11,246 |
| Philippines | 5,700 | 405,008 |

*Source:* Hardie, "Philippine Land Tenure Reform," A2-A3.

Table 7. Owners of farm fands of 24 hectares and above residing outside municipality or province where land is located, Top 10 Philippine provinces, 1951

| Province | Number of Owners | Area (hectares) |
|---|---|---|
| Negros Occidental | 185 | 31,626 |
| Nueva Ecija | 172 | 80,861 |
| Zamboanga | 100 | 9,507 |
| Pangasinan | 83 | 21,164 |
| Tarlac | 68 | 32,743 |
| Pampanga | 38 | 7,379 |
| Quezon | 32 | 3,754 |
| Albay | 28 | 2,899 |
| Negros Oriental | 16 | 4,915 |
| Cotabato | 16 | 1,666 |
| Philippines | 909 | 255,484 |

*Source:* Hardie, "Philippine Land Tenure Reform," A2-A3.

medium-sized landholders did not have its own tensions. Intermittent battles over land ownership in Cotabato and Davao point to their existence. But the absence of feudalism in southern Mindanao proved invaluable to frontier stability throughout the 1950s and into the 1960s. In a feudal social formation, order is preserved through the power a landed elite wields over a peasant majority. It may be superficially less volatile, but the skewed social relationship that elevates the few and leaves the many below subsistence levels often cannot maintain the peace. This is certainly true when profound economic crisis hits the rural community (Scott 1985). Compared to rural underclasses and landed elites, relative parity characterizes the middle layer of landowners that dominated Cotabato and Davao. Order was maintained by the sheer availability of land for owner-cultivators (indigene or settler) who focused on productivity—amidst the constant attacks of rats and locusts, not to mention intermittent droughts—rather than conflict. This was especially true in those sections of the provinces dominated by migrants.

In zones dominated by indigenous groups, especially the Muslims, some qualification is necessary in the light of the presence of traditional elites. Scholars have argued that in the Muslim areas, a form of feudalism antedated colonialism but that the "extensive colonization, large-scale commodity production [and] corporate profiteering" of the American period marginalized this Muslim "variant formation of the feudal type" (Ahmad 1982, 5–6). Scholars of the left, however, contend that Muslim landlordism persisted as local elites began to appropriate communally owned lands from their people, particularly in the postwar period (Mercado 1984, 152). If we base the definition of feudalism on landownership, however, the available evidence from Cotabato does not support the existence of a feudal elite. A rough listing of Magindanao landowners shows that the general pattern of ownership described above also applies to the Muslims. The majority were clumped in the 50–100-hectare range, suggesting that most Magindanaos were small- to medium-sized landowners (table 8).

Furthermore, if we factor in the minimal level of tenancy, we can conclude with a degree of confidence that landlordism did not figure

Table 8. Magindanao landowners, by hectare, Cotabato, 1953

| Hectares Owned | Number of Landowners |
|---|---|
| 1,000 – above | 3 |
| 900 – 999 | 0 |
| 800 – 899 | 1 |
| 700 – 799 | 4 |
| 600 – 699 | 9 |
| 500 – 599 | 4 |
| 400 – 499 | 6 |
| 300 – 399 | 15 |
| 200 – 299 | 38 |
| 101 – 199 | 148 |
| 100 | 80 |
| 90 – 99 | 9 |
| 80 – 89 | 13 |
| 70 – 79 | 29 |
| 60 – 69 | 49 |
| 50 – 59 | 178 |
| 40 and below | 1 |

*Source:* Department of Finance, "Farm Holdings of 50 Hectares or More," 31 December 1953.

prominently among the Magindanaos. Some of the leading Cotabato families did own large land estates, but there is little evidence that they administered their lands through tenancy arrangements.[12] This was a far cry from the feudal social formation that typified highly tenanted areas of the Philippines, like Central Luzon, where peasant resistance was endemic. Where feudal authority was invoked, it had more to do with the nature of these datus' traditional relationships with their constituents than with landownership and the way land and labor were exploited (Abdullah 1989, 21–27).

The availability of land that fostered petty production and minimized social friction in itself made no positive contribution to social peace. In Cotabato, Magindanaos and settlers never really found common ground for long-term peaceful coexistence, while in Davao linguistic differences pitted one migrant group against another from the electoral arena down to daily encounters (*MinT,* 21 June 1951, 15 Jan. and 4 June 1953). Within both indigenous and migrant communities themselves, family and clan interests often displaced community welfare. Yet, despite the social strains, the peace and order condition in these provinces was no worse than in any other province of the Philippines. To further understand why the landscape remained stable, we must look more closely at the character of these communities.

## Community Solidarities and Social Stability

The second factor explaining southern Mindanao's persistent stability was the nature of inter- and intracommunity organization. First, the tense relationship between settlers and indigenes enhanced internal solidarity in the respective communities. Among Muslims, for example, landownership complaints against settlers and the perceived partiality of state officials towards the settlers reinforced a sense of systematic collective marginalization. The cultural overlay of this sentiment was the enduring popular belief that a Catholic Filipino state was determined to destroy Muslim culture and religion (Gowing 1974, 187–91). This sense of discrimination mobilized Muslims around their leaders who used it as an issue to negotiate with the national state and political parties. While invoking the image of the aggrieved Muslim, however, these leaders stopped short of transforming a collective sentiment into a symbol of defiance against the state (Jubaira 1960, 193–97). A strengthened sense of identity did not automatically translate into separatist politics.

Among settlers, a parallel sentiment prevailed, particularly as stories spread of Muslims demanding rent from settlers on the pretext of being owners of the settled lands.[13] New municipalities that emerged out of these settlement areas were unified even at early stages of their establishment by a siege mentality and the belief that local governments were prejudicial toward the Muslims (*MT,* 31 Jan. 1953). As with the Muslims, the feeling of being discriminated against was conveyed through local leaders with ties to the state and party machinery, who ostensibly sought to protect settler rights. These leaders ensured, however, that the mentality did not lead to the initiation of violent actions against the Muslims. Like their Muslim counterparts, settler leaders channeled their followers' anti-Muslim sentiment into electoral support, even at times in alliance with Muslim leaders (*MC,* 28 Apr. 1951). This will be discussed more extensively in the succeeding chapters. For now, it is worth noting that social peace between Muslims and settlers was preserved in part through the mechanism of political links between local leaders with a mass electoral base to offer national parties and state leaders seeking to stabilize the state's presence or expand their own networks in southern Mindanao.

In Davao, where no substantial indigenous community confronted settlers, settler-indigene unease was less marked, making Davao more stable than Cotabato. Here another mechanism of stability can be identified in the migration process itself. Both spontaneous and government-sponsored migrations were movements not merely of individuals or single families but also of groups of families, the majority of whom came from the same villages and municipalities (*MT*, 6 and 21 Jan. 1959; *STM,* 4 Feb, 1953). In a study of a Davao settlement, Simkins and Wernstedt (1971, 57) noted that

> Nearly all sections of the Philippines contributed migrants to the Digos-Padada valley... Yet, despite this broad diversity of birthplaces, the great bulk of the migration to the valley has come from a few places. Of the 523 municipalities of birth represented among valley migrants, 16 municipalities contributed one percent or more of the total movement. These municipalities represent the birthplaces of more than one-half (53 percent) of the total migrant population of the Digos-Padada valley.

A table prepared by the authors is reproduced here to illustrate the tightness of these migrant communities (table 9). It shows that 90 percent of the settlers came from the coastal municipalities of Cebu province. This intimacy was reinforced by the fact that a significant portion of the homesteaders came from Argao and Sibonga in Cebu province, two

Table 9. Percent of total migrants contributed to the Digos-Padada Valley by the 16 leading municipalities (based on homestead applications)

| Municipality | Province | Percent of Migrants | | |
|---|---|---|---|---|
| | | Pre-1942 | 1942 and later | Total |
| Argao | Cebu | 18.2 | 15.1 | 15.8 |
| Sibonga | Cebu | 11.8 | 10.6 | 10.9 |
| Carcar | Cebu | 3.3 | 4.5 | 4.2 |
| Tuburan | Cebu | 3.3 | 3.6 | 3.6 |
| Moalboal | Cebu | 2.0 | 2.3 | 2.2 |
| Tudela | Cebu | 4.0 | 1.5 | 2.1 |
| Barili | Cebu | 1.1 | 2.4 | 2.1 |
| Toledo | Cebu | 1.2 | 2.1 | 1.9 |
| Minglanilla | Cebu | 1.0 | 1.9 | 1.7 |
| Cebu City | Cebu | 1.9 | 1.5 | 1.6 |
| Sogod | Cebu | 0.7 | 1.6 | 1.4 |
| Danao | Cebu | 1.5 | 1.3 | 1.3 |
| Naga | Cebu | 1.0 | 1.4 | 1.3 |
| Catmon | Cebu | 1.7 | 1.0 | 1.2 |
| Dumangas | Cebu | 1.2 | 0.9 | 1.0 |
| Ormoc | Cebu | 0.7 | 1.1 | 1.0 |
| Total | | 53.6 | 52.8 | 53.3 |

*Source:* Simkins and Wernstedt, *Philippine Migration*, 132.

municipalities which became outmigration areas after the land could not sustain the growing postwar population. Poverty kept the people together and this sense of shared deprivation became the means by which solidarity was maintained in their new residence.[14] The authors further noted that there was "very little difference in the patterns of origins of migrants to the Digos-Padada valley through time, i.e., between those who arrived before World War II and those who arrived after." In other words, migrants came from the same specific communities in Cebu, and in the case of the Digos-Padada area, 60 percent were convinced by friends and relatives rather than by government pronouncements (Simkins and Wernstedt 1971, 59, 61–71). The same was true in northern Davao municipalities like Mawab, where the first postwar migrants successfully encouraged more migrants from their home province (Krinks 1970, 86).

Another factor maintaining social cohesion as these communities became accustomed to their new domicile was the migrants' habit of regularly returning to their original provinces. Again, the Simkins and Wernstedt (1971, 137) study is illustrative, showing that over 50 percent of the migrants went back for "home visits." This habit served to maintain community unity in the new home, particularly in the new generations born in Mindanao. Visits preserved cultural attachments which otherwise might be lost through coexistence with other language or ethnic groups on the frontier.

While there have been no case studies of specific Cotabato communities similar to that conducted by Wernstedt and Simkins in Davao, the sense of unity and identity is also evident there. Towns where migration was heaviest developed identities linked to the settlers. The southern portion of Cotabato, for example, became known as "the heart of the Ilonggo Empire" because the majority of settlers came from the western Visayas provinces (*MT,* 6 Feb. 1954). By 1960, "Panay-Hiligaynon" combined with "Aklanon" was the second largest language group in Cotabato after Magindanao (Census of the Philippines 1960).

As with Davao, many migrants moved to Cotabato on the encouragement of those who went before, some of whom started out in government-sponsored colonization programs which moved entire families (*STM,* 7 Feb. 1953). As the programs faltered, leaving those who joined them on the brink of desperation, many survived by finding refuge in the lands of these friends and townmates (*MT,* 29–30 Dec. 1951). And since the majority of these settlers were recruited as families, another survival strategy involved keeping the family units intact; this helped preserve internal unity (Fernandez 1970, 178). As these communities of families and friends overcame their problems, they in turn enjoined more relatives and friends in the Visayas to come to Cotabato, rendering government programs irrelevant. In the municipality of Kidapawan, for example, Sandoval (1957, 501) observed that

> Seventy-three percent of the settlers stated that they had either friends, relatives or neighbors who had moved earlier to the settlement. News of the latter's success played a major role in the increase of settlers... Government and community leaders, in one way or another, influenced the decisions of nine percent of the settlers to go to Mindanao. Eight percent cited newspapers and magazines as responsible for their migration. Only ten percent of the settlers reported no outside influence in their decision to move.

The difference between Cotabato and Davao lay in the relationship between the old hometowns and the new ones. Whereas Visayan settlers in Davao kept ties with their original home provinces as much as possible, Cotabato settlers appeared to consider their migration permanent. Again the Kidapawan study is suggestive. It stated that "[n]one of those who were happy to have settled in the place expressed desire to move back to their home provinces. Only those who were either sorry or of questionable opinion expressed their desires to return to their former homes" (Sandoval 1957, 517). There has been no explanation for the preference of Western Visayan settlers to establish permanence in Cotabato, although economic difficulties in the Visayas as well as in their new municipalities may have prevented such pilgrimages (Townes 1953). The other possible reason was that the Western Visayan provinces were themselves settlement zones in the early part of the century. As such, the sense of being established there was perhaps not as strong as in Bohol or Cebu, most of whose migrants settled in Davao.

## Conclusion

This chapter has examined an understudied episode in southern Mindanao's postwar political development to account for the peculiar stability of this designated frontier. It has argued that amidst the adversities identified with immense demographic change, southern Mindanao communities were able to mitigate the area's potential explosiveness. Stability based on land accessibility and community solidarity, however, was not expected to be a permanent condition. As early as the 1950s, land experts warned, through the Hardie (1951, vi, 9–10) report, that settlement would not only fail to solve the land problem of the Philippines but would even extend it to Mindanao.[15] This report elicited so much resistance from Filipino politicians that it was displaced by one less disruptive of class relations and that continued to promote migration.

Yet as the frontier filled up, the report's prognosis of class stratification and social unrest was only partially correct. As conflict developed in Mindanao, it was at first a struggle over homestead sites in areas where settlers overlapped with indigenes. Only gradually did class stratification begin to erode the frontier's relatively equitable political economy. Even then, what I broadly call community solidarity continued to bolster the island's stability. The final element was politics, i.e., the use of power by local and provincial strong men. These strong men operated on three levels, imposing order in their communities, managing relations between their communities and others, and mediating with the Philippine state. They were integrated into the decentralized, faction-based, patronage-operated process that shaped postwar politics and they found succor in it. This process, to which we turn now, explains why tensions did not explode into widespread confrontation and war during the first two decades of the postwar period.

CHAPTER 6

# State and Society on the Postwar Fron

Southern Mindanao's stability was grounded on a postwar political structure that is generally seen as weak. Scholars are unanimous in describing the nature of the postwar state: riddled with bureaucratic corruption and inefficiency, dependent on the United States, dominated by oligarchic forces that exploited state resources for patrimonial ends, and faced by repeated outbursts of resistance from below. Yet this very same "weak state" presided over a frontier that was stable. Instead of a periphery in turmoil because of the state's inability to assert its authority, southern Mindanao's relationship with Manila was remarkably steadfast. Sporadic resistance, particularly from the Muslim province, occurred, but never seriously threatened political order on the frontier or destabilized the local state.

## The New State Form

Scholars have argued that the Japanese occupation and the subsequent return of the United States did very little to alter the class hierarchy and power structure of the Philippines (McCoy 1985, 4–5). Filipino elites collaborated with the Japanese, and while guerrilla war in the countryside forced many to abandon their estates for the safer confines of the cities, they were not dispossessed of their wealth. They regained their holdings after the war, thanks largely to the use of private armies, local police, and constabulary forces, all of which were used against the threat of an armed, left-influenced peasantry. In the main, this assessment is valid, although it does not apply to all aspects of Philippine politics. In fact, the state itself underwent changes in form and in its ability to exercise power over society.

The late colonial state was not only thoroughly Filipinized by the establishment of the Commonwealth: it was also increasingly centralized under

Manuel L. Quezon. Scholars who argue the Philippine state's weakness as a consequence of the power of the oligarchy often overlook features of state structures that were predisposed to centralization (McCoy 1993; Hutchcroft 1993; Thompson 1995). While the Jones Act of 1916 opened up the colonial state to oligarchic control through Filipinization, it did not modify the executive branch, preserving in the position of governor general the ultimate authority and power in the Philippines. Under Francis Harrison, this provision was set aside because of his close relationship with Filipino leaders and his firm belief in Filipinization. His successor, Leonard Wood, however, committed himself to reversing Harrison's policies and regaining control of the state from Quezon and his allies (Gopinath 1987, 11–12).

Wood and Quezon fought each other with ferocity and we can only speculate how the struggle would have ended had Wood lived longer and Washington subsequently lost interest in reasserting American control (Smith 1969). What Wood did with executive power, however, did not go unappreciated, for once Quezon became president of the Commonwealth, he employed similar tactics to centralize power in his own hands (Gopinath 1987, 39). It was this constitutional authoritarianism that was broken by the Japanese and prevented by Filipino leaders from being restored in the postwar period (McCoy 1989, 117–18). In its stead was established a liberal-democratic regime characterized by "genuine oligarchic competition."[1] Power was formally ascribed to a two-party system which competed for local, provincial, and national legislative seats. Oligarchic power was most concentrated in the national legislature, where provincial and local oligarchies arranged the election of their representatives to ensure the defense and expansion of their patrimonial interests. Politicians installed administrative mechanisms to reinforce this decentralized power structure and preclude the resurrection of Quezon-style one-man rule (Caoili 1986, 16–17). The postwar state was purposely designed to "veer away from the maintenance of a strong, centralized government [and toward] the promotion of greater local autonomy"( De Guzman 1969, 398). Congress passed laws strengthening local government, especially the appointive powers and fiscal prerogatives of provincial, city, and municipal officials. Although these laws were ultimately insufficient to deter a slide into state centralization and authoritarian rule, they were able—in combination with oligarchic control over parties and legislatures, a weak bureaucracy, and an inefficient and corrupt military—to prop up oligarchic democracy for two decades.

Thus, contrary to the continuity argument of many scholars, a break did take place which differentiates the republic from its late colonial counterpart. The strong state that Quezon fashioned under the Commonwealth had ceased to exist, displaced by the weak state that became the idiosyncratic mark of postwar Philippine politics. The leading oligarchic families may have changed little through the colonial, Japanese, and postwar periods, but the manner in which they and their representatives governed reveals variation in the state's centralizing capacity. In Mindanao, the center developed a complex and often contradictory relationship with the frontier. In the following sections, I will examine how this contradiction played out, beginning with the state's development goals for Mindanao.

## Mindanao and National Economic Development

"Genuine oligarchic competition" and the decentralization of power to regional and local forces developed under conditions of profound economic crisis in the new republic. The devastation wrought by American liberation was exacerbated by the slow recovery of the war-ravaged economy, the regressive effects of Philippine-American free trade, and the unbridled plunder of state resources (Valdepeñas and Bautista 1977, 51). The impact of all this on the lower classes was devastating and it helped to sustain the Partido Komunista ng Pilipinas-led peasant rebellion in central Luzon. While an American-orchestrated reformist regime temporarily alleviated the crisis, the administration of Pres. Ramon Magsaysay fell short of reshaping the state into an autonomous, efficient, and coherent apparatus that could move the country away from oligarchic control (Constantino 1992, 262–68).

The Huk rebellion, nevertheless, was a wake-up call for state leaders who realized that the economic development of the country was a prerequisite to political stability. As noted above, however, there was no serious attempt to correct wide income disparities through redistributive policies. Rural development, in particular, was not meant to break up landed estates, but rather to maintain the haciendas through the diversion of landless peasants to newly opened public lands (Licaros 1959, 8). The attempted solution, therefore, was to increase the overall national wealth through the exploitation of untapped resources, which Mindanao possessed in abundance. An early manifestation of this policy was the formation in 1951 of the Mindanao Development Authority (MDA), "a corporate body clothed with the power of government but possessed of the flexibility and initiative of a private enterprise" (Jayme 1961, 328; Maramba 1952, 20–21; *Progress,* 1954, 56–57). The MDA was supposed to be furnished with the necessary powers and wherewithal to spearhead the development of the island. The state allotted the agency a budget of 21 million pesos while granting it power to oversee the economic, infrastructural, educational, health, and social development of Mindanao in coordination with the larger national plan.[2]

But these plans were not implemented. While the MDA was formally created in 1951, it was more than a decade before it was activated (*MT,* 19 June 1963; 11 June 1965). Throughout the 1950s, it remained "a mere symbol or at best a hanging entity" that was repeatedly invoked by politicians and presidents but which never acted (*MT,* 9 Mar. 1964). The agency had no office and its board of directors was never fully constituted. Its budgetary allocation was never released in full, affecting its ability to lobby for infrastructure projects (especially the road system) in congress (Congressional Records, House of Representative 1969, 674). The MDA's most important drawback, however, was that once it received its budget allocation (in 1964), it quickly became an instrument for patronage and patrimonial control. The goal of the agency was to draw local political and business leaders into the project of Mindanao's economic development under its leadership. But the weakness of the MDA's structure and personnel, its long period of hibernation, and its lack of funds caused the opposite to occur. The MDA itself, as well as the direction of Mindanao's development, fell into the hands of local politicians.

From the start, Mindanao politicians were inclined to obstruct the agency's potential to become a powerful and autonomous organization operating outside their control. One salient feature of the MDA that caused considerable apprehension was its commitment to function "as a sort of a third or harmonizing sector to coordinate and/or integrate vigorously the diverse efforts of the public and private sectors for regional development" (Jayme 1961, 328). Although MDA officials gave assurances that it would not "absorb or duplicate the functions of established government agencies," nor compete with private enterprise, local politicians feared their power would be undermined. This could easily happen, for example, were the MDA able to meddle in businesses and industries controlled by politicians in the name of balanced and coordinated development. Beyond its organizational scope, Mindanao politicians also felt threatened by the MDA's potential as a presidential tool (*DM,* 25 July 1961). And infighting at the provincial and local levels of the MDA reinforced suspicion that the agency could be used to advance one faction's interests over another (*Progress* 1960, 200; *MT,* 10 Mar. 1964). Therefore, when the MDA began implementing projects, compliance by local power holders proved impossible to secure.

The case of the MDA illustrates the problems faced by a weak state trying to promote coordinated economic development. The imperative of development called for a comprehensive economic plan designed to enhance state power; to undertake this, a well-organized and effective agency was needed. The structure of postwar Philippine politics, however, was not favorable to such a super agency. Even its basic economic surveys suffered "great delays," as one MDA official pointed out, complaining that the agency "does not possess the coercive powers as to give it authority to demand or obtain data from noncooperative parties" (Manalaysay 1966, 58).

Since other state agencies were even less able to make their presence felt, MDA projects could only be attempted with the help of local politicians—the underwriters of political order in the world of disorder that was Mindanao. But the combination of local hostility and state weakness doomed the MDA's agenda of coordinated economic development.[3] Many projects never reached the first stage of implementation and those that did eventually petered out due to lack of funds. It would take a more interventionist central leadership for the MDA to flex its muscles. This would not come until the mid-1960s with the election of Ferdinand Marcos to the presidency. In the meantime, Mindanao's economic development remained stalled and the frontier was generally left untouched, save for its timber resources.

## Migration and the State

State weakness was evident in another failed project: organized migration to Mindanao. As discussed in chapter 5, the movement of people to the island was mainly in the form of spontaneous private initiative, later considered a major cause of disorder on the frontier. An efficient, well-financed government colonization program might have stemmed this unbridled and uneven peopling of Mindanao. Between 1946 and 1972, five major government colonization programs targeted Mindanao as a major destination. The prewar NLSA was replaced by the Land Settlement and Development Corporation (LASEDECO) in 1950 (Adduru 1952, 62–64; Samson 1957, 16–23). As part of its counterinsurgency program, the government also resettled former communist insurgents in Mindanao under the army-run Economic Development Corporation or EDCOR (*MT,* 11 Dec. 1950). After a change in presidential administrations in 1955, the

National Resettlement and Rehabilitation Administration or NARRA replaced LASEDECO (*MT,* 11 Dec. 1950). NARRA lasted until 1963 when it was replaced by the Land Authority Administration during Marcos's first term (Paderanga 1987, 15–18).

All five set out to provide land to small settlers; none achieved more than minimal success (Paderanga 1987, 2–32). The principal reasons were administrative ineptitude, pervasive corruption, and lackluster support from central state authorities. By the late 1940s, the NLSA had become corrupt and mismanaged, a fiefdom which its autocratic staff looted with impunity. As a presidential agent reported: "Ridiculously incompetent management with a combination of small-time gangsterism and political parasitism has brought the former NLSA to a confused standstill ripe for organized armed trouble" (Marking 1950). Yet its replacement, the ostensibly reform-oriented LASEDECO, became infected with the same "inefficiency, mismanagement, red tape and venality of government officials who are supposed to do everything within their power to encourage and assist homesteaders." EDCOR was likewise called "inefficient and wasteful" and described as "impracticable as an entity and a measure for resolving the landless problems of the populace" (Abbey 10 March 1952). The staff of NARRA, the longest running of all projects (1954–1963), was believed to be exceptional when compared to the venality of its predecessors, but neither was it exempt from corruption (*MinT,* 1 June 1957). Further, its complicated settlement procedures and labyrinthine bureaucracy eroded the agency's morale and efficiency. By its second year, NARRA's sponsor, Magsaysay, was frantically urging its staff to improve its supervision of the colonies (*MT,* 16 Sept. 1954; Pfanner 1958, 107).

The NLSA and LASEDECO were perennially in financial distress, not only because corruption drained revenues but also because of inadequate financing from the central government (Paguia 1948; Wurfel 1960, 452–59). The NLSA was abolished without paying off a 5 million-pesos debt owed to the national government from the colonial and World War II periods. LASEDECO's absorption of the debt limited its operations, particularly its ability to open up new settlements.[4] To cover its arrears, LASEDECO was eventually compelled to pass on the debt payments to its settlers, thus undermining their chance of success (*PFP,* 15 Jan. 1952; Cowen 9–18 Apr. 1952). When it was abolished and replaced by NARRA, LASEDECO was reported to have lost 10–12 million pesos to "malversation, estafa and theft" (*MT,* 22 Jan. 1954). It had gone a further 22,143,342 pesos into debt; much of this money was suspected of having been "embezzled, squandered and left unused" (*PFP,* 29 May 1954). Finally, NARRA and the Land Authority Administration, while not experiencing the same hemorrhage of funds, performed no better than its predecessors. NARRA was forced to scale down its plan to open new settlements because of administrative problems. The Land Authority Administration tried to revive land settlement and managed to bring to Mindanao 674 settler families in its first three years. This figure, however, was deemed "of little significance from the point of view of employment promotion" (*Employment Problems* 1969, 107). Neither was it commensurate to the 23.4 million-pesos budget the Authority was receiving, prompting enemies of the Marcos administration to suspect corruption (*MT,* 29 Jan. 1970).

The inability of the Bureau of Lands to provide support to the colonization schemes was a secondary reason for their failure. As one report noted:

> The most retarding and disorganizing factor in Philippine agriculture had to do with the registration of land titles and the effect this has on the settlement of farmers on new lands. With the sole exception of land tenure problems, more rancor and discomfort arise out of title registration difficulties, particularly on the Island of Mindanao, than from any other source. These difficulties hindered not only the orderly settlement of new lands, but they invite squatting and cause many a great injustice (Report to President of the United States, 9 Oct. 1950, 56).

The situation was aggravated early on by the destruction of records during the war. The task of reconstructing the files was never completed in the disorganized condition of the republic (Wurfel 1960, 396). This in turn created more opportunity for corruption as land sales and ownership were, in effect, opened to the highest bidder. Krinks characterized the political context in these terms: "the work was hampered by the wartime destruction of records, by lack of funds and by illicit intervention of politicians and others in the work of the Bureau. Certain national politicians urged ex-guerrillas to 'hang on to your guns and stick to your land,' even if they were in fact squatters" (Krinks 1970, 9). Another report described the Bureau, responsible for land classification, land title, and credit, as "an agency of incompetent political appointees and corrupters," making the "fast clearance of land titles next to impossible to accomplish" (Abbey 1 Mar. 1951 to 1 Mar. 1952; 23 Nov. 1951). Furthermore, coordination between different offices was minimal, even nonexistent (Pendatun 8 May 1952). The Land Authority Administration's plan to speed up the granting of land patents was frustrated by delayed funding, as well as by jurisdictional disputes with the Bureau of Lands (*MT,* 10 Apr. 1964). Thus, up to the eve of martial law, state land settlement policies were as disorganized and fraudulent as when they were first implemented. The economist Frank Golay (1961, 285) summed up the performance of postwar government-sponsored migration programs:

> The results of the various organized colonization efforts have been disappointing when appraised in terms of economic criteria. Desertion rates and failures have been high. Recruitment policies have been faulty, and site selection has frequently been inappropriate. While these programmes have been set up with revolving funds in which liquidation of settlers' debts would maintain the fund intact and support future colonization, in every case the investment has been dissipated in high administrative costs and settler default. The cost per settler has been excessive by every criterion, but in particular, in terms of the rate of population increase, widespread tenancy, and the public funds available for this type of programme (Golay 1961, 285).

The consequences of failure were disastrous for the settlers enrolled in the projects. Productivity suffered from inadequate farm facilities and lack of government support. In Kidapawan, in north Cotabato, for example, a report cited the following problems: "(1) lack of feeder roads; (2) lack of tools and equipment; (3) lack of work animals; (4) marketing of farm products controlled by aliens; (5) prevalence of plant pests and diseases; and (6) lack of capital for farming operations" (Sandoval 1957, 498). Many settlers fell into debt, while others saw worse (Pfanner 1958, 40–41). When rats devastated agriculture in Cotabato LASEDECO colonies during the 1950s, starvation was reported and LASEDECO officials were helpless to stop it.[5] The decade was half over before LASEDECO—with extensive assistance from the national government and the United States—was able to control the rat plague.[6] Even then, starvation forced over 11,000 families to leave the organized settlements "with despair and disillusionment in their faces."[7] Finally, mention has been made of increasing tension between indigenes and settlers in areas where spontaneous migration was pervasive (chapter 5). Neither were organized settlements able to avoid this problem. In fact, friction in these cases was more pronounced because of heightened Muslim suspicion of government-settler complicity (Majul 1985, 29; George 1980, 114–15). By the late 1950s, NARRA and EDCOR settlements had to be protected by the military as a result of land disputes. By the late 1960s, it was in these government-sponsored colonies that fighting between Muslim rebels and the Philippine army (backed by Filipino paramilitary allies) would be most intense (*MT,* 16 Sept. 1954, 3 Oct. 1955).

The fundamental problem arising from both spontaneous and organized migration was the failure to solve the overall national land problem that catalyzed the rebellions in the north. On the one hand, the uncontrollable rush of immigrants was quickly filling up Mindanao's settlement zones. Wernstedt and Simkins predicted in 1965 that if population growth rate remained steady, "all available farm lands will be occupied by 1972." On the other hand, migrating communities brought not only themselves but also some of the least meritorious features of their home provinces to Mindanao. As person-to-land ratios began to decline, the division between "haves" and "have-nots" eventually reemerged.

Rising land values and shrinking mean farm size made capital formation by tenants and squatters difficult. More and more, available land was bought by nonresidents and wealthy pioneers with large landholdings. These people also obtained land by foreclosing on unredeemed loans to small farmers (Krinks 1974, 4). Stratification and marginalization meant increasing numbers had no chance to own viable farm lots, signalling the beginnings of rural and semirural proletarianization and its accompanying unemployment (Martin 1964; Paderanga 1987, 13–14). The occupation of submarginal and poorer forest lands provided temporary relief, but in the long run low productivity soon took its toll (Davis 1957, 3). In short, instead of helping to solve the country's major source of social unrest, migration to Mindanao had spread it. Although much later than the Hardie report had predicted, migration eventually created a politically fragile context in which communal conflicts as well as class tensions were now imminent. This outcome might have been avoided had the frontier been managed. But the Philippine state, with all its postwar predicaments, was unable to carry out economic development or managed migration. State resources were dissipated by corruption, mismanagement, and the inability of government settlements to take off, undermining the government's reputation and exposing the fundamental inadequacy of the state as an actor in southern Mindanao.

## Security under a Weak State

If the land agencies failed to achieve their goals, so did those agencies responsible for keeping the frontier peaceful and safe. In the postwar period, the republic was expected to take over the responsibility of providing security to its growing constituencies on the frontier. This was made imperative by a lasting legacy of World War II: the proliferation of loose firearms, many of which fell into the hands of bandit groups and local strong men. A U.S. army intelligence report stated that "the most serious situation" in Lanao and Cotabato in 1945 was not hunger, sickness, or poverty but "the Moros [having] obtained thousands of weapons since the Japanese occupation." It added:

> Estimates vary as to the numbers. There must be from 7,000–10,000 guns of all sorts. They have acquired both American and Japanese rifles, pistols and automatic weapons and machine guns. They likewise have plenty of ammunition... The weapons have been obtained by a variety of methods. Many were acquired from the disintegrating USAFFE groups following the Japanese landings in Mindanao. They were found, stolen and purchased. Col. C. W. Hedges, in an account of the 108th Division History, relates how, during the critical period of enemy advance in Dansalan, hundreds of Maranao cargadores hired to carry food and ammunition to the rear areas disappeared like magic.[8]

The Philippine Constabulary (PC) and army units assigned to deal with this situation were ill-equipped and understaffed. Only a small force was assigned to Mindanao in the 1950s, since the bulk of the PC and army was fighting the Huks in Manila and Luzon. In 1953, the Mindanao command of the PC had only 3,344 officers and men (including trainees) distributed unevenly throughout the sixteen provinces and cities of the island (table 10). This was a meager force on an island whose population was climbing toward three million by the end of the decade (JUSMAG, 24 Nov. 1958, 56–66).

In Cotabato, three PC companies and one battalion combat team from the army's 9th Infantry Division covered the whole province (Sinsuat 1952–53, 2–3). These units found themselves overextended as they tried to discharge a variety of duties and to respond to community demands for security.[9] Successes were therefore limited and provincial officials found themselves appealing to Manila for more PC or army units to stem rising criminality (*MCr,* 28 Oct. 1950). Davao was confronted with the same problems. The

Table 10. Military personnel assigned per province and city, IV PC Zone, 1952-53

| Province/City | Constabulary units | | Army units with PC | | Officers (trainees, reservists, etc.) | Total |
|---|---|---|---|---|---|---|
| | Officers | Men | Officers | Men | | |
| Agusan | 0 | 12 | 0 | 0 | 101 | 113 |
| Butuan City | 7 | 65 | 0 | 0 | 0 | 72 |
| Bukidnon | 4 | 79 | 0 | 0 | 41 | 124 |
| Cotabato | 10 | 212 | 1 | 1 | 292 | 516 |
| Davao | 3 | 109 | 2 | 2 | 201 | 317 |
| Davao City | 8 | 55 | 0 | 0 | 0 | 63 |
| Lanao | 15 | 374 | 1 | 1 | 461 | 852 |
| Dansalan | 7 | 78 | 0 | 0 | 0 | 85 |
| Misamis Occ. | 2 | 54 | 2 | 2 | 51 | 111 |
| Ozamiz City | 3 | 32 | 0 | 0 | 0 | 35 |
| Sulu | 21 | 397 | 0 | 0 | 202 | 620 |
| Surigao | 5 | 58 | 0 | 0 | 101 | 164 |
| Zamboanga N. | 6 | 61 | 0 | 0 | 51 | 118 |
| Zamboanga S. | 4 | 98 | 0 | 0 | 1 | 103 |
| Basilan City | 1 | 27 | 0 | 0 | 0 | 28 |
| Zamboanga City | 1 | 22 | 0 | 0 | 0 | 23 |

*Source:* "Appendix M Report, Headquarters of the Philippine Constabulary, 19 December 1953," in *Report of the Commission on Elections to the President of the Philippines and the Congress on the Manner the Elections were held on 10 November 1953* (Manila: Bureau of Printing, 1954), 122-23.

Davao PC had its hands full with responsibilities ranging from antibrigandage operations to mediation of land disputes between settler and indigenous communities. The PC had to appeal for the assistance of the unreliable local police, having in 1950 "only 138 officers and men in the whole province, with only 130 fighting effectives which makes their job of maintaining peace and order a hard thing" (*MinT*, 16 Sept. 1950). The constabulary's biggest success was containing the "revolts" of the Bilaans, one of the indigenous communities threatened by land settlement and the timber industry. But this success was due not so much to the military expertise of the PC as to the feebleness of the Bilaan rebels; most of their acts of rebellion were carried out by small bands with little firepower (*MinT*, 16 Sept. 1950; 6 Apr. 1960).

Moreover, PC incompetence was complicated by reports of strong men coming to the military's rescue (Henderson 1949; Francisco 1950; Foster 1950, 1–4). In deferring to strong men, the PC often became "politicized," i.e., falling under the control of local power-holders and becoming their de facto private security (Rivera 1953). The enforcement of peace and order would then give way to antifirearms operations aimed at weakening the rivals of their patron (*MCr,* 17 Jan. 1959; 20 Apr. 1963). Magindanaos sometimes accused the Cotabato PC of this kind of bias, especially during elections when the military tended to favor ambitious upstarts from the settler areas who were challenging the hegemony of the datus (*MCr,* 22 Oct. 1955). In Davao, the involvement of leading PC officials in land and commodity rackets, as well as their conspicuous support for certain strong men, further tarnished the image of the PC (*MinT,* 3, 21, and 29 Mar. 1951; 18 Mar. 1952; 31 July and 20 Oct. 1958).

All these failings in economic development, organized migration, and frontier security reinforced the image of a weak state with only a marginal presence on the frontier. They likewise bolstered the popular notion in Manila that social and political disharmony was persistent in the south and would likely take a turn for the worse. Yet the anticipated breakdown did not happen. While the state was unable systematically to control such potentially dangerous problems as loose firearms, there was no escalation of confrontations among the different groups—armed and otherwise—in southern Mindanao for over two decades.

Two processes played crucial roles in bringing about this political stability. First was the implementation of popular suffrage in the erstwhile "special province," and the second, a logical offshoot, was the introduction of modern politics and the consequent strengthening of strong man-state ties. The "emblem[s] of full citizenhood in the modern age" created a condition where arms and violent confrontation were supplanted by struggle centering on the ballot and elective seats of office (B. Anderson 1996, 13). As political competition focused on these practices and positions, so were volatile sentiments channeled into more manageable pathways.

## Suffrage and Stability

While Quezon had expanded the rights of Muslims and other non-Christian groups during the Commonwealth, his regime had also continued to treat the districts of the former Moro Province as backward political entities. He granted them representation to the Philippine Assembly and appointed their leaders to provincial and local seats, but limited the exercise of suffrage to the elites. Even Davao remained a "special province," and Dabaweños were in the anomalous position of being Christian Filipinos denied the right to vote (Corcino 1969, 12).

Political independence changed all this as the prerogatives of citizenship were extended and the creation of new constituencies changed the features of southern Mindanao politics.[10] Most significant was the emergence of new electoral "bailiwicks" in an area with a rapidly increasing population. This attracted the attention of national parties seeking to broaden their bases, particularly in Cotabato and Davao, the island's two largest provinces. From areas of relatively minor import, Cotabato and Davao rose to become two much sought-after bailiwicks by the Nacionalista party and its rival Liberal party (Liang 1971, 270–342).

By 1953, Cotabato and Davao were in the top fifteen vote-rich provinces of the Philippines. In terms of registered voters, Davao ranked as high as eighth in 1955, and Cotabato seventh in 1961. Within Mindanao, these two provinces were consistently the top two bailiwicks (with Lanao a distant third) throughout the 1950s.[11] When it came to actual voting, the overall figures were lower and the ranks of both provinces fluctuated from fifth to fifteenth (table 11). Davao reached fifth place in 1953 and settled down to between ninth and fourteenth place in subsequent years, while Cotabato reached eleventh in 1957 and slipped to fifteenth by 1961.[12] The fact that these frontier provinces only a decade earlier did not at all figure in the equation of colonial politics underscores their new importance.

It was, of course, the flood of migrants from the north which considerably increased the number of voters of these provinces. But aggregates were not the most important consideration. Many of the migrants—especially in Davao—maintained ties with their home provinces and were sensitive to the voting preferences of their kinsmen at home. They were also reliable barometers of how a language or ethnic group—wherever it was residing—would vote. A politician devising a plan to win the Visayan vote, therefore, could no longer rely solely on voter turnout in the Visayan-speaking provinces of central Philippines, but would need to keep tabs on the settler provinces of Davao and Cotabato as well (*MinT,* 18 Mar. 1952).

While familiarity with elections was universal among settlers because their home provinces were "regularized" ahead of their new homes, the settlements offered a new electoral context. Notably, the presence of indigenous

Table 11. Provinces with over 100,000 actual voters, 1953-61

| Province | 1953 | 1955 | 1957 | 1959 | 1961 |
|---|---|---|---|---|---|
| Batangas | 121,888 | 146,324 | 151,715 | 181,531 | 194,586 |
| Bohol | 109,566 | 130,946 | 130,601 | 143,986 | 156,408 |
| Bulacan | 143,561 | 167,327 | 158,292 | 198,080 | 202,725 |
| Camarines Sur | 97,196 | 120,834 | 116,907 | 147,114 | 162,265 |
| Cebu | 168,843 | 200,946 | 222,540 | 257,402 | 243,916 |
| Cotabato | 88,261 | 125,429 | 121,999 | 184,040 | 189,173 |
| Davao | 92,411 | 134,106 | 134,092 | 177,030 | 172,118 |
| Iloilo | 153,007 | 183,640 | 188,798 | 211,783 | 217,905 |
| Laguna | 90,153 | 105,291 | 104,343 | 126,050 | 126,096 |
| Leyte | 163,101 | 199,403 | 202,534 | 243,831 | 252,163 |
| Negros Occ. | 128,132 | 153,201 | 159,308 | 181,274 | 202,030 |
| Nueva Ecija | 101,634 | 126,963 | 108,777 | 157,072 | 153,329 |
| Pampanga | 109,017 | 130,511 | 125,618 | 160,037 | 159,421 |
| Pangasinan | 223,108 | 256,721 | 246,596 | 306,684 | 308,646 |
| Quezon | 113,600 | 147,982 | 123,914 | 178,479 | 160,333 |
| Samar | 109,432 | 135,230 | 126,860 | 164,053 | 174,760 |

Sources: *Commission on Elections Reports to the President of the Philippines and the Congress,* various years.

communities and settlers from different parts of the Philippines made ethnicity and language salient factors in determining voting behavior. The different Muslim groups, in particular, were seen to vote in blocs because of the widespread perception that they would follow the instructions of their datu-patrons.[13] While their numbers were not as substantial as the settlers', this bloc voting made them an attractive pool of voters for any candidate aspiring to national office.

Incorporating Muslim communities into electoral bases likewise served to change the range of political options available to a group that was—in the eyes of Manila—prone to rebel. The often-cited role of elections as an alternative to rebellion became a reality in the Muslim provinces after the majority, compelled or convinced by their datu-politicians, accepted the new rules of politics. There continued to be intermittent revolts in Sulu and Lanao, but these were the exception rather than the rule (Mercado 1990, 38–39).

Muslim groups now preferred voting to fighting, and the voting statistics prove it. Anderson's (1996, 14) description of the effect of suffrage applies well to the Muslims of Mindanao:

> On a particular day, determined either by law or by government decision, between hours regulated by the same, at places settled on usually by local authorities [note the state's role in determining when, where, and how the political deed is done], one joins a queue of people whom one does not typically know, to take a turn to enter a solitary space, where one pulls levers or marks pieces of paper, and then leaves the site with the same calm discretion with which one enters it—without questions being asked. It is almost the only political act imaginable in perfect solitude, and it is completely symbolic: It is thus almost the polar opposite of all other forms of personal political participation. Insofar as it has general meaning, it acquires this meaning only by mathematical aggregation. From this perspective, one can readily conclude that, under normal circumstances, the logic of electoralism is in the direction of domestication: distancing, punctuating, isolating. If one asks in whose interest this domestication occurs, one comes immediately to the question of "representation."

In short, I am suggesting that suffrage stabilized the frontier. The state was weak in structure and capacity, but it was an important source of *legitimate political symbols and practices*. Moreover, on this frontier, the only available political mechanism for popular mobilization was the state's electoral system. The Huk movement—then the only viable alternative to the state—failed to expand in southern Mindanao because of organizational weaknesses and a minimal presence among the settler groups. "Rebellious" Muslim groups were, at the time, small armed bands like Hadji Kamlon's in Sulu, aiming to oppose the state's imposition of taxes and the constabulary, with no larger political vision.

## The Politics of Accommodation

The growing electoral importance of southern Mindanao inevitably affected the relationship between state and local strong men. Whereas in the late colonial period, the state (in the person of Quezon) ascribed no serious importance to "Moro Mindanao," links between the two grew stronger after 1946. Henceforth, both the Nacionalista and Liberal parties actively recruited Mindanao leaders, especially those in control of politically strategic provinces like Cotabato and Davao. From all indications, they were successful. All leading Mindanao strong men allied themselves with one of the two parties. To these new politicos, the republic's attraction was what Anderson calls "guaranteed access to national-level political power," the chance to firm up ties with politicians in other provinces and the opportunity to fill the "astonishing proliferation of electoral offices at every level of government" (B. Anderson 1988, 11). Many Mindanao leaders attained national prominence via the decentralized structure of national politics, representing one more provincial bloc or network of clans in congress.[14] Benefits deriving from state access were the main draw for many who ran for office.[15]

Recognizing and participating in the legitimacy of the republic, these leaders were also expected to conform to its norms and practices, as were their constituents. This meant upholding the "emblems" of state rule, of which the most important was pursuing power through the electoral process. The rules of the game now centered on elections, no matter how much a strong man's rise owed to "guns and gold." By opening the state to local strong men via elections, suffrage domesticated their political participation by channeling their energies into legal paths: patronage and connections over weapons and coercion, networks of clients and supporters over retinues of armed men. Henceforth, the ballot, not the bullet, was the main vehicle for local political supremacy.

Adherence to procedure was a strong indication of the domestication of Davao and Cotabato politicians. In Davao, strongmen spent much of their time establishing and consolidating party chapters, dangling patronage benefits to keep supporters loyal and win new adherents. They engaged in factional disputes in conventions and caucuses, protesting nominations, emphasizing the legal way in which candidates were chosen, and negotiating with Manila over positions and resources (*MinT,* 5, 21, 24 July, 23 Aug., 8 Sept. 1951). A 1953 issue of the *Mindanao Times* (16 July 1953), the local Davao newspaper, illustrates how these strong men gave serious attention to playing by the rules:

> [The] following are the developments in the local political front. Defeated Liberal Party aspirant Gregorio Cañeda announced this morning that nominee [Ricardo] Pichon is withdrawing in his favor if he pays expenses amounting to P12,000. "I'll pay him that in cash," Cañeda said. Pichon, on the other hand, declared: "Just look at the face of Cañeda, and judge if he is telling the truth." In a tumultuous caucus at Apo View last

> night, Liberal mayors and leaders informed ex-Senator Salipada Pendatun of their grievances and pledged to support Pichon for congress. Pendatun advised the local Liberals to unite because of the precarious situation of the Liberal Party in Cotabato... The former senator told Pichon to spend the limit to assure his victory and patch up party differences... Meanwhile, the protest of the anti-Veloso bloc against the nomination of the Davao solon as Nacionalista standard bearer is being heard in Manila. [Juan] Pelayo has been chosen as one of the eight aspirants who are definitely to be included in the Nacionalista senatorial line-up together with [Eulogio] Rodriguez, [Lorenzo] Tañada, [Manuel] Cuenco and [Emmanuel] Pelaez.

Strong men also valued election turnout. Despite having often complete control over local police, they rarely used force to ensure electoral victory. Davao was frequently placed under direct constabulary control during elections due to reports of vote-buying, vote-tampering, and voter harassment, yet these incidents were less frequent than might be expected (COMELEC 1959, 25–27). Based on data I have collated, only in early 1951 was there a reported incident in which the incumbent governor publicly admitted using armed former World War II guerrillas to get reelected. This incident sent shockwaves throughout the province and in the following election, the governor was defeated (*MinT,* 22–23 Jan., 27 Sept., 4 Oct. 1951).

Because of the tense relationship among Magindanaos, other indigenous groups, and Christian settlers, we might expect to find Cotabato politics more violence-prone. Yet this was not the case. As in Davao, Cotabato strong men were loyal party officials, engaged actively in similar political practices. Those in power had a substantial arsenal of weapons, but as will be illustrated in the next chapter, they rarely used this coercive tool, relying instead on political and economic control over their voting constituencies to preserve their dominance (Afdal 1949). Statistics on provincial violence bear this out (table 12). A rough compilation of reports of violent acts in Cotabato shows that nonpolitical crimes, from petty theft and cattle-rustling to banditry and murder, occurred frequently, making Cotabato like any other province in the Philippines. What was rare were crimes related to politics and elections. In light of the constabulary's weak presence in the province, peace had to be the outcome of other factors. It was either the result of unusual restraint exercised by the local strong men, or a reflection of their preference for competing in ways other than violent confrontation and in venues other than the battlefield. In this case, the principal arena was electoral politics (Cowen 1950).

Table 12. Types of Violence, Cotabato, 1948-60

| Year | Criminal | Political | Total |
|---|---|---|---|
| 1948 | 4 | 0 | 4 |
| 1949 | 5 | 1 | 6 |
| 1950 | 10 | 1 | 11 |
| 1951 | 2 | 0 | 2 |
| 1952 | 9 | 1 | 10 |
| 1953 | 21 | 1 | 22 |
| 1954 | 21 | 0 | 21 |
| 1955 | 15 | 2 | 17 |
| 1956 | 11 | 0 | 11 |
| 1957* | 6 | 0 | 6 |
| 1958 | 26 | 0 | 26 |
| 1959 | 17 | 0 | 17 |
| 1960 | 15 | 0 | 15 |

Sources: *Mindanao Cross, Daily Mirror* and *Manila Times.*
*No *Mindanao Cross* available

## Conclusion

Herein lay the basis of political stability on the frontier for the first two decades of the republic. Through elections, strong men and state developed a relationship based on mutual interest. Strong men benefited from access to the state and its resources and from the political networks state positions opened up to them. The weak state also found value in the strong men, not only in establishing its authority on the frontier, but in demonstrating that political ambition was best served through the norms, procedures, and practices of the state.

Mutual accommodation does not, of course, rule out contradictions between state and strong man. Inherent features in each sphere, if set alongside each other for long, could produce tension and even conflict. Two of these features are worth mentioning. First, the incompatibility between the innate tendency of the state to centralize and the strong man's instinctive preservation of his autonomy could emerge as the relationship continued. A state seeking to exercise full coercive capacities, to determine the use of natural and human resources, or to reform the electoral system to be more representative of popular aspirations, will inevitably clash with a strong man desiring to preserve his role as the determining power-holder in local society. Strong men could then become obstacles to the "reasons of state" and invite disempowerment or elimination. Given that weakness or strength is historically contingent, there will always be periods in the state's political development when such clashes could occur.

Second, in agreeing to pursue a political career through elections, the strong man puts his own power at risk. He who lives by the ballot may die by the ballot. An electoral defeat would present a variety of options to a strong man intending to remain one, ranging from planning the next campaign to adopting less legal and peaceful means. A state must seek to prevent the strong man's use of coercion, but if it does so while seeking to assert its stateness, the ensuing effort may yield more tension and even outright conflict. Mutual accommodation is therefore a stabilizing relationship but also a balancing act. State and strong men sustained each other, keeping the frontier safe, but their cooperation inevitably involved contradictions that affected their alliance. We will see just how complex this accommodation-*cum*-balancing act was in southern Mindanao in the case histories of Salipada Pendatun of Cotabato and Alejandro Almendras of Davao.

CHAPTER 7

# Local Strong Men: Two Case Studies

## Salipada Pendatun and the Origins of Cotabato Elite Politics

Salipada Pendatun was born 3 December 1910, in Pikit, Cotabato.[1] He traced his lineage to Sharif Kabungsuan, the Islamic teacher from Johore who, according to tradition, founded the Magindanao sultanate.[2] At age sixteen, Pendatun linked the residual value of his lineage to ascendant American power, putting himself under the tutelage of the influential educator, Edward M. Kuder, who gave him a primary education and encouraged him to study further (*PFP,* 5 Aug. 1939). Kuder also shaped his future political career, introducing him to people who influenced colonial politics and protecting him from potential and actual enemies. Pendatun entered the University of the Philippines in 1932 as one of two Muslim pre-law students, finishing his law degree in 1937 and passing the bar in 1938. It was as a law student in Manila that he gained his first political experience as secretary to the Moro representative to the Philippine Assembly, Balabaran Sinsuat (Beckett 1993, 295–97). His ties to the Sinsuats did not last long. Pendatun returned to Cotabato in 1938 to open a law office specializing in landownership cases. One of his first cases involved illegal land acquisition by Balabaran himself. Pendatun won the case, and the court battle marked the beginning of the Pendatun-Sinsuat rivalry with Pendatun vowing "to fight the Sinsuat family in the political arena" (OSS 1945, 3, 7). He became close to the Piangs and helped stage the popular clamor to have Sinsuat replaced by Ugalingan Piang in the Philippine Assembly. Pendatun was elected third member of the Cotabato provincial board in 1938 (Bautista 1939, 279). His alliance with the Piangs was reinforced when he got Ugalingan reappointed to the 1941 assembly (*Seventh and Final Report of the High Commissioner* 1946, 115–16).

If American sponsorship assured him a place in Cotabato politics, fighting the Japanese gave him a berth in the national arena. He kept his anti-Japanese "Bukidnon-Cotabato Force" intact and did not surrender the arms it amassed (Afdal 1949). His coffers were enhanced by war damage payments and guerrilla backpay he and his followers received (Thomas 1971, 316). Finally, guerrilla connections provided access to allies outside Cotabato, from the Fortich family of Bukidnon, who had connections in Manila, to the Liberal presidential candidate Manuel Roxas. With these political assets, Pendatun launched his political career. He joined the Liberal party, was designated campaign manager for Mindanao and Sulu, and won a seat in the first senate of the republic in 1946 (*MT,* 9 Aug 1947).

All this secured more tightly his domination of Cotabato. Governorship of special provinces remained appointive until 1955, and Pendatun took advantage of his Manila connections to award his brother-in-law Udtog Matalam such a position (*MT,* 27 Aug 1947). This period was the high point of Pendatun's political career as he displaced the Piangs and Sinsuats and accumulated wealth far beyond his family's reach during the colonial period.[3] In a 1950 listing of registered Cotabato landowners, the Pendatun family was recorded to have possessed a total of 1,383 hectares (with total assessed value of 113,530 pesos), a figure small by today's standards, but sizable at the time (Department of Finance 1953). His fame brought him controversy, especially in light of the pervasive corruption eating away at the republic in the late 1940s and early 1950s. Like others, however, he survived the allegations (*MCr,* 21 Aug 25 Sept. 1948).

At the height of his power, Pendatun straddled provincial and national politics. At the national level, his membership in the Liberal party, then the dominant national party, and his senate seat gave him access to other political leaders and the presidency, as well as considerable influence over agencies and offices with interests in Cotabato (land settlement, bureau of lands, etc.). At the provincial level, Matalam controlled the local state and used Pendatun's national connections to attract leaders from the settlement areas (*MCr,* 17 July 1948; *MT,* 7 Aug. 1947). The configuration of their power ironically included Pendatun's enemies, the Sinsuats, who were formally linked to the strong man through the Liberal party. Like many political clans that were temporarily eased out of power because of wartime collaboration, the Sinsuats survived politically by distributing family members between the two major parties. This tactic favored Pendatun for a time since his political edge and connections forced the Sinsuats to defer to his authority as provincial party leader.

Pendatun was a fairly active senator, immersed in controversial issues like Japanese collaboration and war damage payments. He was a staunch anticommunist, fought for Mindanao's share in national economic projects, and involved himself in keeping order and stability during the chaotic southern migration (*MT,* 25 Apr., 6 Sept. 1947). Throughout his senate years, he rarely used Islam as a political weapon. Instead, he fashioned himself as a national leader whose religion was incidental. When the sporadic conflict between settlers and Magindanaos was debated on the senate floor, Pendatun was careful not to frame it in terms of a religious war, focusing his remarks instead on the inability of the police to solve the conflict (*MCr,* 20 Mar. 1948).

## Provincial Strains

Two threats confronted Pendatun at the provincial level: the repercussion of massive unorganized migration to Cotabato and the political recovery of the Sinsuats. The massive inflow of people was altering the social and demographic balance, and the Cotabato government, plagued with inefficiency, corruption, and an inability to collect taxes, was in no position to deal with the problem (Sinsuat 1950–51; *MCr,* 28 Apr. 1951). With neither government safety net nor protection, it fell on self-appointed leaders of the settlements to maintain order and defend settler lands against Magindanaos and other indigenous communities. Settler-indigene tensions grew as more migrants arrived (Majul 1985, 31). Feeling outnumbered and marginalized, Magindanaos fought back, but their resistance was hampered by ignorance of land laws and deficient agricultural experience. A lack of professional Magindanaos who could interpret laws and apply them favorably also cost the community many legal battles over land. In the meanwhile, more literate Christians began to enter the local bureaucracy and state agencies, increasing anxieties that a plot to take over Magindanao lands was in the offing (Hunt 1957, 201).

All this had an impact on local politics. Because they constituted the fastest growing populations of the province, the settlers were becoming more important. Cotabato politicians realized that their political calculations had to accommodate the leaders of these new constituent groups on equal terms as their Magindanao allies (*MCr,* 30 Apr. 1950; *DM,* 2 Apr. 1953; *MT,* 1 Oct. 1953). From the early 1950s, Pendatun and Matalam began successfully reaching out to these new leaders. Pork barrel and connections with the settlers' patrons in congress facilitated the new political alliance. If Pendatun could court settlers, however, so could the Sinsuats (*MCr,* 2 Feb 1953). Within three years of their

1946 defeat, they had recovered their influence and rekindled connections with national leaders. The Sinsuats also augmented their firepower by purchasing some of the weapons proliferating in Mindanao.[4] Most important, they brought some of the new settlement leaders onto their side by promising to work for the creation of a new province out of settler-dominated southern Cotabato (*MCr,* 4 Apr. 1953). This alliance broke down quickly when the Sinsuats reneged on their promise (*MCr,* 1 Mar 1952). But the settlement leaders gained an important political education that gave them confidence to test the political waters, setting up their own coalition in the 1953 elections. This fledgling association failed, largely because of inexperience, disunity, and inadequate financial and coercive resources. Yet some of their relatively unknown candidates performed well against Pendatun's and Sinsuat's candidates, giving notice of the settlers' growing political importance (*MCr,* 24 Oct. and 14 Nov. 1953).

## National Pressures

These two problems might have been mitigated had Pendatun been able to retain power on the national level. Pendatun's influence in the senate was based mainly on alliances in the legislative body and in the Liberal party. His faction was the most powerful in these two bodies, counting as its leader Senate President Jose Avelino. In 1948, however, Avelino went to war against President Elpidio Quirino, and Pendatun, loyal to his patron, joined the fray (Lockett Dec. 15 1948; *Memoirs of Elpidio Quirino* 1990, 120–35). The fight led to Avelino's suspension as senate president and for backing the losing side, Pendatun was deprived of the patronage funds necessary to run a nationwide campaign. In 1948, he lost his re-election bid. With the Sinsuats upstaging him in Cotabato, Pendatun tried to reconcile with Quirino, but the latter was not forgiving. Quirino appointed Duma Sinsuat, the eldest son of Pendatun's old enemy, to replace Matalam as provincial governor and helped revive the Piang family's fortunes (*MCr,* 7 Jan. 1950; 15 Apr. 1949). Pendatun then came under a barrage of graft and corruption charges, as Quirino's allies orchestrated a campaign to publicly disgrace him *(* Feb. 10 and 20 Apr. 1949). Especially harmful for Pendatun politically was the revelation that he had defrauded 1,000 Muslim pilgrims who were left stranded and suffering in Mecca for failure to pay pilgrimage taxes and other obligations to the Saudi government.[5] Pendatun was also assailed for his failure to distribute war backpay to some of his followers; his critics suggested that he pocketed the money (*MinT,* 21 Aug 1951; *MT,* 28 Jan. and 23 Feb. 1948).

These attacks weakened Pendatun, forcing him to capitulate to Quirino who then took steps to further limit his maneuverability. Quirino made Pendatun "presidential technical assistant," a largely ceremonial position that was used by presidents to keep their opponents virtually imprisoned in the presidential palace. Pendatun was now consigned to the role of a presidential hanger-on (Cowen 6 July 1949; *MCr,* 9 Apr. 1949). One of his duties was to write reports to the president on conditions in Mindanao and Sulu. The tone of his reports convey his political isolation and helplessness:

> For quite some time now I have been trying to force myself to be quiet by withholding some information and complaints because I do not want to add more problems to the President. I have realized the gravity of the complicated problems facing the President but I do believe that I will be doing some injustice to the country and to His Excellency and to myself if I do not disclose the true picture of Mindanao and Sulu's situations, particularly on the question of peace and order (Pendatun to Quirino 17 Oct. 1950).

So frustrated was Pendatun that at one point he privately threatened to use his army against Quirino allies and the Constabulary in Cotabato (Cowen 4 Apr. 1950). However, these were empty threats as he was momentarily without power in Cotabato, watching helplessly as the Sinsuats reestablished their hold over the province (*MCr,* 22 Apr. 1950). In a local interview, Datu Duma Sinsuat, now leader of the clan, described Pendatun as "a dying gladiator... mortally wounded [and] forced against the wall by the onslaught of his more superior opponents" (*MCr,* 22 Sept. 1951).

But the Sinsuats' power was no more secure. Even as they defeated Pendatun and Matalam in the 1951 and 1953 elections, their stature was considerably tarnished by their failure to control the rat plague, effectively mediate land disputes, and contain reports of abuse of authority (*MCr,* 18 Apr. 1950, 18 Sept. 1954; *DM,* 28 Sept. 1953). The Sinsuats were also blamed for the deterioration of peace and order and the transformation of the province into a hot bed demanding tighter military control (*MT,* 30 Jan. 1954; *MCr,* 28 Feb., 7 and 21 Mar, 1953; *DM,* 4 Dec. 1953). These failures would cost the Sinsuats their hold on the province; the 1953 election of a Pendatun ally to congress signaled the turning of the tide (*MCr,* 11 Apr. 1953; Sinsuat 23 Feb. 1952).

The waning of the Sinsuats and resurrection of Pendatun were also aided by the shifting support of the settlement communities. The Sinsuats' failure to prevent land conflict and the spread of religious enmity brought the leaders of the settler zones back to Pendatun and Matalam, who had a history of facilitating peace between indigenes and settlers. These leaders, however, were not the weak settlement leadership that had first backed the Pendatun-Matalam bloc. They had learned from past mistakes and strengthened unity within their ranks. Thus, although Pendatun successfully restored his power on the local level, his position was more tenuous than in the 1940s.

It was not long before another national level threat to Pendatun's power appeared, this time in the guise of a reformist regime in Manila. Political parties had tolerated fights among their members—particularly at the provincial level—because these did not affect the parties' electoral success. Quirino could depend on the Sinsuats to control Cotabato when he undermined Pendatun, while Pendatun's conflict with the Sinsuats never threatened Liberal party control of Cotabato. However, this rivalry within the party became problematic in the mid-1950s when a new presidential administration of the Nacionalista party became directly involved in Cotabato's politics. Ramon Magsaysay defeated Quirino on a platform of reform, vowing, among other things, to end the communist threat through land reform and resettlement and to rid the government of corruption and inefficiency (Abueva 1971; Starner 1961). As part of his development agenda, Magsaysay was committed to using Mindanao's huge empty spaces for settlement from the north. EDCOR became the centerpiece of his resettlement program, while he expanded his jurisdiction of the NLSA and LASEDECO.

Cotabato was foremost in Magsaysay's mind because he saw its turbulent politics as a test case for his reform administration and an opportunity to break the control of the Liberals and the Pendatun-Matalam cabal (*MT,* 30 Jan. 1954). He aimed to do this by creating his own network of local allies, mainly among the settlers, who were the most receptive to his land for the landless program. Magsaysay wasted no time, appointing an outsider, Col. Primitivo Buagas, to succeed Duma Sinsuat as governor in 1954 (*MCr,* 21 Nov. 1953). Buagas cast himself as the "Magsaysay of Cotabato," promising reforms and an end to disorder (*MT,* 24 Apr. 1954). He focused his concern on the settlement zones to show that he was a leader capable of invigorating their political stature. Buagas's appointment was backed by an unprecedented flow of funds from Manila for infrastructure development, settlement rehabilitation, and even reduction of the provincial deficit (*MCr,* 4 Apr. 1953; 26 Mar. and 8 May 1954). Magsaysay also protected Buagas by deploying more troops in Cotabato and intervening in local clan disputes (*MCr,* 23 Jan.

1954; *MT,* 27 July 1954). For the first time since the Quezon era, Manila had intervened actively to alter Cotabato's politics. Whether Magsaysay's motive was patronage politics or sincere reformism is beside the point. The most important thing was that Buagas had the force and resources of the central state behind him. With the Sinsuats in retreat once more, it was left to Pendatun to deal with Manila's intrusiveness. Already familiar with the techniques of patronage politics, Pendatun sought to moderate the state's assault by instructing his allies to join Magsaysay's party, ingratiate themselves with the president, and convince Manila that peace and order could best be achieved by a Buagas-Pendatun-Matalam alliance *(MCr,* 16 Jan. 1954). The strategy did not work. Magsaysay remained committed to Buagas as the new leader of the province and supported his efforts to set up networks independent of the datus, networks that became conduits for largesse from Manila (*MCr,* 31 July 1954).

In 1955, however, fortunes changed again. An overconfident Buagas challenged the Magindanao leaders when the office of governor became elective, running as the official Nacionalista candidate (*MCr,* 30 June 1955). In response, the Sinsuats, Matalam, and Pendatun formed a tactical alliance, branding Buagas's "anti-Muslim." While the alliance did not last long (the Sinsuats quickly withdrew), it galvanized a unified Magindanao vote. Buagas also fell victim to his own reformism, alienating his settler constituents by zealously exposing the corruption of their leaders. The final blow to Buagas's ambitions came when the Nacionalista leadership dumped him after striking a secret deal with Pendatun, who agreed to switch parties and deliver the Magindanao vote to the Nacionalistas (*MCr,* 24 July, 11, 18, and 20 Sept., 16 and 30 Oct. and 6 Nov. 1954). Matalam was elected governor in a campaign characterized by violence and rampant irregularities; Buagas conceded defeat and returned to Manila (*MCr,* 1, 15 and 29 Oct. 1955).

With Matalam's victory, Pendatun appeared to have recovered fully from 1948. His restored power, however, was substantially different. In 1946, Pendatun and Matalam were virtually unchallenged; in 1953, migration, the Sinsuats, and the new possibility of state-supported challengers like Buagas complicated the political landscape. There was growing political aggressiveness in the settler zones, manifested not only in electoral challenges at the municipal, town, and provincial levels, but also in a growing ability to operate as a bloc (*MCr,* 11 Feb. 1956). How this alteration in the structure of political bases and networks in Cotabato would affect Magindanao politics became more apparent as Pendatun renewed his quest to return to the national arena and reclaim the lost power and prestige he had enjoyed in the senate.

In 1957, Pendatun won the congressional seat for Cotabato, attributing his victory to the restoration of harmony between settlers and Magindanaos after the Buagas period and to an unprecedented unity among the Magindanaos that he claimed to have brokered (*MCr,* 2 Dec. 1957). This was not the complete story. Pendatun won because he did not rely solely on his provincial base, but was backed by the Nacionalista leadership and by the Mindanao-Sulu-Palawan Association (MINSUPALA), a bloc of Mindanao political leaders whose purpose was to "get concessions from both the ruling party and the Nacionalista administration of [new president] Carlos Garcia" (*MT,* 26 Mar. 1960; *PFP,* 1 and 29 June 1957). In congress, Pendatun gained leverage when he was chosen house majority floor leader courtesy of the Mindanao bloc (*MCr,* 13 Sept. 1958). With his new alliance and influence, he was able get Matalam reelected as governor in 1959, despite strong opposition from the Sinsuats. He also was able to establish a modus vivendi with the settler communities with the help of MINSUPALA leaders (*MCr,* 1 Jan. 1959).

Their success, however, was fragile. Pendatun's and Matalam's victories came at a time when Cotabato was already considerably changed by migration, by the worsening ferocity of factional politics, and by the growing presence of the Manila government (*MCr,* 17 Jan. 1950). They had regained power not through a combination of solid support from below and patronage from above, but because Pendatun staked his fortunes on national politics and its many shifting coalitions. Social and intraethnic tensions at the provincial level had a lot to do with this tactical shift. The Magindanaos were divided into two factions, weakening their position vis-à-vis the settlers who, sensing their growing power, became more hostile toward Magindanao leaders (*MT,* 26 Mar. 1960). Thus, Pendatun and Matalam came to rely on Manila to maintain their position in Cotabato.

As the Magindanaos felt increasingly marginalized by the settlers, and as their fear of government complicity in their fate spread, Pendatun found himself in a bind. To consolidate power in Cotabato he could have reached out to the settlement zones, continuing to demonstrate that he and Matalam were leaders of a diverse province, with the ability to unite its disparate and contentious communities. But to do so risked alienating the Magindanaos who increasingly saw the turbulence in Cotabato in ethnoreligious terms and who were becoming suspicious of the compromises made by Pendatun. The alternative was to accept the altered sociopolitical landscape, acknowledge his waning influence in the settlement zones, and preserve his influence among the Magindanaos. This path risked his standing in Manila, which preferred

"Filipino-Muslim unity" and expected Magindanao politicians to maintain alliances with their Christian counterparts. Nevertheless, Pendatun chose the latter option, hoping that by focusing on a single constituency he could get out of the situation of utter dependence on Manila. By narrowing his concerns, Pendatun was able to get himself reelected in 1959 and throughout the 1960s (*MCr,* 18 Nov. 1961). He also made religion and identity truly significant in Cotabato politics for the first time in Philippine postwar political development.

## The Resurrection of the "Moro Problem"

Amidst growing religious tension, calls to defend and preserve the "Muslim community" began to be heard in the political arena. Because of their high visibility, Muslim politicians—notably Pendatun—were easily identified as the purveyors of such sentiments (*Congressional Records* 1950, 568–72). Instead of presenting themselves as national statesmen, Pendatun and other leaders recast themselves as Muslim leaders, now engaged in the resolution of the "Moro Problem." This time, however, it was not the "Moros" who *were* the problem, but the "Moros" who *had* the problem: their growing isolation from an anti-Muslim state. As this theme was expounded, the rich tradition of Moro resistance to a prejudicial state became a dominant theme in their political discourse (*TWM,* 15 Sept. 1957). If Muslims were to preserve their identity, it became important for them to unite as one ethnoreligious group. For only from a position of unity could the Muslims effectively resist the state and its allies. Organization followed rhetoric soon enough. Pendatun helped transform the Muslim Association of the Philippines (MAP) into a bloc to fight for "Muslim interests" within MINSUPALA.[6] MAP's and MINSUPALA's intensive lobbying eventually led the government to create a Commission on National Integration (CNI) whose official responsibility was to design a comprehensive development plan for the national minorities and hasten their integration (Salgado 1989, 83).

Pendatun's ethnicization of Cotabato politics set a precedent for the leaders of the settlement communities to use religion and identity as well. Seeing how these issues had united the Magindanaos and revived Pendatun's career, settler leaders began to cast themselves as defenders of the "embattled Christian settler." They played on the fears of their constituents and encouraged a more bellicose attitude toward Magindanaos (*MCr,* 28 Apr. 1956). When combined with issues like land for the landless and a portrayal of the small settler under constant harassment by well-connected Magindanaos, religion proved very potent. Preventing religious war became the new justification for dividing Cotabato and creating a settler-majority province (*MT,* 22 Feb. 1957). Thus the Magindanaos' assertion of "Muslim resistance" was matched by the defense of "Christianity" in the settler communities. Using religion as the mobilizing theme, both sides added a volatile element to their already brewing hostility.

Pendatun's strategy of confining his local concerns to the Magindanaos, however, did not draw all Muslims to his side. In fact, it spawned some criticism from young educated Muslims who assailed him and other leaders for using Islam to advance their traditional politics. In 1957, an essay appeared in the MAP magazine openly criticizing Muslim politicians:

> Pseudo-Muslim leaders in their mad scramble for political recognition, made a mountain out of a mole hill, so to speak, of minor incidents in the Muslim provinces and exaggerated the not-too-repulsive traits of their brother Muslims. In a nutshell, the world is misinformed that in the Muslim area different kinds of people have different moral, economic, social and political outlooks. Hence, [they] should be treated differently—with unlimited patience, understanding and sympathy… The difference, if any, lies in our pretentious Muslim leaders who are counterfeit gods with feet of clay, politically built on stilts that do not fit them. I'd like to see the day when I can proudly shout my voice hoarse to all and sundry, that "there goes a genuine Muslim leader, the man after my heart." Indisputably there are no so-called Moro problems, just as there are no Muslim leaders yet (*CR,* 1957, 3).

As president of MINSUPALA and executive board member of the MAP, Pendatun was singled out as the quintessential patronage politician, a creature of the system of compromises, backroom deals, and political pragmatism. Muslim intellectuals admired his political skills, but to some he was much more a Filipino politician than a serious defender of Muslim interests (Glang 1969, 61). These critics gained little ground while the datus remained preeminent (*CR* 1958, 3). They nevertheless foretold future difficulties as the political conflict in Cotabato worsened.

In his second appearance on the national stage, Pendatun had become the consummate political survivor, adeptly switching political parties when electoral tides turned. Taking advantage of Magsaysay's death, Pendatun had switched parties to give Garcia a win in Cotabato and was awarded the position of house majority floor leader. He held this post until 1960, when Liberal party leader Diosdado Macapagal defeated Garcia. The majority floor leader, Matalam, and their followers immediately returned to their old party. Shifting political allegiance again proved a wise move, for Pendatun was reelected to congress in 1961 (*MCr,* 3 and 30 Mar 1962). Social and economic conditions, however, continued to change.

By 1960, scholars and policymakers observed that the Mindanao frontier was filling up fast, and unless the government responded to it, land-related conflict would become more violent (Costello 1984, 2–9). The signs were already there. Settlers continued to force non-Muslim indigenous groups out of the hinterlands, and there was a notable rise in banditry all over Mindanao and Sulu.[7] Corporate investments, though still limited, were starting to grow, signaling the entry of a new player in the island's politics (Tadem 1992, 6). Their wealth and the potential benefits they could bring made them a valuable source of political support. When Castle and Cooke, Inc. opened an 8,000-hectare pineapple plantation worth 80 million pesos in Polomolok, southern Cotabato, it elevated the political status of the leaders of the predominantly settler communities of that municipality (*MCr,* 14 Nov. 1963). It also served to accentuate the diminishing political clout of Magindanao politicians in the settler towns (*MCr,* 8 Jan. 1966).

Within Magindanao society, Pendatun brokered a reconciliation with the Sinsuats which was again short-lived as violent incidents between the two camps soon resumed (*MT,* 27 May 1961, 13 Feb., 8 Aug., 1962; 20 Apr. 1963). Failing to unify the Magindanaos, Pendatun shifted his attention back to national politics, a move which surprised observers. The dominant explanation at the time was that Pendatun trusted his ally Matalam to mind the provincial store vigorously and with a heightened sense of vigilance. The real reason, however, was that Pendatun was forced to make backroom compromises because of the Sinsuat connections in the Liberal party and in congress. One major concession was his support for fellow Liberal Mando Sinsuat's candidacy for mayor of Cotabato City, a move that had serious implications for Pendatun's own network (*MCr,* 24 June 1963). In exchange, Pendatun became Speaker Pro-tempore in congress, a largely ceremonial title that placed him in the line of succession to the Speaker should a reorganization in the lower house occur. This compromise would end up costing Pendatun a lot.

The most immediate repercussion of Pendatun's concession was a fallout with Matalam. For a long time Matalam had been in the forefront of the struggle against the Sinsuats and he now refused to abide by the compromise. Supporting his own candidate, a Liberal leader from the settlement communities, Matalam openly criticized the party and Pendatun's pact with the Sinsuats (*MCr,* 22 and 27 Feb. 1963). The *Mindanao Cross* (10 Oct. 1963) observed: "And so it has to be, Pendatun and Matalam in politics which have been inseparable as turtle to a shell are parting ways to support their own candidates... For Matalam, no Sinsuat is acceptable as a candidate. Pendatun, on the other hand, had to play national politics. He can support only [Liberal party] candidates." The rift worsened on election day, sending reverberations throughout the Magindanao community (*MCr,* 19 Oct. 1963). It marked the beginning of the decline of Pendatun as a local power in Cotabato, a decline aggravated by the presidential election of Ferdinand Marcos in 1964.

Salipada Pendatun's career has shown the complexity of the life of a postwar Cotabato strong man. That he had a Janus-faced political persona was never in doubt. What is notable about his politics is how he shifted from one public position to another: national statesman-senator, then local patronage politician with national connections, and finally defender of the Muslims. While he remained the dominant Magindanao politician throughout the 1960s, Pendatun's career indicates a steady decline in influence and power, reflecting the ever-narrowing space in which he operated. Postwar changes that fundamentally altered Cotabato's political landscape—inmigration, intensification of factional battles, new settler-based strong men, a more intrusive national government—made his standing precarious and his public positions evanescent. Thus, while he appeared to pull himself out of political purgatory and once more plant his feet in both provincial and national politics, Pendatun was actually growing weaker.

Pendatun's political journey reflected one type of pilgrimage that Filipino strong men made in the postwar period. This was by no means the only way of accumulating, preserving, and defending one's power. Other strong men took different routes, starting as small-town local leaders and ascending slowly to provincial and eventually national politics. And they proved more successful in the long run than Pendatun was. This was true in the case of Alejandro Almendras and his political hegemony over adjoining Davao province.

## "Landring" Almendras and the Stability of Davao Politics

Almendras, whose last resumé described him as "businessman, farmer, congressman," was born in Danao City, Cebu province. His father Paulo was a powerful figure in Danao politics during the Commonwealth period, but his power waned in the 1940s when his ambitious brother-in-law, Ramon Durano, broke ties with the Almendras family, and, with the help of the powerful Cuenco family of Cebu City, seized control of Danao (Sidel 1993, 401). Almendras's brother, Jovenal, was elected congressman of the first district of Cebu in 1946, but he was unable to arrest the expanding power of his uncle. The family's status was further weakened when Landring migrated to Davao (Cullinane 1993, 171, 174, 217). In Davao Landring settled in Sta. Cruz, a municipality south of the city.

He could not have chosen a better town to start his political career. Sta. Cruz adjoined a string of settler municipalities along the Padada Valley that were dominated by Cebuanos and Boholanos. Landring was at home with his language and regional group. Further, these municipalities were noted for their enduring political loyalties. The settlers of Sta. Cruz and other communities of the valley were supporters of the Cebuano leader and former Commonwealth president Sergio Osmeña and maintained their support when they moved to Davao. Landring, whose family was allied with the Osmeñas, found a sympathetic community in the Cebuano settlers, while they, knowing the name Almendras, saw in the young businessman a potential leader. This plurality of pro-Osmeña Cebuanos explains why Almendras chose Sta. Cruz over Davao City. Although Cebuanos and Boholanos also dominated Davao, which in turn controlled provincial politics, Landring's political potential would have been constrained. Because its top positions remained appointive, Landring would have been vulnerable to attack from his family's Cebu rivals who were major players in national politics (Sidel 1995, 408–11). In Sta. Cruz he had a supportive constituency, and the municipality's elective posts gave him the opportunity to build a local base.

Being a municipal resident also kept Landring out of factional battles in Davao City. Jockeying for positions was intense there as appointed officials constantly negotiated their fate with Manila. Appointees were also less dependent on electoral bases and easily broke away from or remained autonomous of elected provincial bosses. City politicians from both parties were thus engaged in incessant internal disagreement. As early as 1948, "many claims to the leadership" divided the city's Liberals, while similar dissension affected the Nacionalistas (*MinT,* 19 June 1951). Landring was not immune to these battles, but because he was the leader of a municipality consisting mainly of people loyal to him, he was not exposed to their negative consequences as often as his fellow Nacionalistas. He managed to preserve an independent posture vis-à-vis the fights in Davao City.

Landring came on the scene at the point when migration was transforming Davao into an opposition bailiwick. From 1946 until the election of Ramon Magsaysay in 1951, the Liberal party dominated Philippine politics. In Davao, however, the loyalty of Cebuano and Boholano settlers to the Nacionalistas proved enduring. A confidential memorandum from a Liberal supporter to President Quirino noted that Davao's Cebuanos voted Nacionalista "due to the fact that the rank and file have not forgotten President Osmeña" (De Jesus 1952, 2). Landring, however, had to bide his time in Sta. Cruz. His family's opponents were in control of national and Cebu power, and Davao was under the thumb of Ismael Veloso, a former protégé of the Japanese during the Commonwealth period whose fortune was revived through Liberal party membership. In 1946, Veloso was elected Davao's lone representative to congress and anchored his dominance through connections with Manila. In this way he became Davao's patron, bringing in pork barrel funds as well as facilitating the settlement of the frontier (*Congressional Record* 12 Mar. 1953, 875; *MCh*, 2 Feb. 1958).

In November 1948, the Liberals asserted their domination by winning elections for governor, provincial board, Davao City council, and the mayoralties of most municipalities. Their victory, however, was not total. Veloso, sensitive to the weakness of his local mass base, had defected to the Nacionalistas and begun to court Almendras and other leaders of the Cebuano-Boholano-Samar-Leyte faction. Veloso's local vulnerability was something Landring would exploit in the future, but in the meantime, he quietly built his own base and played the loyal ally. Veloso defeated his Liberal rival handily, and while incumbent Liberal governor Ricardo Miranda managed to retain his seat, he did so only by intimidation and fraud (*MinT,* 22 Feb. 1951). The clearest sign that the Liberals were not safely ensconced in power was the defeat of Liberal presidential and senatorial candidates in Davao. Liberals blamed the loss on inadequate assistance from the national party and divisions within the local leadership; another factor was clearly the rejuvenation of the local Nacionalista machine (Confidential Letter to Quirino 4 Dec. 1949, Villafuerte 8 Aug. 1950). To fight back, the Liberal-controlled national administration used pork barrel to weaken Veloso and strengthen Miranda (*MinT,* 6 July, 14 and 16 Aug. 1950). The provincial government likewise capitalized on the migration rush to public lands in the Padada valley and northern Davao by encouraging indiscriminate settlement, thus disrupting social life in these Nacionalista municipalities (*MinT,* 1 Feb. 1951). Finally, the Liberals tried to win back defectors to tighten their grip on municipalities under their control (*MinT,* 7 Apr. 1951).

Incessant divisions within the Liberal leadership negated these efforts (*MinT,* 17 Mar. 7, 9 and 26 June 1951). The Liberals were also unable to solve land disputes in the settlement areas and even aggravated the problem (*MinT,* 6 Aug. 1950). They thus failed to counter the Nacionalista resurgence. While Nacionalistas themselves were not without internal disputes, with many still suspicious of Veloso, these fissures remained under control as long as the party was in opposition (*MinT,* 10 Oct. 1941). They were also mitigated by the continuing growth of the party network, thanks to the support Almendras drew from Cebuano and Boholano settlers and squatters, as well as former guerrillas and veterans. Moreover, since Veloso was the only link they had with the national government, warring Nacionalistas were pragmatic enough to rally behind their patron. Keeping their differences under control, the Nacionalistas prepared for the 1951 provincial and city council elections (*MinT,* 19 and 23 Feb. 1951).

This election marked the appearance of Almendras as a leader in provincial politics. Going into the convention, he was not even considered a candidate for the provincial slate. He was young and was regarded as a political novice, though also recognized as someone "to reckon with in Davao politics especially in the southern towns" (*MinT,* 7 Oct. 1950). When placed on Veloso's slate as provincial board member, Almendras was forced to withdraw when older members demanded priority (*MinT,* 28 June 1951). Anti-Veloso factions, however, then set up their own list and immediately added him to it, threatening disunity among the ranks. Intervention by Manila Nacionalistas averted the rift, and a compromise list nominated Almendras as the dark horse candidate for governor (*MinT,* 7 Oct. 1950; 21 June, 1 and 3 July and 7 Aug. 1951). Despite this recognition of Almendras's potential, Veloso remained the patron and leader of the fight against the Liberals (*MinT,* 30 Aug. and 4–10 Sept. 1951. Almendras resented his patron's control but understood that his time had not yet come. Meanwhile, continuing disunity wracked the Liberals' organization, made worse by Manila's mistrust of the local Liberals (*MinT,* 23 and 25 Feb., 1951; Villafuerte 8 Aug. 1950). This spelled their ruin. In November 1951, the Nacionalistas defeated the Liberals and governor-elect Almendras now had the opportunity to extend his influence beyond Sta. Cruz (*MinT,* 29 Nov. 1951).

For the next six years, the Veloso-Almendras bloc ruled Davao, with the exception of Davao City which remained in Liberal hands until 1954. Veloso took care of national connections, while Almendras supervised the provincial network (*MinT,* 17 June 1952). Their partnership drew strength from Davao's position as an opposition province. The Liberal-controlled national government showed little interest in Davao, and this contrived negligence became an issue to rally supporters. Almendras continued to defer to Veloso, but also tended to his own base. He avoided the battles that had destroyed his family's ambitions in Cebu. He instead established close ties with Davao relatives of his Danao opponents, notably Gabino Sepulveda, the brother of a Durano protégé, and Vicente Duterte, a cousin of Durano's wife (Cullinane 1993: 172). Almendras also kept close ties with the Philippine Veterans League (PVL), an association that became important because of land conflicts (Harrington 5 June 1951, 1). When fights over public land erupted between these veterans and the government, Almendras consistently supported the PVL, even when many of its members turned out to be squatters (*MinT,* 25 Mar. and 6 May 1952). In return, the veterans backed Almendras.

Squatting, in fact, became an opportunity for Almendras to expand his mass base. Employing the same strategy that fortified his support among the veterans, Almendras drew organized groups of settler-squatters into his fold by defending them against government attempts to evict them.[8] He mediated between community and state, as well as among squatter groups, carefully cultivating the profile of an impartial arbiter (*MinT,* 6 Jan., 3 Mar., 8–29 May, 17 June, and 11 Sept. 1952). Also important to Almendras were the municipal mayors, and he took advantage of proximity to foster close ties (U.S. Embassy to Department of State, 11 May 1951, 2). (Mayors were more accessible to a governor than to a senator or congressman who divided his time between Manila, Davao City, and the municipalities.) Language and regional ties facilitated his relationship with the mayors from Cebu and Bohol, while non-Visayans were courted with patronage resources through Veloso (*MinT,* 8 Jan. 1953).

As Almendras tightened his control over local constituents, he also made connections with forces outside the province. The growing importance of Davao as an electoral bailiwick put Almendras in touch with important committees within the Nacionalista party. Regional powerbrokers from the Visayas who wanted to retain influence over the settler communities asked Almendras to facilitate their contacts, to the growing consternation of Veloso (*MinT,* 12 Mar. 1953; 6 Nov. 1954). Almendras especially tried to keep Veloso out of the loop in his dealings with Cebuano leaders. He hammered out alliances with rising politicians like Congressman Filemon Kintanar and continued to maintain close ties with the Osmeñas (*MinT,* 8 Mar. and 8 Apr.

1952). These connections complemented his alliances in Davao, which always remained his priority.

As a result of these networks, Almendras was able to cast himself as the quintessential Davao leader. Through antigraft campaigns and an apparent concern for peace and order, he was able to project a public image of the clean politico—the antithesis of most Davao politicians, including Veloso (*MinT,* 9 May 1951; 24 and 29 July 1952; 29 Jan. 1953). Occasionally, the darker side of his character slipped out. In 1952, the *Mindanao Times* (26 and 29 July, 30 Sept. 1952) reported the dismissal on technical grounds of an assault case filed against Almendras by a local bureaucrat. It was reported that the graft-busting governor ordered an investigation of anomalies allegedly committed by the bureaucrat, and when this did not bear fruit, had his protagonist re-assigned to dangerous Lanao del Norte and Lanao del Sur provinces. Evidence of the Almendras temper also appeared, particularly during party debates. Once, as an exchange turned bitter, Almendras stood up to "challenge by fist or pistol" those who impugned his political position (*MinT,* 20 June 1953). His image as an honest leader was also blemished when an overzealous land investigation committee exposed the extent to which he had accumulated land while in office (*MinT,* 19, 23 and 26 June 1954). These defects, however, were not enough to derail his popularity in local and national politics. In 1953, President Magsaysay appointed Almendras to the Nacionalista national committee assigned to screen candidates for the next election (*MinT,* 16 June 1953). The governor had taken the first step into national politics.

## The New Patron

The Nacionalistas continued their electoral victory in 1955 with Almendras winning reelection by a wide margin (*MinT,* 12 Nov. 1955). The 1955 election was also meaningful because it was the first general election for all Davao City positions. Veloso and Almendras, given a free hand by the president to run the province and Davao City, imposed their will on the city's rebellious factions and chose the candidates for city positions (*MinT,* 12 Dec. 1953). Their interference drew stiff opposition from city Nacionalistas in alliance with Manila leaders who prized Davao for their own political ends (*MinT,* 22 May 1954). Veloso and Almendras fought off challenges from three city factions before assuming control of the city.[9] They won the battle, and their candidates for mayor and councilors swept the elections. The Veloso-

Almendras alliance, however, began to break down as each used the occasion to outmaneuver the other for control of the province and the city.

The trouble began when Veloso unilaterally decided to choose a long-time Almendras opponent as candidate for mayor. Despite his suspicion that Veloso was promoting a new protégé, Almendras supported Carmelo Porras' candidacy (*MinT,* 28 May, 16 June and 7 July 1955). But Veloso did not stop with Porras. He also began to usurp Almendras' position as defender of settlers and squatters against the government and influential people (*MinT,* 13 Apr. 1955). Almendras yielded publicly to Veloso, but continued quietly to act as mediator for the squatters, sending the message that he would not relinquish the role completely (*MinT,* 23 June, 11 and 21 July, 17 and Oct. 1956). Two incidents led to an open break. Porras, beginning to appreciate his power as mayor, attacked Almendras, criticizing his dictatorial rule of the Davao Nacionalistas and exposing his connection with gambling dens in the city (*MinT,* 17 Nov. 1956). While Porras was attacking, Veloso was coercing municipal mayors to sever ties with Almendras under threat of sanctions from the party center and denial of pork barrel funds and election support. This proved a miscalculation. The majority of the mayors not only rejected the congressman's overture, but also demanded that Almendras split from Veloso (*MinT,* 19 June 1957). It was not clear whether Almendras had a hand in the mayors' response, but in picking up the cudgels for him, the mayors gave Almendras's anti-Veloso response a popular cast. This was all Almendras needed to portray himself as an embattled leader assailed by a more powerful patron. It was a good tactical move.

On 21 June 1957, Almendras publicly broke with Veloso, citing public clamor for him to do so (*MinT,* 22 June and 24 Aug. 1957). Fifteen of the twenty-five municipal mayors and two of the three Davao city factions openly supported his move (*MinT,* 13 July 1957). No amount of mediation by provincial or Manila envoys could mend the split (*MinT*, 20 July 1957). The next move was to challenge Veloso in the upcoming congressional elections. For this Almendras picked Gabino Sepulveda, an illiterate but reliable ally, if only to emphasize that anyone could defeat the "orator" Veloso (*MinT,* 24 Aug. 1957). Almendras was given a further boost when, in exchange for his promise to deliver Davao to Nacionalista presidential candidate Carlos P. Garcia, party leaders declared Sepulveda the official candidate over Veloso and refused Veloso's request to make the entire province a free zone (*MinT,* 6 June and 21 Aug. 1957). Almendras also received unexpected support from an old family ally, the Osmeñas of Cebu, who, despite being Liberals, directed their Davao supporters to back Almendras (*MinT,* 20 Nov. 1957). What followed was a campaign characterized by the systematic cutting down of Veloso and Porras by Almendras's allies at the *Mindanao Times*. On election day, Sepulveda defeated Veloso, and Almendras's candidates swept the elections (*MinT,* 13 Nov. 1957).

Veloso's defeat showed how the patient building of an extensive provincial network could pay off. It also illustrated that a secure local base was necessary for long-term survival as a major player in national politics. Veloso was not bereft of power himself, possessing more resources and having powerful connections in the capital. In a decentralized, regional power bloc-based electoral system like the Philippines, however, relying on power at the center was precarious. For the center itself was always shifting with the constant reconfiguration of political factions and forces. Almendras, perhaps learning his initial political lessons in Danao, acknowledged the power emanating from the center, but also saw its dependence on regional and provincial blocs. By preserving, defending, and expanding his local network, Almendras had more options than Veloso. He could live his political life within Davao, sure of widespread support. He could also use that base to propel himself into national politics and to bargain for support from national leaders. Almendras thus straddled the provincial and national spheres more comfortably than Pendatun because of his entrenched control of local politics. After his triumph over Veloso, and with a new presidential administration grateful for his campaigning in Davao, Almendras was ready for bigger things. On 3 May 1958, he became secretary of the newly created Department of General Services that oversaw personnel management for the state bureaucracy (American Consul, Cebu, 1 July 1959). He used his position against his rivals, pulling strings from afar, settling feuds, organizing candidate lists, and even managing municipal campaigns (*MinT*, 21 and 24 May, 18 June, 12 July and 6 Aug. 1958). But he did not remain secretary for long. On 8 August 1959, he was chosen to represent Mindanao on the Nacionalista senate slate. With huge numbers voting for him in the Visayas and Mindanao, he won handily over a Mindanao rival. His chosen successor, cousin Vicente Duterte, also prevented Veloso's comeback attempt and won the governorship. Almendras's victory was spoiled only by his failure to dislodge Porras from Davao City (*MinT,* 11, 14 and 18 Nov. 1959). The losses, however, were minor. Almendras was now senator, and with his new powers he was hardly held back by the local trifle that was Carmelo Porras.

## Conclusion

The stories of Pendatun and Almendras show how mutual accommodation with the state brought strong men to power and helped the state govern Mindanao. They also demonstrate how tenuous that accommodation was. Strong men had to continually balance their power between Manila and Mindanao to accomplish their objectives both as local leaders and as representatives of the state. Provincial problems, lack of attention to a local power base, and changing politics at the center all affected the ability of the strong man, and thus the state, to govern. This is reflected in the ultimate success of Almendras and failure of Pendatun in maintaining that balance and their power.

While religion was a factor in Cotabato which was absent in Davao, other factors were more important in explaining the different outcomes in these two men's political careers. Foremost of these was their choice of path to national power. While both were protégés of local leaders and first established their presence locally, Pendatun capitalized on his guerrilla record to set himself up quickly as a national leader, while Almendras used his family's stature in Cebu to create a local network. Pendatun's priority was politics at the state center, subordinating his local political network to this primary goal. As a consequence, Pendatun relied on allies and subordinates to maintain his provincial network. Thus the Cotabato strong man immediately engaged in a balancing act between provincial and national spheres. He failed to understand that the provincial governor's "office has been the stepping-stone of almost everyone of the small group of men who have reached the inner seats of power in the national government" (Hayden 1942, 28). Pendatun clearly regarded himself as a patron, concerned with representing and negotiating for his province at the center. After he lost his senate seat and had to go home, his disengagement from the nuances of provincial politics caused him difficulty. When he did win a legislative seat again, his preference for national politics was evident in his involvement in MINSUPALA. Almendras, in contrast, carefully molded and consolidated a local power base before making a successful bid for national prominence. He willingly subordinated himself to patrons like Ismael Veloso, who gave him both cover for the building of local alliances and a connection to the national side of the political equation. Pendatun walked on two legs, while Almendras used the "bottom up" approach to power.

Almendras's power was fundamentally different from Pendatun's in the configuration of priorities and political alliances. His connections were not only multi-faceted and evenly distributed; he was also the center through which the various actors were linked to one another. Just as Pendatun relied on Matalam, Veloso had to go through Almendras to reach his Davao constituents. Unlike Matalam, however, Almendras was an arbitrator who strategically deferred to his patron while quietly expanding his own power. Finally, while Almendras's and Pendatun's local bases appeared similarly constructed of ethnic/linguistic allies, the crucial difference was in their maintenance. Pendatun coursed all local affairs through his brother-in-law; when he interceded in provincial matters, he did so through his Manila connections. Almendras, in contrast, relied on a wide variety of local leaders, from squatters and ex-soldiers to municipal mayors; this extensive network became an asset to him in national politics. Almendras was the better coalition-builder, and it was because of his local success that his foray into national politics in the mid-1950s stood on firmer ground.

CHAPTER 8

# Centralizing State, Weakening Strong Men, and a Frontier in Crisis

If the late 1950s saw the height of strong-man power in southern Mindanao, the 1960s marked its waning as the national government once more tried to assert its presence on the frontier. This time, under Ferdinand Marcos, the state was more successful. By strengthening the office of the president, Marcos, not unlike Quezon, undercut strong-man power in southern Mindanao, especially as the political and economic value of the region became more pronounced. Under Marcos, state centralization affected the manner in which regional and provincial strong men went about their politics. Pendatun's decline was hastened as his constant shifting between provincial and national politics dissipated his resources, while Almendras, now immersed in Manila as an ally of Marcos, left Davao to subordinates and also saw his local power decline.

A related factor in the eclipse of the Mindanao strong men was the appearance of new rivals. Pendatun and Almendras were able to combat opponents who fought within the framework of party-patronage politics, but social and educational changes in the 1960s culminated in the rise of new forces in Mindanao. Inspired by anti-American nationalism and religious radicalisms within and outside the Philippines, a younger generation began to engage in popular organization locally and nationally. In Davao, vowing to end the American imperialist stranglehold over Philippine society and to overthrow comprador-capitalists, bureaucrat-capitalists, and landlords, these forces compensated for their deficiency in resources with astute propaganda and organizing. In Cotabato, young Muslim intellectuals influenced by Nasserite nationalism and student radicalism in Manila advocated a militant, antistate, anti-Filipino nationalism among Muslim communities. They were able to utilize splits among Muslim politicians to advance their goals. By the 1970s, both forces had shifted the provincial limelight away from the old strong men.

These changes occurred as southern Mindanao moved into its final phase of demographic change. Although the frontier was considered filled, migration actually surged, with now predictable results. Landownership disputes became more frequent and in Cotabato took on religious and ethnic overtones. In Davao, the emergence of class stratification in settlement towns foretold wider and more serious social strife. In the main arena of political contestation—elections—these polarizations had a profound impact on strong men. The continued consolidation of settlement towns in both provinces produced new electoral rivals. Pendatun and Almendras thus faced unprecedented challenges on the local level just when the national state became more interventionist. The following sections trace the impact of these conflicting political and demographic trends especially their repercussions on the political lives of Salipada Pendatun and Alejandro Almendras.

## Ferdinand Marcos

The association of Marcos with dictatorship and patrimonial plunder has often obscured the fact that he also represented a new breed of Filipino politician. While sharing the landed origins of his political counterparts, Marcos did not found his power exclusively on the traditional bases of economic and political influence—control of land and vital export crops. Instead, he combined control over his local bailiwick (and language group, the Ilocanos) with connections established in college as a member of an elite fraternity. His putative war record as a leader of an anti-Japanese guerrilla group enhanced this language-*cum*-education base during World War II (Spence 1979, 174–76). Like Salipada Pendatun, Marcos's war record gave him an added layer of fame and set him apart from many fellow politicians who collaborated with the Japanese (McDougald 1987, 89).

What most distinguished Marcos (and to a certain extent, his presidential predecessor Diosdado Macapagal) from other postwar leaders was his ability to combine the traditional use of patronage with more modern mechanisms of winning elections and sustaining power. Marcos won the presidency through vote-buying, electoral fraud, and a modicum of coercion—all the oft-cited means by which Filipino politicians gain power. But he also used the media to tap into the popular mind and gain electoral support (Liang 1970, 391). When he became president, Marcos kept up this image of the modern leader, anchoring his economic program in a modernization project centered on infrastructure, communications and technological development (Doronila 1992, 132–33).

Initial reception of this developmentalist ideology and program was positive; by the time Marcos was elected in 1964, oligarchic politics had begun to decline (Nowak and Snyder, in Kerkvliet 1974, 153–241; Nowak 1974). Elections had become bloody and fraudulent, and there was general skepticism over the ability of congress to enact laws to clean up corruption or improve tax collection and social welfare. Criminality had worsened: smuggling cost the country an estimated 800 million pesos annually and a new breed of criminals had emerged —the children of the economic and political elite (Liang 1970, 385, 389, 395; Gleeck 1987, 47, 66–67). All this was taking place in an economy experiencing "tight credit, a deteriorating peso, rising prices of commodities and possible rice shortage" (*PFP,* 8 Feb. 1964). Cracks within oligarchic democracy revealed that the elite's public standing was beginning to unravel because of its rapacity (Liang 1970, 402). Public cynicism and mistrust created spaces for third party initiatives by reformist politicians which, while not succeeding in dislodging the Nacionalistas and the Liberals, did develop a following among segments of the population disenchanted with the existing political process.

The reformist and developmentalist presidency that Marcos projected was thus partly in response to prevailing popular sentiment. It also facilitated Marcos's efforts to centralize the state. Lacking the political and economic capital of older elite families made Marcos more willing to tap resources other than these traditional bases of power. One such resource was the state and the various modes of acquiring state power. Previously, the centralizing capacity of the executive agencies of the state was weak, held hostage to the power of the oligarchy that dominated congress and kept power decentralized. Marcos remained part of this system, but he was also

> the first elite Filipino politician who saw the possibilities of reversing the traditional flow of power. All his predecessors had lived out the genealogy of mestizo supremacy—from private wealth to state power, from provincial bossism to national hegemony. But almost from the beginning of his presidency in 1965, Marcos had moved out of the nineteenth century, and understood that in our time wealth serves power, and that the key card is the state. Manila's Louis Napoleon (B. Anderson 1988, 20).

Marcos moved to take control of what he regarded as essential agencies of the state. He centralized economic planning with handpicked, American-educated technocrats who, amply funded by the president's office and multilateral lending agencies sympathetic to their programs, began implementing development goals in a well-coordinated manner (Ocampo 1971, 31–64; Rodriguez 1985, 24–25). By the end of his first term, Marcos could boast of a series of infrastructure and impact projects to show how earnest his national development program was (Liang 1970, 406). Marcos also sought to get the Armed Forces of the Philippines (AFP) on his side by exercising more actively the constitutional powers granted the presidency in relation to the military, integrating the military into his development project, appealing to the military's disaffection with elite politics, and most important of all, cultivating his own cabal of favorite officers, many of them from Ilocos (Rodriguez 1986, 32–33; *MB*, 24 Jan. 1966). The AFP responded positively to Marcos's overtures, especially when its inclusion in the presidential national development plan expanded its area of operations and brought it special support and patronage from the presidency (Hernandez 1979, 160–61).

Along the way, Marcos sought to undermine congress, depicting it as a major obstacle to the goals of reform and development. This popular move was reinforced by numerous disclosures of congressional corruption and related debaucheries (*PFP*, 17 June 1967). Declaring his intention to fight the oligarchy and hasten national development, Marcos began to develop a national network parallel to and immune from congressional influence by opening direct links between himself and "the rural masses" (Stauffer 1975, 32). He revived old executive agencies and sent their personnel directly to towns and municipalities over the heads of local politicians. Use of the military in the infrastructure program was a prime example; Marcos cited an urgent need for civic action to divert army money and personnel to road-building (Caoili 1986, 21). In doing all this, Marcos required neither congressional approval nor allocation. To sidestep congress's power to impede the release of funds, Marcos created his own financial base, obtaining funds from both internal and external sources. Monies were then concentrated in the Presidential Arm for Community Development (PACD), which became the symbol of Marcos's commitment to national growth (Spence 1979, 327).

With his expanding network and purse, Marcos became more confrontational with congress, vetoing laws it passed for its own benefit (such as increasing congressional allowances), while exposing its members' lack of moral rectitude, for example, the protection of politicians' children involved in criminal activities (Gleeck 1987, 67). The opposition in congress fought back against this increasingly dominant presidency. It battled Marcos over policy—including his broken promise not to send Filipino troops to Vietnam—and retaliated with its own exposés of corruption and venality in the presidential palace. The conflict escalated after Marcos was reelected to the presidency through massive fraud and coercion. Marcos, of course, remained a politico at heart and his actions were designed to expand his own power. Scholars, however, tend to focus too much on this rapaciousness and ambition, understating the degree to which Marcos's drive for power revitalized the state's centralizing capacities. What is important to stress here is that patrimonial intentions and state centralization meshed quite well for Marcos, so that he achieved the peculiar status of being both exemplar of patrimonialism and vanguard of state modernization (Hutchcroft 1991, 414–50). This was Marcos's contradictory legacy.

This interlacing of patrimonial intent and state centralization had a major impact on Mindanao. The island fitted well into the national development agenda and the political ambition of Marcos. It was rich but undeveloped and had a diverse population to mobilize for development. If the country were to maximize the exploitation of its resources, Mindanao—with its huge timber and agricultural lands, mineral and fishing resources, and a growing population—would be crucial. Besides, no politician developing new networks could afford to ignore Mindanao's potentially vote rich provinces.

Marcos thus focused his attention on Mindanao to showcase his reformist plans and consolidate his influence. He activated the Mindanao Development Authority (MDA) and made it a conduit for industrial and economic support to deserving communities. He also used the agency to award positions to political associates and subordinates (*STM,* 2 Feb. 1961). Marcos knew that to counter the powerful regional politicians of the central Philippines, especially the Osmeña family of Cebu and the sugar-based Lopez family of Negros Oriental, he needed to tap Mindanao's growing population. Marcos thus developed and nurtured ties with Mindanao leaders whom he targeted as allies and moved against those who had fought him in the past or whom he perceived as future threats. In southern Mindanao, these moves came as the frontier was experiencing significant internal pressure.

## Social Tensions

Two trends had become manifest in southern Mindanao by the 1960s: the filling up of the frontier and a consequent rise in conflict among settlers and indigenes over remaining available public land. The entire island was witnessing much more dramatic population growth than in the previous two decades. While the population rose from 2.9 million to 3.5 million from 1948 to 1958, it jumped to over 5.3 million (Census of the Philippines 1961, 2) in the following years. This trend was most apparent in the settlement zones of Agusan, Bukidnon, Cotabato, and Davao (table 13).

Table 13. Population in Cotabato, Davao and Mindanao, 1948-1960

| Province | 1948 | 1958 | 1960 |
|---|---|---|---|
| Agusan | 126,448 | 152,010 | 271,010* |
| Bukidnon | 63,470 | 76,300 | 194,368 |
| Cotabato | 439,669 | 528,540 | 1,029,119+ |
| Davao | 364,854 | 438,610 | 893,023‡ |
| Mindanao Total | 2,943,324 | 3,538,300 | 5,338,447 |

*combined population of Agusan del Norte and Agusan del Sur after division
+combined population of Cotabato and South Cotabato after division
‡combined population of Davao del Norte, Davao del Sur and Davao Oriental after division

Source: *Census of the Republic of the Philippines* (Manila: Bureau of Printing, 1954, 1959, 1960).

Within these aggregates was a distinct shift in demographic composition, especially in the Muslim provinces, where Christian settlers were becoming the majority. In Cotabato, for example, the 1960 census showed that Magindanao-speaking communities comprised only 30 percent, while those speaking the two leading languages of the central Philippines (Ilonggo and Cebuano) comprised 37 percent of the provincial population (Census of the Philippines 1960, 19). This change in composition hastened the marginalization of indigenous groups as settlers continued to arrive and as the older migrants' children reached adult age and formed their own native families. Majul (1985, 31) observed that in these "traditional areas, the Muslim population had all but disappeared by the 1960s." In Mindanao as a whole, the Muslim population declined from 31 percent in 1903 to less than 20 percent in 1960, largely as a result of Christian migration (Wernstedt and Simkins 1965, 101; O'Shaughnessy 1975, 376–82). The government attempted to correct this imbalance, but its policies were either implemented halfheartedly or were just cosmetic solutions (Santos 1962).

This process would have an impact on politics in Cotabato. Although Pendatun and other Magindanao leaders were still dominant, voter turnout showed the settler communities emerging as a substantial voting bloc within the province. A rough calculation of voting preferences from 1949 to 1967 showed that starting 1963, non-Magindanao and settler candidates received at least 30 percent of the vote (*Census of the Republic of the Philippines*, 1954, 1959, 1960). In settler municipalities, these candidates received as many or more votes than their Pendatun-supported Magindanao rivals. In 1963, for example, in sixteen of the twenty-four municipalities of Cotabato, non-Magindanao candidates running for congress and the provincial governorship received 50 to 90 percent of the vote (*MC,* 1 Dec. 1963). In 1965, when Pendatun ran for congress, his Christian opponent, Melquiades Sucaldito, won in seven municipalities, lost by only 10 percentage points or less in seven others, and grabbed between 30 and 40 percent of the votes in ten out of forty-two municipalities (table 14). For a relatively unknown rival pitted against the strong man of Cotabato, this showing attested to the growing political clout of the settlement zones (*MC,* 29 May and 17 July 1965).

The most significant consequence of frontier closure and demographic shift was a surge in land conflict between indigenes and settlers. At the same time, disputes over land took on a new character. Struggles that had once involved only individuals or families now broadened to entangle entire communities.[1] In certain instances, state intervention even aggravated the situation because authorities in Manila were ignorant of what was happening in the settlements. Marcos's development projects and assertions of central control, for example, precipitated hostilities between state agencies and local communities, particularly the Muslims (Gowing 1979, 310).

Davao did not face as serious a situation as Cotabato, but it nevertheless began to experience social problems as the state centralized and the frontier filled up. While economic development sped up under Marcos, it failed to eliminate the social tensions that had existed since the early postwar period (National Economic Council Nov. 1960, 2). Land conflicts persisted between indigenous groups and the settlers who continued to pour into the province (*MT,* 27 May 1963; 1 Sept. and 8 Oct. 1966; 2 Apr. 1968). In fact, indigenous groups like the Atas, Bilaans, and Mandayas were more belligerent in defending their lands, and

Table 14. Congressional Election Results, Cotabato, 1965

| Municipality | Pendatun | Sucaldito | Total | % Sucaldito |
|---|---|---|---|---|
| Upi | 1,360 | 2,286 | 3,646 | 62.6 |
| Tacurong | 1,608 | 2,647 | 4,255 | 62.2 |
| Koronadal | 3,024 | 4,542 | 7,566 | 60.0 |
| Surallah | 1,771 | 2,288 | 4,059 | 56.3 |
| Libungan | 1,690 | 1,987 | 3,677 | 54.0 |
| Tupi | 1,151 | 1,335 | 2,486 | 53.7 |
| Polomolok | 1,389 | 1,558 | 2,947 | 52.8 |
| Dinaig | 6,901 | 6,704 | 13,605 | 49.2 |
| Tangtangan | 1,334 | 1,227 | 2,561 | 47.9 |
| Pigkawayan | 1,884 | 1,613 | 3,497 | 46.1 |
| Tulonan | 1,681 | 1,354 | 3,035 | 44.6 |
| Kidapawan | 4,013 | 3,181 | 7,194 | 44.2 |
| Mlang | 3,362 | 2,630 | 5,956 | 44.1 |
| Makilala | 2,389 | 1,744 | 4,133 | 42.1 |
| Lebak | 1,579 | 1,046 | 2,625 | 39.8 |
| Glan | 2,128 | 1,358 | 3,486 | 38.9 |
| Parang | 4,895 | 3,109 | 8,004 | 38.8 |
| Tampakan | 959 | 558 | 1,517 | 36.7 |
| Midsayap | 3,635 | 2,020 | 5,655 | 35.7 |
| Magpet | 990 | 480 | 1,470 | 32.6 |
| Kabacan | 2,568 | 1,084 | 3,652 | 29.6 |
| Maasim | 939 | 395 | 1,334 | 29.6 |
| Palimbang | 2,472 | 1,040 | 3,512 | 29.6 |
| Kiamba | 1,897 | 704 | 2,601 | 27.0 |
| Maitum | 1,487 | 469 | 1,956 | 23.9 |
| Matalam | 3,150 | 979 | 4,129 | 23.7 |
| S. Barongis | 5,191 | 1,319 | 6,510 | 20.2 |
| Buldon | 6,297 | 1,355 | 7,652 | 17.7 |
| Carmen | 5,431 | 677 | 6,108 | 11.0 |
| Ampatuan | 6,798 | 557 | 7,335 | 7.5 |
| Columbio | 3,067 | 170 | 3,237 | 5.2 |
| Buluan | 8,565 | 398 | 8,963 | 4.4 |
| Tumbao | 2,443 | 105 | 2,548 | 4.1 |
| Pikit | 13,361 | 97 | 13,458 | 0.7 |
| Nuling | 7,803 | 32 | 7,835 | 0.4 |
| Datu Piang | 7,703 | 12 | 7,715 | 0.1 |
| Maganoy | 6,701 | 0 | 6,701 | 0.0 |
| Pagalungan | 7,994 | 0 | 7,994 | 0.0 |

*Source: Mindanao Cross*, 18 November 1965.

reports of "Bilaan outlaws" attacking settlers increased in the 1960s.[2] Generally, though, life in the settlements became more stable than in the late 1950s. The resolution of most land title disputes, the implementation (no matter how skewed) of land for the landless programs, and the peace contrived by Almendras while he was governor led to a certain amount of normalcy.

But tension and conflict among local politicians did not disappear. In the 1960s, it became discernible in the intense jockeying for position among local leaders as Almendras's power continued to slip and Vicente Duterte was unable to wield effective authority. More towns were placed under constabulary control than in the previous decade as incumbents and their challengers resorted to more aggressive means of competition.[3] By 1970, reports of election fraud (vote-buying, vote-tampering, stealing of ballot boxes, etc.) had become customary, spiced up by accounts of assaults and political assassinations (*MT,* 2 Sept. 1970; 14 Jan. 1971; *MinT,* 3 Sept. 1970). Davao's image as an economic growth region was eventually canceled out by its notoriety as the new Mindanao "hotspot." In reality, Davao was less unstable than Cotabato, but recurring reports of constabulary control, Bilaan uprisings, smuggling and brigandage were enough to renew the image of a volatile frontier province.[4]

Such was the context in which the interaction between southern Mindanao strongmen and the centralizing national state would take place in the 1960s. The difference between the pre-Marcos and the Marcos periods became increasingly stark, as conditions turned less congenial for the exercise of local power and mutual accommodation with the central state. The maneuvering room for local strong men narrowed considerably and their options dwindled. For many of southern Mindanao's strong men, the balancing act between local and national politics became more precarious.

## Marcos and Pendatun

Marcos and Pendatun had disliked each other since Marcos defected to the Nacionalistas and used the party to launch his presidential bid. Enmity grew after Pendatun ensured that Marcos would not win Cotabato, though this did not prevent him from winning nationally (*DM,* 29 Mar. 1965). After the election, Marcos upped the ante by removing Pendatun's cronies from the MDA board of directors, calling Pendatun an obstacle to development after the latter threatened to use the Mindanao bloc to thwart Marcos's plans (*MT,* 10 Mar. 1964). Marcos also used his presidential prerogatives to deliver infrastructure funds to settler communities over Pendatun's head (Lane 19 Oct 1965, 2; *Variety Magazine*, 29 Sept. 1968). Marcos thus offered these communities an alternative source of patronage funds that had previously been controlled totally by Pendatun and distributed mainly to municipalities that supported him (*Progress*, 1960, 200–1). Finally, Marcos revived the flagging careers of Pendatun's principal enemies, the Sinsuats, by once more infusing the remaining areas they controlled with presidential funds. In due time Marcos fashioned a united front to challenge Pendatun and Matalam who had arrived at a fragile reconcilation in the face of this new threat (*MC*, 13 May 1967).

Saddled with problems even before Marcos came to power, Pendatun responded to this concerted assault by cutting his losses and consolidating his strengths. In 1965, despite opposition from his Magindanao allies, Pendatun supported the division of Cotabato into two provinces, hoping to eliminate the competing pulls of Muslim and Christian constituencies.[5] Ostensibly to improve governability, Southern Cotabato (where Christians had become a majority) and Northern Cotabato (where Muslims still had an edge) were formally created in 1967 (George 1980, 145). Marcos appointed leaders from the settler communities and the Sinsuats to the provincial leaderships of the new provinces. Unable to do anything in the transition, Pendatun awaited the elections that followed the division. His problems continued to multiply.

The division of Cotabato may have clarified Pendatun's constituencies, but it also constricted his political arena and the resources available to him. With Marcos in control of new funds and his own largesse limited to congressional pork barrel allocations, Pendatun had fewer assets to distribute to his followers. The division also intensified local rivalries among Pendatun's allies, who were now jockeying for position in the new, smaller province. The conflict between his Magindanao and Christian municipal allies in North Cotabato became acute; ill will was generated by allegations that Muslims lacked governing skills as well as by disagreements over allocations. Yet even among the Magindanaos, Pendatun looked weak for failing to mobilize effective opposition and ultimately acquiescing to the provincial division. His standing among his communities was put in further doubt when Marcos was able to organize an opposition right under Pendatun's nose.

Backed by the Marcos-Sinsuat alliance, Sinsuat supporter Abdulla Sangki ran for governor of North Cotabato in the 1967 local elections, a direct challenge to the Pendatun-Matalam bloc. Interpreting the Sangki candidacy as an escalation of the battle, Pendatun met the challenge head-on by running for governor himself, even while remaining an active member of congress. With frenetic energy, he brokered electoral coalitions with new groups, rekindled ties with the Piangs (abandoned a decade earlier), and granted concessions to leaders of settlement communities to gain their support (*MC,* 9 Sept. 1967). He also began to cast his candidacy in cultural terms, presenting himself as the only true defender of Magindanaos against Manila's machinations to constrict their world through impositions like the division of Cotabato (*MC,* 18 Nov. 1967). Surprisingly, Pendatun gave little attention to Matalam.

Pendatun was elected governor by a narrow margin and at a considerable cost (*MC,* 30 Dec. 1967). His decision to run for local office while still serving in Manila opened him up to the criticism that he was power-hungry, a trait that made him look more and more like the other "crocodiles" in congress (*MC,* 30 Mar. 1968; *Anatomy of Philippine Muslim Affairs* 1971, 220). Pendatun's invocation of Magindanao identity was even viewed with suspicion, as it appeared to be used solely for election purposes. Pendatun's continuing characterization of Magindanaos as "backward" also cast doubt on the sincerity of his Muslim identity. He never stopped portraying the Magindanaos as culturally lagging behind the rest of the Philippines:

> [My] people are still ignorant. They are not in consonance with the progress of civilization. They are in fact the most backward and illiterate minority group in the country today. They feel like they are second class citizens. Whether right or wrong, that is their feeling. But what is wrong would be to force them to reject and keep rejecting changes for the betterment of their life, like sanitation and health services. Certainly not our customs and traditions because those are things we would never let go. But they must change in order to be able to participate and help in the country's progress. Until such time, Muslims have no right to ask for equal justice (*PP,* 29 Aug. 1971).

At a time when uncontrolled migration and land tension made Magindanaos more apprehensive about their fate, Pendatun's patronizing view of "his people" did not bode well. Finally, Pendatun's victory increased the distance between him and the aging Matalam. Pendatun's political bargaining with the younger Piangs and the settlers aroused Matalam's suspicion that his ally was losing confidence in him and was easing him out in favor of new partners (*MC,* 7 Sept. 1968). Estranged but still unable to break from Pendatun due to conjugal ties, Matalam opted to retire from politics. The bitterness lingered and would resurface in a more contentious form a few months later (George 1980, 131–32).

Pendatun's victory did not bring back normalcy to Cotabato. Peace and order continued to deteriorate as reports of increased clashes between Muslims and settlers captured national attention (*Commerce,* 12 Oct. 1968; George 1980, 140). Marcos inflamed conditions with his continued interference. To undermine Pendatun, Marcos brought in the military as a foil to the area's private armies and as a new conduit of economic development (*MT,* 20 Jan. 1966). Marcos also continued to increase aid to settlement communities through the PACD and other development agencies (*MT,* 25 Mar. 1967; *MC,* 18 May 1968). Pendatun viewed these actions with concern but did little in response, choosing instead to shift his attention back to congress.

In 1968, deteriorating Muslim-Christian relations took a critical turn when the media exposed a massacre of Muslim military trainees in a secret training camp just outside Manila. The Jabidah massacre increased Muslim animosity against what was seen as a deliberate plan by a pro-Christian government to eliminate their "way of life" (Majul, 1985, 40–43). Among younger Muslims, sentiment was growing in favor of separating Mindanao from the Philippines to preserve Muslim identity and put a stop to the "oppression of Muslims." Muslim politicians deplored the massacre but characteristically restrained popular hostility to the government. Pendatun and other anti-Marcos Muslims in congress demanded an investigation and warned of the damaging impact the massacre would have on Muslim allegiance to the Philippine state. But they stopped short of mobilizing their constituents, preferring to fight the issue within the legislature and against Marcos rather than against the entire government. Pendatun's general identification with the Philippine state made the latter option distasteful, and he also saw the issue as a means of recovering ground lost to Marcos in the provincial elections (Mastura 1984, 39). Other Muslim politicians remained loyal to Marcos, resulting in a split in the Muslim Association of the Philippines (MAP) and the creation of a new pro-Marcos association (Dimaporo 1970, 3–4).

These politicians' exploitation of the Jabidah massacre for their own personal ends was clearly out of step with popular sentiment in the provinces. The MAP split and the attempt by Pendatun and others to use the massacre to score points against Marcos increased the public's alienation from its traditional leaders. The creation of the CNI (see chapter 7) further eroded the politicians' standing. The CNI was an attempt by the Marcos government to address the deterioration of majority-minority relations in places like Mindanao. Although its resources were limited, one of the benefits it brought to Mindanao was its role as a public forum for cultural communities' grievances. Stories of eviction and land-grabbing in the areas reserved for minorities not only exposed the seamier side of provincial politics, but also testified to the failure of local leaders to guarantee peace in their domain. Despite its circumscribed ability to influence policy, the fact that the CNI had to mediate in land disputes suggested to the public that this national state agency was more effective than local officials in addressing the problems of the masses (*MT,* 19 Sept. 1961).

This situation created an opportunity for a new kind of leadership to emerge in the Muslim communities from a younger generation which had benefited from the massive expansion of English-language education in the late 1950s and 1960s (B. Anderson 1988, 19). Many earned their degrees at the University of the Philippines, while others were beneficiaries of scholarships given to Muslim Filipinos by private and religious institutions of Islamic countries like Egypt (*MM,* 2 Sept. 1967). The government envisioned them to become an embryonic Muslim middle class that would energize Muslim participation in the Philippine economy and society and become the next generation of Muslim political leaders (Cayongat 1986, 80). Instead, they were drawn into opposition politics in their schools in both Manila and Cairo. Many became attracted to the resurgence of nationalism and radicalism among young Filipinos. Vietnam, the Great Proletarian Revolution, and Nasserite nationalism also radicalized them (*MC,* 20 Sept. 1967).

Confined initially to the universities, these young radicals began to search for ways to reach the Muslim masses to give substance to their revolution. After the Jabidah massacre, that opportunity appeared as Muslim sentiment against the government became widespread. The opportunism of Muslim politicians emboldened the radicals to provide an alternative leadership. Radical idealism, however, was tempered by the reality that to reach the masses, they still had to go through the local politicians they despised. In Cotabato this was precisely the dilemma the new group faced. They were fortunate then to find an ally in the alienated Matalam, whose political prospects had dimmed after Pendatun abandoned him. The result was a marriage of convenience between radicals seeking the fastest means to mobilize the Magindanao masses and a strong man recognizing a way out of political purgatory (George 1980, 197; Majul 1985, 45; Mastura 1984, 136; Cayongat 1986, 86). In May 1968, four months after the Jabidah massacre, Matalam came out of retirement and announced the formation of the Muslim Independence Movement (MIM). The MIM vowed to "struggle for national recognition, justice and equality," because the "more affluent cultural majority and the government had failed to listen to the Muslims" (*STM,* 16 June 1968; *MC,* 30 July 1968; Abubakar 1973, 125). It also promised to rally the different Muslim groups together to form an independent Islamic state separate from the republic (*STM,* 11 Aug. 1968).

Pendatun initially ignored the MIM and even denied its existence. Despite the settlers' growing concern about the MIM's radicalism, he saw no threat from an aging ally and his group of young, politically inexperienced ideologues (*MC,* 3 Aug. 1968). Pendatun instead focused on the Nacionalista threat from Marcos and the Sinsuats in the upcoming (1969) congressional elections (*MC,* 7 Sept. 1968). True enough, his enemies once again launched a vigorous and vicious campaign to unseat him after he proclaimed support for Marcos's presidential opponent, Sergio Osmeña Jr. This time they centered their attention on expanding settler support in Pendatun's domain. These groups had become receptive to the idea of further subdividing North Cotabato and creating a new province in which Christians would be the majority (*MC,* 15 Feb., 29 Mar., 23 May, and 6 Sept. 1969). Fearful of losing the support of this voting bloc, especially after Marcos and Matalam employed religious differences as a campaign weapon, Pendatun abandoned identity politics and tried to resurrect his old image as the leader of all Cotabato communities (*MC,* 13 Sept. 1969).

Pendatun was reelected in 1969, but he won victory by threatening to use force and by resorting to massive electoral fraud (*DM,* 4 Mar. 1969; *MC,* 15 and 20 Nov. 1969; 24 Jan. 1970). He also won without the support of Matalam, who kept his distance from the traditional politics of his brother-in-law upon the advice of his radical allies (*MC,* 8 Nov. 1969). In the meantime, the MIM was becoming more active. In its propaganda, it demanded that public lands in Muslim provinces be open to settlement only by Muslim and indigenous communities. It attacked the fascist tactics of the military and warned that the "impatience of the people has reached a point which will survive the upheaval and the rise of an imminent revolution [led by a new] Muslim grouping in the south." (*MC,* 14 Feb. and 16 May 1970). The MIM also quietly built up its armed forces, especially after a number of its leaders returned from military training in Malaysia (Mercado 1984, 157).

Propaganda and military training were eventually complemented by the formation of mass organizations in schools and mosques. While these associations were poor counterparts to the better-organized left-wing organizations (see below), their presence nevertheless revealed the extent to which the young radicals had changed Cotabato politics. On 9 April 1970, students in Cotabato held a protest rally demanding political reforms and peace in Mindanao. The "Student Organized Reform Movement," an organization formed by MIM activists and sympathizers, led the protest. The protest was historic for introducing a different form of politics and showing the extent to which Islamic radicalism had already upstaged traditional politics (*MC,* 11 Apr. 1970).

The expansion of the MIM not only attracted government attention, but also began to evoke fear among settler communities that a religious war was in the offing (*MC,* 24 Aug. 1968; *MT,* 18 Aug. 1968). The ensuing tension began to take on more religious coloring than ever before in Mindanao's history. All that was needed was a spark to set Magindanao-settler conflict aflame. That spark came from a self-proclaimed vigilante called "Kumander Toothpick," who, after his family was massacred by Magindanaos identified with the Sinsuats, formed an armed band vowing to kill all Magindanaos. Toothpick called his gang "Ilaga," the Visayan word for rat, alluding to the devastation he would inflict on the Magindanaos, just as rats had devastated the farms of settlers in the 1950s (George 1980, 147).

Toothpick kept his word and his retaliation against Magindanaos was brutal. To the settlers, he was a folk hero, fighting their battles and protecting them against the Muslims (*DM,* 10 Aug. 1970; *MT,* 12 Aug., 14 and 16 Sept. and 1 Oct. 1970). He also gained the attention of seven Christian mayors who saw in him a chance to break the hold of the Magindanao leaders over the province (Glang 1972). The secret support of Marcos for the mayors' plan to use Toothpick against the Magindanaos closed the deal. With arms and funding from the mayors and Marcos, Ilaga attacks on Magindanaos became more frequent and ferocious (Majul 1985, 47–48). Their towns deserted by people seeking refuge from Cotabato, Magindanao leaders responded in kind. With Matalam and the MIM's assistance, Magindanao mayors formed an army called the "Barracudas" which engaged the Ilagas in open warfare (Mercado 1984, 158–59). As fighting between the two groups spread from Cotabato to other Muslim provinces, the government joined the fray, increasing its military presence and concentrating its guns on the Barracudas.

Before long the entire province was engulfed in war, causing more concern in Manila (*DM,* 18 Nov. and 4 Dec. 1970). The Ilaga-Barracuda war provided material for legislative privilege speeches and press conferences for Pendatun, but once again, he kept himself immersed in congressional politics rather than attending to the crisis at home (*MT,* 19–20 Sept. 1968). The split among Muslim politicians over the government's handling of the "Moro Problem," however, revealed the absence of any serious consideration on their part of the consequences of "pocket wars" in Mindanao. This failure exposed them as paragons of self-interest whose actions were guided only by political ambition (Mastura 1984, 180; Stewart 1988, 108). In Cotabato, Magindanaos were incensed at the attention given by Pendatun and the Sinsuats to their own rivalry and their use of the war for patronage and electoral battles (*MC,* 8 and 15 Mar. 1969; 7 Mar. 1970). Popular alienation from politicos increased, as war spread in the municipalities (*MT,* 16 Sept. and 3 Oct. 1970). Preparing for the 1971 elections instead of finding a resolution to the war proved that Pendatun had failed his people, who then felt justified in switching to the MIM (*MC,* 29 Aug., 12, 17 and 19 Sept. and 7 Nov. 1970).

On 24 September 1970, Pendatun survived an ambush on his way to congress. Marcos later used the ambush as an excuse to send more troops to Cotabato, purportedly to deter conflict, but actually to strengthen the state's presence in the war-torn province. That the military was perceived as partial to Toothpick and his settler allies naturally worsened conditions, reinforcing Magindanao fears of a joint Ilaga-military campaign to annihilate them as a people. More joined the Barracudas and the war in Cotabato escalated (*Solidarity,* 1972, 6–8). The ambush and consequent military deployment made Pendatun finally realize how serious conditions had become in Cotabato (*PP,* 29 Aug. 1971). He shifted course again, now offering to assist the MIM with arms and resources. He also attempted to unite the smaller private armies of his remaining confederates that, in turn, prompted anti-Pendatun Christian mayors to reinforce their armies and seek closer ties with the military (*MT,* 27 Oct. 1970). These were actions that came too late, however. Islamic radicalism had achieved unprecedented hegemony in Magindanao politics, and began openly challenging the preeminence of datu-politicians (*WM,* 14 Mar. 1970).

Polarization and the worsening conflict had simplified the issue for Pendatun (Gowing 1979, 46–54; Committee on National Minorities 1971, 1–26). But by the time he realized it, he had already become a secondary actor in Cotabato politics. His marginalization was underscored when he ran for a senate seat in November 1971, invoking "religious rather than regional voting affiliations." This religious conversion did not prevent a poor electoral performance, as he placed fifteenth even in Cotabato (U.S. Embassy 22 Nov. 1971, 4; *MT,* 13 May 1972). After losing, Pendatun moved back to Cotabato and continued his attempt to ingratiate himself with the MIM. That organization, however, had already amassed ample man- and firepower and had little need for the erstwhile strong man (Abat 1993, xix). Nine months later Marcos placed the country under martial law. At the time of the declaration, Pendatun was in the Middle East "on vacation" and would remain there until 1978. In exile, he could only watch helplessly as his province plunged into war (Abat 1993, 28–29).

## Marcos and Almendras

When he became senator in 1959, Almendras reached the high point of his political career, but it also marked the beginning of new battles. Almendras was elected just as his Nacionalista party lost the presidency and became locked in an impasse with the Liberals in the senate (*MT,* 5 Nov. 1958). He joined a senate presided over by Nacionalista Eulogio Rodriguez, who had once tried to dislodge him from Davao in favor of his brother, former mayor Julian Rodriguez. In the senate, Rodriguez lost no opportunity to make life difficult for Almendras and quietly supported his provincial enemies (*MinT,* 15 Aug. 1963). In 1961, with Rodriguez's assistance, Ismael Veloso and Carmelo Porras won the congressional and Davao City mayoral seats, respectively, defeating Almendras's candidates. Veloso then proceeded to use the lower house as a pulpit to attack the senator, while Porras kept Almendras supporters neutralized in the city council (*MT,* 12 and 30 Dec. 1961). In Manila, the senate leader stood by when President Diosdado Macapagal began to exert pressure on Almendras to switch parties to end the year-long impasse. In his first year in office, too, Almendras spent his time fending off a succession of exposés of tax evasion, hidden wealth, graft, and corruption with little help from his party leadership.[6]

Almendras survived, thanks mainly to his acquaintance with a rising star, fellow senator Ferdinand Marcos. Though in opposing parties, Almendras and Marcos had been friends since they met in the house of representatives in 1955 (Spence 1979, 303). Their camaraderie proved propitious for both. When Macapagal instigated attacks on Almendras, Marcos, as Liberal party president, stepped in to stop the attacks and limit the damage (*MT,* 7 Mar. 1963). A month later, Almendras returned the favor, casting his vote for Marcos as senate president and ousting Rodriguez (*MinT,* 1 Apr. and 16 May 1963; *MT,* 7 Apr. 1963). When Marcos switched to the Nacionalistas to run for president of the Philippines, Almendras defended his switch to party members who resisted accepting Marcos (Spence 1979, 306). The high point of the friendship came when Marcos became president and Almendras was reelected with the second highest vote count in the 1965 elections (*MT,* 17 Nov. 1965). The American consul in Cebu wrote that Almendras "presumably will enjoy considerable influence in the new administration" (Lane 1965, 4). And he did. Marcos gave Landring control over the MDA, facilitated development aid from presidential coffers to Davao, and protected Almendras's flank when Davao and Mindanao politicians attacked him as a Marcos crony.[7] Almendras was also appointed chief of the Mindanao Nacionalistas and took over the leadership of the MINSUPALA from the ousted Pendatun.

The assaults of Rodriguez and Macapagal, however, had caused cracks in Almendras's provincial armor. Veloso's political resurrection and Porras's mayoralty attested to this. These cracks also facilitated the rise of new local rivals, of whom the most prominent were Gaudencio Antonino and Lorenzo Sarmiento. Beneficiaries of Davao's timber resources, these businessmen-turned-politicians were able to create their own power bases and connect to the national party systems independently. Antonino used his timber money to run successfully for senator. He became an occasional opponent of Almendras in the senate debates, but concerned himself mainly with national affairs and less with Davao (*MinT,* 29 July 1950; *MT,* 12 Feb. 1963). The more serious contender was Sarmiento, who used his fortune to take over the weakened Davao Liberal chapter and carve out a turf in northern Davao where his timber enterprises were located. Sarmiento immediately showed his mettle by challenging Almendras's candidate for congress in 1963 (*MinT,* 15 and 22 Nov. 1963; Valenzuela 1968, 66–68). He lost but returned in 1965 to defeat Almendras's candidate Manuel Sotto. This victory was significant because it coincided with Almendras's reelection and Marcos's win and thus demonstrated that Almendras's success in national politics did not necessarily translate into complete control of the province (*MT,* 20 Dec. 1963; *MinT,* 6 Nov. 1965).

The more Almendras immersed himself in the dazzle of national politics, the more he lost control of the Davao Nacionalistas. Veloso's resurrection, for example, showed that the old rival still had enough Nacionalista support to get himself reelected. Despite Governor Vicente Duterte's effort to duplicate his patron's past exploits, it was clear that Almendras's successor lacked the ability to unite the fractious Nacionalistas at the municipal level (*Philippine News Digest* 5 July 1960). By 1961, two years after Almendras became senator, internal squabbles had caused the party to lose the mayoralties of fourteen of the thirty municipalities to Sarmiento's Liberals (COMELEC 1962, 12–14). These defeats opened Duterte to challenges by other leaders, including some of Almendras's relatives who felt Duterte did not have the ability to lead. Almendras, overwhelmed by his own battles in the senate, stepped in too late to stem the defeats (*MinT,* 11 July, 5, 8, 26 and 28 Sept. 1963). In 1963, despite a minor recovery by Nacionalistas in the November elections, the Liberals maintained their control of the municipalities won in 1961 (*MinT,* 15 Dec. 1963).

Sarmiento's victories and Nacionalista disarray ultimately convinced Almendras to agree to a division of Davao into smaller provinces (*MT,* 2 Jan. 1964). Where Pendatun saw a chance to consolidate his strength, Almendras regarded division as a way of foiling the expansion of Sarmiento's influence. Having more positions to dispense to his followers because of the division, Almendras hoped to appease local leaders who felt that the positions and paths open to them were inadequate (*MM,* 16 Sept. 1967). The ruse worked; Almendras mollified his local allies with appointments and opportunities to become kingpins of the new provinces (*MT,* 3 and 13 June 1966). It did not stop Sarmiento, however, who responded by switching parties. As a Nacionalista he put himself in a position to compete with Almendras as a dispenser of spoils (*MM,* 18 Feb. 1967; *MinT,* 23 Feb. 1967). While Sarmiento's defection weakened the Davao Liberals organizationally, his move also occasioned a mass migration of his followers, thus giving him a ready-made bloc within his new party (*MinT,* 16 Feb. 1967).

Davao was divided into the provinces of Davao del Norte, Davao Oriental, and Davao del Sur in July 1967. Almendras, with Marcos's blessing, handpicked their first leaders and thus held the initial upper hand over Sarmiento (*DM,* 14 Apr. 1967). But not for long. Even before the inaugural ribbons were cut, the Nacionalistas were at each other's throats over the candidate lists for the 1967 elections. Whereas in previous years Almendras had resolved the factional fights easily, the task proved more difficult with Sarmiento and the new, ambitious kingpins of the three provinces involved. Almendras played one supporter off against another while making deals with Sarmiento over the lists (*MM,* 29 Sept. 1967). Almendras even exploited his protégé, Duterte (who had ambitions of becoming congressman), secretly abandoning him in favor of a younger supporter, Artemio Loyola, only to switch back to Duterte at the last minute (*MM,* 23 Sept. 1967). In shifting his support back to Duterte, Almendras alienated Loyola, who then sought the help of Sarmiento, who used Loyola's defection to break his agreement with Almendras (*MinT,* 23 Nov. 1967). These "political double-crossings and [not-so] clandestine deals" resulted in election victories for Loyola and Sarmiento's people in the three provinces. The only victory Almendras could claim was in Davao City, where his candidate, Elias Lopez, ousted Porras (*MinT,* 28 Dec. 1967). With this realignment of forces in Sarmiento's favor, Almendras was forced to conciliate with and make concessions to new leaders like Loyola (*MinT,* 4 Jan. 1968).

Yet the changing social and political landscape of Davao hardly concerned Almendras. Despite numerous land disputes, the reappearance of class hierarchies in the settlement zones, and growing popular disenchantment with local politics, Almendras remained impervious to the changing context of his battle with Sarmiento. The more he tried to undermine Sarmiento, the more he found himself relying on Marcos rather than on his own fractious provincial base. In 1969, he once again asked Marcos's help to get his new ally Loyola reelected against an abandoned ally, former Davao City police chief Luis Santos (*MinT,* 10 Mar. 1966; 6 July 1967; *MM,* 4 Nov. 1967). Loyola won but not without a strong fight from Santos, who used his private army to intimidate Almendras's candidate (*MinT,* 25 Sept., 16 Oct. and 13 Nov. 1969). Two years later Santos ran again (this time against Almendras's candidate for Davao City mayor, the incumbent Elias Lopez) and won (*MinT,* 11 Nov. 1971). While echoes of Porras can be seen in Santos's fierce opposition to Almendras, the police chief was notable for two reasons. First, unlike Porras, who still depended on his party faction, Santos challenged the Almendras machine single-handedly, using his own resources. He showed that he did not need the Nacionalista machine and could take on the kingpin of Davao himself. This showed Santos's ability and also hinted at the extent to which Almendras had lost his grip on Davao politics (*MinT,* 2 Oct. and 10 Oct. 1969).

Second, when Santos won the Davao City mayoral seat in 1971, he not only matched Almendras force for force, but also was able to mobilize voters by tapping into the increasingly antipolitico public mood. By the late 1960s, it was clear that popular resentment had grown against graft and corruption, the worsening moral ills of local society, and the inability of local leaders to guarantee peace and order.[8] This was reinforced by a perception that local governance had grown more incompetent and that government positions were only political booty for self-proclaimed leaders. Santos, who was ousted several times as Davao City police chief by local politicians who regarded him as a threat, appeared to be the only exception (*MinT,* 17 Mar., 17 Apr., 1 and 10 Dec. 1966). He seemed to give due attention to the problems of the city. In his first week in office as mayor, he dismissed known corrupt city officials and embarrassed them in public. Santos also raided gambling dens and made public spectacles of slain criminals and bandits by displaying their bodies in the public park (*MinT,* 23 and

30 Jan. 1969). These were obviously political exhibitions of power by Santos, who advertised himself as a peace and order toughie, but they had the effect of assuring an apprehensive public that stability was at hand with Santos at the helm (U.S. Embassy 16 Nov. 1971, 3–4, 6).

Public cynicism towards politicians and demands for political reform also led to the appearance of Christian student activist-led social movements in the Davao provinces. In 1969, a group of settlers filed a claim to 10,000 hectares of public land in Davao Oriental. Unlike similar claims in the past, this action was organized and led by two organizations, the Federated Movements for Social Justice and Reforms (FMSJR) and the Khi Rho (*MT,* 16 Oct. 1969). Assisted by local religious, these reformist organizations launched a systematic organizing campaign among settlers while publicly assailing social problems like rampant land-grabbing (*Development Potentials,* 1969). A major target were properties of the Almendras family which FMSJR and Khi Rho claimed were illegally acquired. Almendras was caught off guard by these new forces and was initially unable to respond when confronted by novel actions like sit-ins, demonstrations and pickets as well as the astute use of political propaganda in national and provincial dailies (*MinT,* 12 Mar. 1970; *MT,* 17 June, 17 Sept., 12, 19, and 25 Nov. 1970). Criticism of land-grabbers gave stimulus to settler and indigene complaints and brought public attention back to land problems in the Davao provinces.[9] Soon after, the radical student group Kabataang Makabayan (Nationalist Youth or KM) followed its reformist counterparts in Davao, matching the latters' rhetoric and organizing ability (*MinT,* 9, 23 and 30 Apr. 1970). By 1971, other radical groups set up chapters and with the KM began to snatch student leadership from the FMSJR and the Khi Rho. The radicals also seized the political arena from the politicians, and the first cells of the new Communist Party of the Philippines were formed to lead the Davao mass movement (Ating Walong Taong Pakikibaka 1992, 1–3).

While the KM and its allied organizations held their widely publicized Mindanao regional congress in Davao, Almendras was in the middle of a reelection campaign (*MinT,* 11 Nov. 1971). In an election that showed deep voter dissatisfaction with Marcos and sympathy for opposition Liberal party candidates who had survived a grenade attack during their *miting de avance* (proclamation rally), Almendras won by a slim margin only after special elections were held in four municipalities in war-torn Lanao del Sur. In Davao, he only placed fifth in the total eight slates open for election (*MinT,* 30 Nov. 1971; 22 June 1972). His own candidates lost badly in the local polls in the three provinces, including even in his own bailiwick of Davao del Sur (U.S. Embassy 22 Nov. 1971, 3–4, 6). Sensing that his stature diminished significantly with his poor electoral showing, the reelected senator wasted no time trying to recover. Turning to Marcos once again for succor, he was soon bringing pork barrel funds into the three provinces (*MinT,* 24 Aug. 1972).

This was, however, Almendras's last public act. Political attention in the Davao provinces shifted to a new problem: On 8 June 1972, an armed propaganda unit of the CPP's New People's Army attacked a military outpost in northern Davao, prompting the military to launch a manhunt. The revolution had arrived in the Davao provinces and signaled the emergence of a different type of politics (*MinT,* 8 June 1972). A few months later, warning of impending political breakdown and a dual threat from rightists and the CPP, President Marcos declared martial law. Among the first acts of the new order were the abolition of congress and the virtual political disenfranchisement of all politicians. Divested of his powers, Almendras retired to his farm in Sta. Cruz to await the call for his services in Marcos's "New Society." Marcos, meanwhile, had found a new set of Davao cronies.

## Conclusion

Ferdinand Marcos's ultimate purpose was to centralize state power for patrimonial reasons, and his actions had a profound impact on the provincial politics in the 1960s. State centralization became a weapon with which Marcos destroyed enemies like Pendatun, pushing him into the arms of the MIM, which ultimately rejected him. The growing importance of politics in the center likewise made Almendras devote more attention to Manila, causing him to become fatally dependent on Marcos. Both strong men were undermined in their provinces through the shifting balance of center and provincial politics.

This suggests that national and provincial arenas may complement each other and help propel an ambitious strong man to positions of power and influence in both arenas. But it also shows that this interconnection is fraught with danger, especially for someone who intends to work both spheres. Pendatun and Almendras were ultimately banking on the complementary character of the two spheres. This led to downfall when each sphere developed its own dynamics that profoundly altered the balance between them. For Pendatun, the growth of settler communities, and for Almendras, the rise of a wealthy independent leadership interacted with Marcos's centralization of power to diminish the strong men's ability to maintain control of their provinces. Mutual accommodation between strong man and state (or central leadership) to ensure governance was not easy to maintain and stability could only be ensured if the strongman favored one sphere over the other, as Almendras showed in the early part of his political career. To be ambitious and play both spheres seem to have invited political asymmetry, and once the balance was lost, it proved difficult to return to preeminence. When martial law was declared, all Pendatun and Almendras had were their names and perhaps the most loyal of their allies; they were a far cry from their old selves.

When a balance between national and provincial politics was achieved, however, mutual accommodation between strong man and central state did work. In these times, two notable characteristics of Cotabato and Davao politics were their general stability and the degree to which their strong men practiced politics within the bounds of the law. At the apex of their powers, Pendatun and Almendras presided over generally peaceful domains and immersed themselves in party and factional politics, resorting to force and coercion only to a minimal degree. Both even ensured that the conduct of provincial politics followed procedures like conventions and debates, and they respected election outcomes (albeit tolerating a certain amount of electoral fraud). This is not to say that Pendatun and Almendras were totally law-abiding politicians who never resorted to compulsion. Yet, it cannot be ignored that these strong men were equally concerned with looking legitimate and proving themselves capable of governing according to the rules. It was when the province and the center went out of balance, especially under Marcos, that more coercive means were utilized and even preferred. By this time, of course, the armed capacity of Pendatun and Almendras was not enough to ensure their continued hegemony. They lost out both to a more centralized and better armed state and to radical groups which declared war on strong-man "politics as usual."

CHAPTER 9

# Lessons from the Periphery

The declaration of martial law, the rebellions of the MNLF and CPP, and the eclipse of southern Mindanao's strong men represented a shift in the political development of the region. While elements of postwar constitutional government did persist, martial law temporarily suspended electoral politics, offering us a vantage point from which to assess how Cotabato's and Davao's political histories relate to larger questions of state formation, state capacity, and local power. This chapter therefore closes the study by reflecting on a number of issues which I hope will lay as basis for dialogue and debate among those interested in southern Mindanao's political development.

## Philippine State Formation Reconsidered

The scholarly consensus on the modern state in the Philippines assumes that despite variations in state form—colonial and postcolonial, American and Filipino, cacique democratic and authoritarian—one single process of state formation transpired over a territory unproblematically understood as "the Philippines." These assumptions are not justified. The Americans did not inherit from Spain a consolidated Philippines, but encountered what McCoy and De Jesus describe (1982, 4) as an "intensely dynamic society, or series of societies" that were in a state of flux at the turn-of-the century (McCoy and De Jesus 1982, 4). The colonial state that was established in the first decade of American rule reflected a fragmented effort by the new colonizers to deal with these societies. The best evidence of this fragmentary nature was the military regimes of the Moro Province and the Mountain Province. In these areas, autonomous and powerful army administrations built the colonial state on the premise that the "non-Christian tribes" were different from the Christian population (Finin 1991,

31–102; Jenista 1987). The Americans knew that, historically, they had never been integrated into the Philippines, and until their transformation into "civilized subjects" was achieved, they were to be secluded and protected from the "more civilized" Filipinos. In these provinces, the army-run regimes exercised authoritarian control, limiting indigenous participation in local administrative affairs (Hayden 1942, 318–19; Cullinane 1971, 13–76).

Moreover, their distance from the colonial capital helped the "special provinces" fend off Manila's centralizing advances. Believing that its assignment to civilize the non-Christians would be of long duration, the military went to the extent of advocating Mindanao separatism. Seeking support for this position from their Muslim wards, army officers reinforced the significance of what they considered historic suspicions and antagonisms. These views were part of the philosophy behind the army's campaign to develop a loyal following among the Magindanaos of Cotabato, and the effect, predictably, was not integration into the larger colonial body politic, but preservation of the tendency toward autonomy.

In Davao, the indigenous population was sparse and the army's main concern was to fill up the far-flung district. This emptiness, along with Davao's distance from Manila and the provincial capital, Zamboanga, also encouraged separatism. Taking on the anti-Filipino, anti-Manila role were army officials and American settlers who saw Davao as the final stop on the drive to the American western frontier.[1] Many also saw the district as a future model of prosperity, progress, and civilization for neighboring indigenous communities. As in the Muslim areas, settlers and their military governors were committed to keeping southern Mindanao separate.

All this changed with Filipinization. Quezon's success in ending army rule and eliminating threats to his power also centralized state control, strengthened the territorial unity of the colonial geo-body, and redefined the linkage between center and periphery. Southern Mindanao remained the frontier, but now in relation to Manila. In Cotabato, the centralization of state power laid the foundation for long-term accommodation between a changing Muslim political elite and the Filipinized colonial state. Quezon never relaxed his control over the Muslim provinces, but he expanded "Moro participation" in colonial politics, appointing datus to positions in the municipalities, provinces, and national assembly, and inviting them to join the Nacionalista party to see the benefits of patronage politics. The aging datus who had worked with the Americans gave way to a new generation whose political perspectives and ambitions were firmly located within the framework of the Philippine state. Several years and a war would pass before these "Muslim-Filipinos" could participate fully, but it was clear that their political evolution strongly resembled that of their Christian counterparts.

Meanwhile, the failure of the American dream in Davao set the stage for the Japanese takeover of that province's abaca plantations. Davao's integration into the Filipinized colonial state was faster and less problematic than that of Cotabato because there was no "Moro problem," only relations between Filipinos and the new settlers, whose plantations were proving a windfall for farmers and the state alike. The Japanese protected their investments by playing the patronage game with emerging Filipino politicians, who in turn protected the hemp plantations while remaining extremely loyal to Quezon. This relationship made the question of autonomy from Manila superfluous. With southern Mindanao now an intrinsic part of the colonial body politic, the Philippines came under the *effective* control of *one* state and a unitary process of state formation became the conventional framework for discussing Philippine political development (Quirino 1971, 92).

That the postwar republic reproduced many features of the Filipinized colonial state is another convention of Philippine political history (B. Anderson 1988; Guerrero 1971). Local elites, whether collaborators or resistance leaders, dominated the politics of the postwar era, joined by parvenu strong men who had amassed weapons, power, and influence during the war.[2] In the absence of long-entrenched landed families and clans, southern Mindanao's political environment was conducive to the emergence of such parvenu strong men.[3] The continuous inflow of migrants from the north also created the opportunity for ambitious upstarts to build political careers as patrons and defenders of the settlers. Salipada Pendatun and Alejandro Almendras were two such strong men who rose to power with the birth of the republic Quezon did not live to see. But whereas the Commonwealth's unity was based on Quezon's powerful hold on party and bureaucracy, the decentralized politics of the republican period saw provincial clans, families, and strong men in the ascendance over a "weak state," which they exploited for patrimonial ends.[4] Pendatun and Almendras built their local and national power on this political configuration, setting themselves up as kingpins in their provinces and joining a national network of politicians which dominated the party system, legislature, and presidency. Their political prominence was mainly due to these arrangements, not to an identification with ethnic or religious causes.

Ferdinand Marcos altered this political configuration when he sought to fulfill his own ambition by concentrating state power in the hands of the executive. As diffuse and localized power gave way to dominating central state leadership, the continuing process of state formation moved out of the legislature and party system, out of the houses of provincial caciques and the patios of local strong men. It went back to the presidential palace where Marcos revived Quezon's centralist dreams. In southern Mindanao, Marcos's centralization of the state likewise brought down the strong men, first those who opposed him, like Pendatun, and eventually even his allies, like Almendras, who had become fatally dependent on Manila. The simultaneous rise of new challengers who identified themselves by ethnicity and religion was clear evidence that the postwar balance between local strong man power and central state authority had given way to more polarized politics.

## How Weak States Govern

Contradictions in state formation and local power and diversity in social identification lead to the question of state capacity. Scholars have been partial to Weber's notion of the state and measure the capacity of postcolonial states by the degree to which they achieve this Weberian ideal. Badie and Birnbaum (1983, 60), for example, argue that "the true state is one that has achieved a certain level of differentiation, autonomy, universality and institutionalization." Merilee Grindle (1996, 4, 7) defines state capacity as the "ability [of a state] to set the terms of interaction and to carry out the functions assigned to them." Out of these features, Ali Kazancigil (1994, 216) concludes that "a taxonomy takes shape, in which states are categorized from strong state or high stateness, to weak states or low stateness" (Kazancigil 1994, 216). In short, the social modernization of the postcolonial state has been judged by its resemblance to "that of the modern state, that is, the tandem of bureaucracy and capitalism" (Balakrishnan 1996, 282).

Southern Mindanao, however, suggests that overreliance on the Weberian ideal, particularly the often unstated hope to see that ideal succeed, can restrict one's understanding of state capacity in postcolonial societies. These states seem to be examined not only because of their analytical worth, but also because of the desire to pinpoint weaknesses and obstacles to realizing the myriad of activities that represent the raison d'etre. The three major perspectives on postcolonial politics—modernization, dependency, and state theories—share this desire for postcolonial states to attain "high stateness," even as they differ in analyses and arguments.

In southern Mindanao, we see that state capacity was not based on its ability to rise above and impose its hegemony on civil society. Rather, its influence lay in defining the parameters of doing politics. A prominent feature of postwar southern Mindanao was a fairly high degree of electoral participation. I have argued that this signified acceptance by newly declared "citizens" of the state's lawful avenues of political participation. It also indicates that a weak state can compensate for its institutional weakness by providing focus in a region lacking an "institutional core" (Wiebe 1975, 7). John Bodnar's (1992, 22) observation of the nineteenth-century United States political system reminds us of southern Mindanao in the postwar period: "the state, as a symbol and as a political structure, exerted considerable influence over politics and culture in the nineteenth century. This influence was tenuous and often challenged by a variety of vernacular interests but was very real both because the nation-state was viewed as a resource for the attainment of leverage by various smaller interests from time to time and because it sometimes gathered a force and power of its own that could not be easily resisted" (Bodnar 1992, 22).

Local strong men surrendered some of their power by accepting the state's political parameters and thereby brought stability to their regions, as the case of Almendras illustrates. For all the commotion caused by massive inmigration, land conflict, armed banditry, rebellious Bilaans, and the tumult of elections, postwar Davao was quite stable (Garcia 1947, 1). Much of that stability was due to Almendras, a quintessential strong man around whom local politics evolved, and whom national and regional state leaders had to accommodate. Almendras drew the boundaries within which the groups forming his political base negotiated and vied with each other. And, significantly, Almendras accorded great importance to fighting within the legal framework laid down by the state. He fought battles in the electoral arena, in party back rooms, in the courts, and in other agencies of arbitration. While he had coercive resources and was sometimes accused of employing them, Almendras was largely a law-abiding strong man.

An instrumentalist perspective would argue that Almendras conformed to state norms in order to access the resources and prestige of the state for his own needs. Such has often been the case in the Philippines and various studies have suggested it (Kerkvliet and Mojares 1991). I would add, however, that strong men like Almendras also worked within the law because they included in their political ambition the exercise of state power. They were strong men whose powers derived in part from the state. Almendras saw himself as a political boss *and* governor of Davao; working within the law was as much a fundamental attribute as was his private army, his share in the illegal economy, and his network of patrons and clients.

Thus, to evaluate state capacity solely on the basis of institutional autonomy undervalues the compensating effect of powerful rituals of mobilization and participation. This cultural capital cannot be ignored, for it, perhaps more than anything else, helps us understand how weak states maintain themselves despite their structural fragility. Further, the mutual accommodation reached by the state and the wielders of local power compels the latter to act as effective agents of the state, at least as much as it compels the state to scale back its policies and goals. I have attempted to show that strong men valued and recognized the responsibility of being a state official. The story of Almendras, as well as that of Pendatun, while abounding in episodes of patronage, backroom deals, corruption, and threats of coercion, are also replete with compromise, reliance on party networks, and other evidence of mutual accommodation. In short, strong men also made sacrifices to facilitate state formation.

Southern Mindanao politics shows that in structurally weak states like the Philippines, state capacity is defined by an exchange between state and society, through the mediations of regional and local strongmen. Samuel Huntington (1968) may be correct in asserting that what is at issue is not modernization, but the ability to govern. Unlike Huntington, however, I would argue that the ability to govern means finding a middle ground with other centers of power. The issue students of postcolonial states may want to reconsider, therefore, is not so much the capacity of a state to exercise hegemony, but its ability to compromise with societal forces. Saddled with budget deficits, patronage politics, administrative inefficiency, patrimonial plunder, political apathy, and perhaps even resistance, these states may realistically aspire to less ambitious objectives than the Weberian ideal. A realistic goal might be to achieve a level of governance consistent with a certain degree of political stability. State scholars may see this as a predicament that obstructs the flowering of the state in a Weberian manner, as well as the development and progress of a society. On the ground, however, this may be the only way a state like the Philippines can endure and exercise its authority *qua* state.

While to conceptually distinguish state from society (or economy) remains a valuable tool of analysis, the intimate and often intense bonding between these two categories, not to mention the (mal)development of state structures, serves to caution us about the limits of this heuristic distinction. For one, it draws our attention away from the most dominant spaces in political systems—the realm where state and society commingle. In this political "netherworld" (at least from the perspective of the conceptual dichotomy) where state meets society, the parameters of governance are negotiated and determined. Pendatun and Almendras exemplified the administrative capability of this political fusion by their respective roles as strongmen and state actors, here defending their local turf, there executing imperatives of state on their constituencies. Southern Mindanao, whose image as a frontier was fraught with political, economic, and military uncertainty, was thus rendered governable because of this interlacing of two spheres (B. Anderson 1990, 46–58; Wolters 1994, 13; Mamdami 1996, 60).

I am not suggesting that accommodation was the only mechanism operating in this sphere. On the contrary, as a realm mixing state and societal concerns, it also became an arena of growing dissonance. Economic crisis, the emergence of a developmentalist agenda, and the state's instinctive disposition to centralize worked to destabilize the overall harmony of this netherworld and bring to the fore the contradictions inherent in it (B. Anderson 1991, 67–82). In the same vein, a strong man seeking to expand or salvage his local power might resort to means detrimental to governance and state power, and thus precipitate conflict between center and periphery. Southern Mindanao during the Marcos period exhibited both of these phenomena, resulting in the fragmentation of the frontier's social and political landscape, the breakdown of governance by both state and strong men, and the emergence of antistate insurgencies.

An appropriate way of picturing this political realm is to imagine two overlapping circles, whose intersection contains these interlacing identities and responsibilities. There is also tension because the nonoverlapping areas of the circles create centrifugal pressures to break the link. The strains on the relationship arise from the inherent characteristics of each side, as well as from the presence of social forces within them, that favor delinking rather than mutual accommodation. On the one hand, local constituencies pressed their strong men to minimize state intrusions. One example of this arose from the persistent Magindanao apprehension that the government's development and security programs were actually meant to destroy "Muslim culture." This kept leaders like Pendatun attuned to local sentiments even as they played politics in Manila. Provincial infighting among his wards likewise acted as a form of deterrence that impeded Almendras's ambition to become a full-blown national leader.

On the other hand, certain state agencies took their responsibility of making the state effective quite seriously, pushing for the detachment of the state from what they perceived as unproductive links with antireform strong men at the local level. Technocrats working for Marcos located in strategic planning offices advocated greater centralization and the diminution of local power in the name of better "national economic development" (Ocampo 1971, 31–64). These advocates of a centralized state received support from groups receptive to reform and critical of patronage politics. Together, they formed the centrifugal part of the state circle, which exerted pressure on the state to disengage from society and rule in accordance with its essence as a state. The crisis of the 1970s cannot be fully understood without considering this tension.[5]

## State Formation and Social Identities

The unevenness of a state's development and the variable impact it has on society also affect the manner in which identities associated with the state (citizen, "tribal ward," colonial subject, etc.) are intermeshed with those existing in civil society. Political leaders are aware that the success of state formation depends in part on their ability to erase or minimize social identities that embolden resistance against the state in favor of identities that strengthen the state's legitimacy. This, however, is the ideal situation; in reality state-linked identities find themselves coexisting or overlapping with society-based identities they seek to displace. In southern Mindanao, this was a dilemma that both colonial state builders and their postcolonial successors faced (Kaviraj, 1995, 118–9).

This complex interlacing of identities was pronounced during the different phases of the American colonial period. While U.S. army and Filipino elites agreed that Muslims were "uncivilized," they differed significantly in dealing with their "backwardness." Americans wanted to protect the Muslims from cultural corruption by the Filipinos. They regarded their continued control of southern Mindanao in dual but contradictory terms: as a civilizing process and as a way of preserving the Muslims in a pristine ethnic state. In contrast, Filipino leaders regarded "Muslim identity" as an intrinsic part of being Filipino and thus advocated integration alongside civilization. Organizational fiat eventually resolved the debate, and the Filipinized colonial state's policy towards "the Moros" became the blueprint for subsequent dealings with the Muslims.

With independence, the granting of full suffrage was seen as a way of hastening southern Mindanao's integration. Elections and related exercises, as well as the expansion of access to state positions, however, did not eliminate other identities. On the contrary, Muslim politicians utilized preexisting identities and blended them with more modern ones to achieve and maintain power. Citizenship became mixed with ethnic, religious and linguistic affiliations, as local leaders straddled the two spheres. Which identity was emphasized varied: citizens dominated during periods of stability, while anti-Manila "Muslims" took precedence in times of social stress. Let me elaborate on this by examining more closely the character of the "Moro elite."

Scholars studying this elite have emphasized the blending of a traditional system of authority with the structures and processes of the modern nation-state, a combination that became a political asset for its practitioners. As Mednick (1971, 146) observed, "the sultan-mayor becomes powerful precisely because he controls the local police and the enforcement of settlements is at his discretion. Other title holders are forced to become subordinate to the mayor and such other political figures if they wish to have access to the power which is so necessary to their continuing function as mediators."

Datus got "opportunities for advancement to which they were indebted, and with greater exposure to national problems, these Muslim leaders developed an affinity with the national body politic."[6] Traditional authority thus served as a gateway to modern politics as datus gained access to positions in the modern state and learned the art of doing politics: from competing over resources and allocations to fashioning laws and forming political factions (De los Santos 1975, 32). These exercises, in turn, strengthened the leading Muslim families of Mindanao:

> The Alontos of Lanao, the Pendatuns, Sinsuats and Ampatuans of Cotabato, and the Abu Bakrs of Sulu are all of royal blood; although occasionally in distantly collateral line. Their gradually waning traditional influence is now rather significantly buttressed, if slightly in nature, by the considerable resources of the constitutional system (such as patronage, public works funds, police systems, etc.). The datu class now controls sizable blocs of votes, which are often the basis of constantly shifting political alliances. It appears to be a fact that the most effective leaders are those who combine both traditional and constitutional authority (Saber 1962, 14).

These assessments, however, are also mixed with criticism. Scholars who praised the blending of the two systems also cautioned that the "introduction of new modes of achieving power" stunted the ability of the national structure to accomplish its programs in the Muslim area while causing dislocation and strain within traditional authority (Mednick, as quoted by Thomas 1971, 311).

Furthermore, by introducing patronage to Muslim leaders, political blending reinforced their local power and curtailed the growth of real democratic processes among their constituents (Bentley 1985, 68). While Muslims were already feeling estranged from the state because of the state's perceived pro-Christian bias, patronage politics tended to enhance that alienation (Majul 1985, 29). Increasingly reliant on the "higher officials of the bureaucracy" and on the national party system, Muslim leaders were sometimes perceived as operating "contrary to the wishes and interests" of their constituents (Bentley 1985, 69). A more serious criticism, however, was that datu involvement in postwar politics all but eliminated their distinction as Muslim politicians and subordinated Islam to the dominant political identities of party and factional affiliation:

> In the wake of republic-hood, datus were initially full of doubts, then found it easy to have the best of both worlds. Theoretically, their position was threatened by such novel and evidently alien concepts as adult franchise and elective posts. But the more enterprising discovered that all they had to do was to tolerate the nuisance. Datus got elected as mayors, governors and congressmen. They were "predetermined leaders." However, the addition of a democratic feather to their hereditary cap did not improve the quality of their leadership. The facility with which they took to politics showed that there was no difference between Muslims and Christians in the operative side of public life in the Philippines. They became subjects to the same inner logic that seemed to motivate all politicians, looking upon power as an end in itself (George 1980, 99–100).

These portraits and criticisms of the Muslim politician confirm parallel findings by scholars looking at the interaction between traditional structures and authorities and the modern state in other postcolonial societies. Their discussions, in fact, point to something unnoted in the Philippine debate: the creation of an interface between the strong man's community and the nation-state. A datu-politician representing the interests of both state and community may thus be likened to a "Janus-faced gentry" who occupies the interstices between state and society and engages in a balancing act to mediate between these two often contradictory spheres (Shue 1988, 89). In metaphorical terms, the Muslim politician possessed two public masks that he donned for different audiences. A traditional mask embodied his "Muslim-ness" and the "authority" conferred by his specific ethnic group, and his "modern" mask symbolized his standing as representative of the modern-state. He employed these masks with his two constituencies: the communities under his jurisdiction and the larger national audience which was concerned with his territory. It might be assumed that the traditional mask was directed to the local community, while the modern mask was reserved for politics in the capital.

I think the contrary was more often the case. Datus invoked their Muslim identity when addressing national audiences (from party networks to the legislature) as a means of claiming their right to represent, defend, and speak for their communities. Their traditional authority gave them this advantage which the nation-state, generally unfamiliar with and lacking access to the Muslim community, had to rely on. At home, the modern mask was donned for the datu's own ethnic group and the larger Muslim community. What scholars have noted as the excessive concern of Muslim leaders to sound and act like Filipino politicians can also be interpreted as presenting their credentials as representatives of the modern nation-state. This mask demonstrated that they could bring the benefits of the modern state to their constituents: from patronage funds to new programs and even the latest political gossip from the capital. These conventions of modern politics augmented the datu-politicians' standing with their local constituents.

The utility of this "Janus-faced" persona—modified (see chaper 1)—explains the political value of blending traditional and modern authority systems. Datus could be palace advisers, heirs to Magindanao royalty, defenders of Islam, and protectors of the nation-state, all at the same time. Invoking tradition or subsuming it to modern politics was not the issue. Instead, both types of authority became tools in the Muslim politician's search for power. In a way, datus were indeed like other Filipino politicians: "local patrimonial lords" who possessed "economic power, assume[d] quasi-military and quasi-judicial functions in their localities, and [were] represented at the national level in a powerful legislature" (Hutchcroft 1992, 17). What gave them added leverage, in their heyday, was the way they lightly wore their identity. Within the larger national political system, it afforded them more material control over their own communities, which in turn translated into the delivery of a unified "Moro" vote and a stable frontier (Hutchcroft 1992, 17). The state, therefore, did not seek to eliminate competing social identities in favor of the broader nationality, but actually made use of them to preserve its own authority.

## Conclusion

A weak, accommodating state must tolerate multiple identities, but a postcolonial state that is overdeveloped and has feeble ties with the communities under its jurisdiction likewise finds itself unable to homogenize civil society into the ideal subject population. Southern Mindanao's political landscape was able to maintain its stability until the 1960s because the Philippine state obliged these intertwined identities as part of the mutual accommodation it made with the region's local strong men. Through this ambiguity, state formation in this periphery of the body politic continued with minimum complication until the late 1960s when the frontier filled up and Marcos changed the rules. When those in control of the state decided to alter the relationship, the nature of local politics on the frontier also changed. Peace and order in Cotabato and Davao began to break down and the fragmented landscape that many erroneously associated with frontier Mindanao came to pass.

# NOTES

## Notes to Chapter 1 (pages 1–16)

1. Laitin in Evans et al. 1985, 286–87; Hobsbawm and Ranger 1983, 1–14; Brass 1991, 247–99; Breuilly 1993, 1–2, 257–68.

2. Tadem 1980; Tiglao 1981; Salgado 1989, 77–96; Silva 1979, 55–63; *Mindanao Focus* 18, 30–43; Collier in Turner et al. 1992, 203–10.

3. For example, Zartman 1995.

## Notes to Chapter 2 (pages 17–44)

1. This section is based on chapter 2 of my dissertation (Abinales 1997b).

2. On 1 June 1903, the Philippine Commission, the highest colonial policy-making body, passed Act No. 787 creating the Moro Province as "the framework within which transition from military to civilian rule in Moroland would take place wherever and whenever the duly constituted authorities felt it was indicated" (*RGMP* 1904, 113–21).

3. Cotabato was 11,786 square miles; Davao, 9,707 square miles; Zamboanga, 5,591 square miles; Lanao, 3,900 square miles; and Sulu, 1,039 square miles (*ARWD* 1909, 412–23).

4. *Census of the Philippines* 1903, Vol. 2, 123–37, 400–7. In his last year as governor, Pershing even transferred policing duties to the datus to show that "peace prevail[ed]" in the province (*PFP*, 18 Nov. 1911; Hobbs 1962, 189–91).

5. The phrase "reach of the state" was coined by Shue (1988).

6. Coats 1968, 361; Roth 1981, 30–37, 148–54; Thompson 1975, 55–56; Funtecha 1979, 59; *ARWD* 1902, 2127; Hurley 1936, 178–79.

7. Gowing 1983, 228–29; *RGMP* 1904, 13; *RPC* 1906, part 3, 118; *RGMP* 1906, 340.

8. Collections in the Zamboanga port totaled 82,240.40 pesos in 1904; 108,719.86 pesos in 1905 and increased to 178,818.95 pesos in 1906 (*MH,* 15 Sept. 1906).

9. Hartley 1983, 38, 44–45; *MH,* 30 June 1906. The eventual foundering of the rubber industry was a setback, but even its stunted growth kept investors interested (see Hartley 1983, 44–46).

10. See various annual reports, *RGMP* 1903–1913.

11. The Muslims were not even considered because military officials felt that they were not ready to be handed administrative responsibilities beyond the tribal ward system (*MH,* 2 Mar. 1909; *RGMP* 1909, 8).

12. *RPC* 1901, 32. The significance of the 1902 and 1904 municipal and provincial elections and the 1906 elections to the Philippine Assembly for the evolution of Filipino political power within the colonial state has been discussed by scholars elsewhere. Here I only focus on their impact on southern Mindanao. On the growing power of Filipinos, see Golay 1998; Stanley 1974; May in Paredes 1989, 13–40; Cullinane 1981, 79–80; Cullinane 1989, 227, 251–56, 273–87.

13. See, for example, the proceedings in *JPC* 1911, 770–71 and *JPC* 1913, 765.

14. Gowing 1983, 194, 220–21; *RGMP* 1908, 373; *RGMP* 1910, 7; and *RPC* 1902, 360–61.

15. In provinces like Bukidnon and Agusan, this was exactly what happened. Manuel Fortich, a former constabulary man from Cebu and a prominent Nacionalista, established the dominant role his family enjoys to this day in Bukidnon (*RF,* May 19; Lao 1987, 325–26; Lao 1985, 70–77). And Guingona, whose initial wealth came from cattle-raising and land-owning in Agusan, Bukidnon, Lanao, and Cotabato, likewise established a patronage network before being promoted to Carpenter's side as secretary-treasurer (*PFP,* 28 Oct. 1933; *MB,* 26 Aug. 1934).

16. *MB,* 4 Jan., 5 Feb., 6 May and 5 June 1919; *MB,* 2 May 1916; *PFP,* 8 May 1915 and 4 Aug. 1917.

17. In 1917, these were cited as reasons for low voter turnout in Muslim areas (Carpenter 1917, 79).

18. On the datus' visits, see *MB,* 26 Jan., 6 May and 15 Oct. 1915; *PFP,* 6 Feb. 1916 and 19 Oct. 1918.

19. *MB,* 15, 18, 22–23, 25–27 Oct. 1915; Elequin 1981–82, 85.

20. Quezon 1940, 124–26; Guinto 24 June 1934.

21. Guingona 1935; *MB,* 10 Oct. 1936 and 1 Jan. 1937.

## Notes to Chapter 3 (pages 45–68)

1. This section on Magindanao in Southeast Asian society is a version of an essay titled "From Orang Besar to Colonial Big Man," which will appear in *Lives at the margins: Biographies of obscured Filipinos*, edited by Alfred McCoy (forthcoming).

2. Reid 1988 and 1993; Kathirithamby-Wells and Villiers 1990; Gowing 1979, 89; Loyre 1991. In fact, the seventeenth-century Magindanao Sultanate emerged as part of a "new generation of port-states [whose role] was to keep the indigenous network of trade alive in the face of European challenges" (Kathirithamby-Wells and Villiers 1990, 120). The Magindanaos, and later the different Sulu groups, participated in this new link. They supplied its trading centers with a variety of forest and sea products, and most important, with slaves for the pepper plantations set up all over Southeast Asia (Villiers 1990, 151).

3. Kudrat spoke Spanish "as fluently as if it were his mother tongue. He also spoke, in addition to his native Magindanao, Chinese, English and Dutch" (Laarhoven 1990, 163).

4. Laarhoven (1990, 179); Warren 1977, 67–78; Majul 1973, 311–14.

5. The extent to which the once powerful Magindanao sultanate had declined was vividly captured by a contemporary report, which observed that the Sultan of Magindanao, "whose ancestors were once the most powerful chieftains of the Island of Mindanao, is utterly without means of support. Though having no following, he is respected by the Moros on account of his 'royal' birth, and is virtually living the life of a tramp. Having no home of his own he spends his time visiting the various chieftains, stopping at each place until his presence ceases to be a novelty, [then] he moves in on some neighboring chieftain" (*MH,* 17 June 1905).

6. Andaya 1993, 37; Laarhoven 1990, 168.

7. I argued in my dissertation that Ali's revolt was the last attempt of a Southeast Asian orang besar to maintain his regional identity. It was not a nationalist revolt as Mapanao (Mapanao 1985, ix, 2) contends (see Abinales 1997b, chapter 3).

8. *MH,* 4 and 25 Aug. 1906; Gowing 1983, 183. Mastula's appointment not only enhanced Piang's standing among the Magindanaos (for restoring some credibility to the old sultan), but also fit well with the American intention to use Magindanao royal families for pacification purposes (*MH*, 17 June 1905).

9. Gullick 1958, 13; Wilkinson 1923, 124–40. Abdullah's actions occurred at almost the same time as Piang and Ali sought Spanish aid to undermine the Datu of Buayan (Ileto 1971, 62–63).

10. This section is derived from my article The "Muslim-Filipino" and the state, *Public Policy: A University of the Philippines Quarterly* 2(2), Apr.-June 1998, 37–69.

11. Letter of Datus Guiambangan et al., JRH Box 27–32; see also file on Sunset Cox and the Piangs, 18 Nov. 1926, JRH Box 28–24.

12. Among the "nationalist" datus of Lanao were Sultan Benito and Datus Tiburon, Dianalan, Nadankup, and Dimacota (see Carpenter 1917, 295; *MB,* 4 July and 4 Aug. 1931; *MTr,* 28 Sept. 1931).

13. The idea of administrative "pilgrimage" having a role in the creation of nations is from Anderson 1991, 132.

14. Gutierrez 1934, JRH Box 27–31.

15. Meeting with municipal presidents, Mindanao Special Province, 24 Feb. 1938. See also Kasilag 1938, 12–23; Quezon 1940, 24–26.

## Notes to Chapter 4 (pages 69–93)

1. *Independent*, 23 Aug. 1900; *Outlook*, 20 Mar. 1901; *MH*, 29 Apr. 1905.

2. *MH*, 8 Apr. 1905. Provincial authorities also asked for a law that would allow "settlers to have a good title to their land that would run for twenty-five years, with the privilege of renewal for another twenty-five years, long before which period shall have expired the land laws will undoubtedly have been adjusted to suit the convenience of all who desire to settle and afford ample protection from the native" (*RGMP* 1905: 6).

3. Settlers who "occupied and cultivated unappropriated, unreserved public lands since August 1, 1898," or who, if settling before that date, had "continuously occupied and cultivated such land for three years" were granted free patents (*MH,* 30 Dec. 1905).

4. The first quotation is from *RGMP* 1 Sept. 1904, 22; the second is from *MT*, 30 Mar. 1905.

5. See, for example, the case of settler Henry Pahl, in *ACCJ* 1926, 26. Two prominent "corporations" that were forced to go into receivership due to lack of capital were the Butalaki Hemp Company and the Mindanao Agricultural and Commercial Company (*PFP,* 9 Apr. 1910; *MT,* 2 Apr. 1910).

6. This section is an abridged version of the essay "Davao-kuo: The Political Economy of a Japanese Settler Zone in Philippine Colonial Society," published in *Journal of American-East Asian Relations* 6, 1 (Spring 1997), 59–82.

7. The Japanese first acquired land through individual purchase and lease and also by marrying indigenous women who had the right to purchase or lease lands from the government (*PFP*, 4 Oct. 1930).

8. Rent was later increased to 10 and then 15 percent as the companies' capitalization grew.

9. Hayase 1984, 2–13. Furiya gives the figure 14,029 for 1936 (see Furiya 1993, 155).

10. Jose 1992, 65. In 1931, trade between the Philippines and Japan amounted to $17 million.

11. Memorandum of J. C. Early; profile of Sebastian Generoso, JRH Box 27–3. At one time, Generoso was suspended for "irregularities" and unprofessional conduct as a public official (see third endorsement of secretary of interior, JRH Box 27–5; note of J. C. Early on meeting with secretary of interior, 26 June 1931, JRH Box 28–3).

12. Friend 1965, 180–81.

13. *Proceedings of the Constitutional Conventional Convention* 1935, 70, 183–84; letter of secretary of agriculture to J.R. Hayden, 26 Mar. 1935, JRH Box 4; *Commonwealth Advocate* 16 Apr. 1936 and 15 May 1936. These criticisms became strident when the Japanese seized Manchuria in 1931–1932. Filipino writers issued warnings that Southeast Asia and the Philippines would be the next targets of Japanese expansionism (*Commonwealth Advocate,* July 1935).

14. The act granted leases totaling 10,204 hectares to eighteen Japanese corporations (see Hayase 1984, 165–66, and also *MH,* 9 Apr. 1936; *MB,* 11 and 23 Apr. 1936).

15. Quezon, "Speech before the Philippine Assembly, June 23, 1936," *National Archives, Bureau of Insular Affairs*, File Number 17073, 456; *The Filipino People,* April 1936, 16–17.

## Notes to Chapter 5 (pages 94–114)

1. Haggerty 1946, 9; Conditions affecting Domestic Order in the Moro Provinces of Mindanao and Sulu. Prepared by the Philippine Research and Information Section, Counter-Intelligence, GHQ, AFPAC, APO 500, 28 August 1945 – Confidential" (JRH Box 42–20: 2–3); Memorandum of Lt. Col. J.R. Grinstead to Lt. Col. Robert V. Bowler, CO, A Corps, 10th Military District, USAF, 5 February 1944 (JRH Box 42–26): 2; Hartendorp 1967 (2), 293; Keats 1963, 74.

2. Baclagon 1963, 74; Haggerty 1946, 23; Quirino 1984, 29–41, 43–44, 51–62; Keats 1963, 371.

3. The quote is from Baclagon 1963, 288–89; see also Morison 1963, 240.

4. In fact, when the Japanese forces concentrated in the coastal towns flexed their muscles against the guerrillas, the latter were easily routed. This

counteroffensive, however, came too late—the Pacific War was already turning in the Americans' favor (Baclagon 1963, 292–94).

5. "The Government of the 'New Philippines': A Study of the Present Puppet Government of the Philippines," Office of Strategic Services, Report No. 1752, 15 May 1944, 41–44; *Historical Bulletin* 1972, 343; Baclagon 1988, 80, 88–89.

6. Third Annual Report of U.S. High Commissioner 1943, 58; Santos 1934–35 in JRH Box 29–6; *The Philippine Policy* 1939, 111; Rodriguez 1938, 3–12.

7. *Commonwealth Advocate,* Oct.-Nov. 1935, 52; Mar. 1937, 57; *PM,* Feb. 1938, 82–83; Feb. 1939, 85.

8. *MB,* 24 and 27 Feb., 3, 10, 13, 15 and 24 Mar., 1, 25 and 26 Apr. 1939; 12 and 17 Apr. 1940; 19 Feb. 1941.

9. I am grateful to Alfred McCoy for this insight.

10. *MT,* 24 Mar. 1947; Magsalin 1948 in Elpidio Quirino Papers; Congressional Records April 1950, 1326; *MinT,* 12 June 1951.

11. Sanders 1953, 5; *MT,* 3 Jan. 1952 and 8, 10, 12 and 13 Nov. 1956; *DM,* 7 Nov. 1956.

12. The economic arrangements between these families and their subalterns are an area in Magindanao studies that remains unexplored.

13. *MT,* 3 Oct. 1955; 5 Feb. 1956; 4 May 1956; 15 Dec. 1957; 8 Dec. 1960.

14. I thank Michael Cullinane for this information (personal communication, 2 Jan. 1997). According to him, Argao and Sibonga were part of a string of municipalities on the southeastern coast of Cebu that were traditionally densely populated with limited land productivity.

15. McCoy 1982, 311–26. McCoy (private communication, Jan. 1997) likewise suggests that the slow and infrequent boats from Negros to Cotabato, the long waiting period to accumulate cargo and passengers, the distance between Cotabato or Koronadal and western towns like Iloilo (compared to the proximity of Bohol or Cebu to Davao) were obstacles that a poor settler lacked the resources to endure.

## Notes to Chapter 6 (pages 115–133)

1. I am grateful to Ben Anderson for suggesting this phrase.

2. *DM,* 18 Jan. and 30 Mar. 1961; *MT,* 17 July 1961; *STM,* 2 Apr. 1961; *PH,* 20 Jan. 1961.

3. *MT,* 3 Feb., and 12 Dec. 1959; 20 Feb., 26 and 31 Mar. 1960; *DM,* 18 Jan. 1961.

4. *MB,* 1 Jan. 1952; *PFP,* 15 Mar. 1952; *MT,* 3 Jan. 1952; *DM,* 9 Jan. 1952.

5. Sarmiento 1953; *MB,* 9 Sept. 1953; Dougherty 1953.

6. U.S. Embassy to Department of State, 13 Mar. 1953; 4 Mar. 1953.

7. *TW,* 11 Nov. 1956; *MT,* 18 Jan. 1953; *PH,* 29 Sept. 1953; *MCh,* 6 June 1956.

8. Philippine Research Information Section, 28 Aug. 1945.

9. *MCr,* 16 Sept., and 15 Oct. 1950; 18 Sept. 1954; 4 Apr. 1956; Stewart 1977, 52.

10. Davao and Cotabato were not yet formally regular provinces. The Revised Administrative Code's Charter 63 accorded them full suffrage rights but certain provisions from the colonial charter remained. In Davao's case, provincial officials were still appointed by Manila until 1953, when another charter change made them elective. *MinT*, 18 Oct. 1952.

11. *Commission on Elections Reports to the President of the Philippines and the Congress*, various years.

12. The figures included voters from Cotabato and Davao cities.

13. This was the case in Jolo, and there is no reason to assume the practice differed in Cotabato and other Muslim provinces (Youngblood 1966, 129).

14. Among the prominent Muslim politicians elected during this period were Salipada Pendatun (Cotabato), elected senator in 1946, congressman in 1957–69; Domocao Alonto (Lanao), elected congressman in 1953, senator in 1955; Gumbay Piang (Cotabato), elected congressman in 1946; Blah Sinsuat (Cotabato), elected congressman in 1949; Datu Luminog Mangelen (Cotabato), elected congressman in 1953; Mohammad Ali Dimaporo (Lanao), elected congressman in 1959; Omar Amilbangsa (Sulu), elected congressman in 1946, 1953, and 1957; and Hadji Gulamu Rasul (Sulu), elected congressman in 1949. In Davao, Alejandro Almendras, originally of Cebu, was elected senator in 1949; Ismael Veloso of Iloilo was elected congressman in 1949, 1953, and 1961; and Gabino Sepulveda, from Cebu, was elected congressman in 1957.

15. This description of the value of politics to Maranao leaders could apply to any Mindanao strong man: "By aligning themselves with the more powerful party in exchange, a few Maranao political leaders and attorneys profited handsomely... Maranao lawyers use [their] connection to gain official appointments by which they enhance their personal status" (Bentley 1985, 70; see also *MinT,* 7 June 1951).

## Notes to Chapter 7 (pages 134–154)

1. Pendatun was actually born 3 Dec. 1912, but the earlier date was used to "enable him to make the statutory age required to run for the Philippine Senate in the first election held after the war" (Baclagon 1988, 39).

2. While still popularly revered, being of royal blood, the Magindanao Sultanate had become largely ceremonial since the arrival of the Americans and had little influence on local colonial politics.

3. Access to state power endowed him with timber concessions as well as pivotal roles in negotiating land sales and facilitating farmer loans from the Philippine National Bank (*MCr*, 20 Mar., 28 Aug. 1948).

4. "Conditions affecting Domestic Order in the Moro Provinces of Mindanao and Sulu, 28 August 1945—Confidential," JRH Box 42–20, 9.

5. *MCr,* 10 Dec. 1949, 26 Aug. 1950; *MT,* 12 Mar. 1950; Cowen 1950b.

6. *Proceedings of the Second National Muslim Conference* 1956; Mastura 1984, 100.

7. *MT,* 8 Dec. 1958; *PFP,* 16 July 1960, 15 Dec. 1962; *Report of Senate Committee* 1960, 63.

8. On the prevalence of squatting in postwar Davao, see Abinales 1997b.

9. *MinT*, 12 and 22 Jan., 22–23 Feb. and 17 Aug. 1955. This included surviving a later mandate from Manila declaring Davao City a "free zone" open to any Nacionalista faction (*MinT,* 5 Oct. 1955).

## Notes to Chapter 8 (pages 155–177)

1. *DM,* 22 Nov. 1951; *MT,* 8 Feb. 1957, 23 Mar., 27 and 30 July 1959, and compare with *MS,* 27 Nov. 1972; *DM,* 25 Feb. 1972.

2. *MT,* 1 and 9 Mar. 1961; 7 Nov. 1962; 27 May 1963; 2 May 1964; 20 and 22 Apr. 1967; *MinT,* 22 Apr. 1966.

3. *MT*, 18 Aug. 1960; 21, 24 and 27 Oct. 1961; 30 Mar. and 17 Nov. 1962; 25 Sept., 2, 11, and 23 Oct. 1963; *MinT,* 20 June 1963.

4. *MT,* 20 July 1963; *MinT,* 27 Jan. and 12 Oct. 1966; 9 May, 8 and 14 Aug. and 22 Nov. 1968; 18 May, 1 and 12 June, and 20 July 1967; 21 Mar. and 12 Dec. 1968.

5. *MC,* 13, 18 and 20 Nov. 1965. Marcos signed the law dividing the province a few months after he assumed the presidency (see also *MT,* 16 July 1966).

6. *MT,* 19 Mar. and 22 Mar. 1962; *DM,* 15–16 Oct., 11–12 Nov., and 26 Dec. 1962; *PFP,* 27 Oct. 1962.

7. *MT,* 25 May 1966; 28 Feb. 1968; *MinT,* 10 Feb. 1966; 16 Mar. 1967.

8. *MinT,* 7 and 13 Aug. 1970; *DM* 15 Mar. 1971; Local Government Research Team 1970, 7–9, 13–14, 52.

9. *MT,* 28 July, 20 Aug., 9 Sept., 23 and 31 Dec. 1970; *MinT,* 10 Oct. 1970.

## Notes to Chapter 9 (pages 178–189)

1. March 1899; Tate 1965, 278–79; Carano and Sanchez 1964, 169–222.

2. McCoy 1985, 4–5; Silverstein 1966; Benda 1968, 65–79; Agoncillo 1965; Baclagon 1952; Keats 1963; Hartendorp 1967 (vol. 1), 282–96; Ancheta 1982, 193–240; Morison 1963.

3. "The Government of the 'New Philippines': A Study of the Present Puppet Government of the Philippines," Office of Strategic Services, Report No. 1752, 15 May 1944; Baclagon 1988; Haggerty 1946; Quirino 1984, 29–41, 43–44, 51–62.

4. Caoili 1986; Hutchcroft 1991; Lacaba 1995; Lande 1964; and McCoy 1993.

5. For analogous cases, see Shefter 1987, 13–104; Shefter 1994, 169–94.

6. Majul 1985, 29. This affinity made Carl Lande conclude that "it is not Muslims against non-Muslims but rather Muslim Liberals against Muslim Nacionalistas… The party system, rather than exacerbating regional or cultural differences, exerts a unifying influence by bringing together within each party politicians from all islands, whose constituencies include voters representing every type of crop, industry, linguistic or religious minority" (Lande 1964, 40).

# REFERENCES CITED

## Abbreviations Used

| | |
|---|---|
| *ABK* | *Ang Bag-ong Kusog* |
| *ACCJ* | *American Chamber of Commerce Journal* |
| *ARWD* | *Annual Report of the War Department* |
| *C-A* | *Cablenews-American* |
| *DM* | *Daily Mirror* |
| *ET* | *El Tiempo* |
| *JPC* | *Journal of the Philippine Commission* |
| *JPL* | *Jose P. Laurel Papers* |
| *JRH* | *Joseph Ralston Hayden Collection* |
| *M-A* | *Manila-American* |
| *MB* | *Manila Bulletin* |
| *MCh* | *Manila Chronicle* |
| *MCr* | *Mindanao Cross* |
| *MH* | *Mindanao Herald* |
| *MM* | *Mindanao Mail* |
| *MN* | *Mindanao News* |
| *MS* | *Mindanao Star* |
| *MT* | *Manila Times* |
| *MTr* | *Manila Tribune* |
| *MinT* | *Mindanao Times* |
| *PFP* | *Philippines Free Press* |
| *PH* | *Philippines Herald* |
| *PM* | *Philippine Magazine* |
| *PP* | *Philippine Panorama* |
| *PR* | *Philippine Review* |
| *RF* | *Revista Filipina* |
| *RGGPI* | *Report of the Governor-General of the Philippine Islands* |
| *RGMP* | *Report of the Governor of the Moro Province* |
| *RPC* | *Report of the Philippine Commission* |
| *STM* | *Sunday Times Magazine* |
| *TW* | *This Week* |
| *TWM* | *The Weekly Magazine* |
| *WM* | *Weekend Mirror* |

Abat, Fortunato U. 1993.The day we nearly lost Mindanao: The Armed Forces of the Philippines Central Mindanao Command story. Manila: n.p.

Abbey, Merill N. 1951. Memorandum to the Department of State. Subject: Land settlement, Bureau of Lands procedure, 23 November. United States, Department of State central file, The Philippine Republic, internal and foreign affairs.

———. 1951–52. Report to the Department of State. Subject: Philippine annual agricultural policy report, 1 March 1951–1 March 1952, 10 March 1952. United States, Department of State central files: The Philippine Republic, internal and foreign affairs.

Abdullah, Inutas. 1989. Land ownership dispute and its settlement among Maranaos. *Moro Kurier* 4, 1–2 (January-June).

Abinales, Patricio N. 1997a. Davao-kuo: The political economy of a Japanese settler zone in Philippine colonial society. *The Journal of American-East Asian Relations* 6, 1 (Spring).

———. 1997b. State authority and local power in Southern Philippines, 1900–1972. Ph.D. diss., Cornell University.

———. 1998a. The "Muslim-Filipino" and the state. *Public Policy: A University of the Philippines Quarterly* 2, 2 (April-June): 37–69.

———. 1998b. Early American colonial state-building in the Philippines: A reconsideration. Symposium on *Revisiting the birth of our century: The meaning of 1898*, 30–31 October 1998. Center for Latin American Studies, Tulane University, New Orleans.

Abubakar, Asiri. 1973. Muslim Philippines: With reference to the Sulus, Muslim-Christian contradictions and the Mindanao crisis. *Asian Studies* 11, 1 (April).

Abueva, Jose V. 1971. *Ramon Magsaysay: A political biography*. Manila: Solidaridad Publishing House.

Acuña, Rodolfo. 1974. *Sonoran strong man: Ignacio Pesqueira and his times*. Tucson, Arizona: The University of Arizona Press.

Adduru, Marcelo. History of the LASEDECO. 1952. *Commerce: The Voice of Philippine Business* 47 (September-October).

Afdal, Samoan. 1949. Report of the operations intelligence officer, Cotabato, to the chief of the Philippine Constabulary, GHQ, Camp Crame. In Elpidio Quirino Papers.

*Affairs of the Philippine Islands: Hearings of the senate committee on the Philippines*. 1900. 10 April 1902. Washington: General Printing Office.

Agoncillo, Teodoro A. 1965. *The fateful years: Japan's adventure in the Philippines, 1941–45*. Quezon City: R.P. Garcia Publishing.

Ahmad, Aijaz. 1982. Class and colony in Mindanao. *Southeast Asia Chronicle* 82 (February).

Alonto, Abdul Khayr. 1977. Speech of the vice-chairman of the Moro National Liberation Front. Delivered at the general conference of the Ansar El Islam, 28–30 January.

Amendments introduced by the Committee on Mindanao and the Special Provinces 1946. 1st Cong. of the Republic of the Philippines, 1st regular sess., 1, 4.

American Consul, Cebu, to the Department of State. 1959.General impression on Davao City, 1 July. United States, Department of State central files: The Philippine Republic, internal and foreign affairs.

Amoroso, Donna J. 1996. Traditionalism and the ascendancy of the Malay ruling class in colonial Malaya. Ph.D. diss., Cornell University.

———. 1997. Inheriting the Moro problem: Muslim authority and colonial rule in British Malaya and the Philippines. Association for Asian Studies, 1997 Annual Meeting, 13–16 March, Chicago.

*An anatomy of Philippine Muslim affairs: A study in-depth on Muslim affairs in the Philippines.* 1971. Manila: Filipinas Foundation, Inc.

Ancheta, Celedonio A. 1982. *The Wainwright papers.* Vol. 3. Quezon City: New Day Publishers.

Andaya, Barbara Watson. 1993. Cash cropping and upstream-downstream tensions: The case of Jambi in the seventeenth and eighteenth centuries. In *Southeast Asia in the early modern era: Trade, power and belief*, edited by Anthony Reid. Ithaca and London: Cornell University Press.

Anderson, Benedict. 1988. Cacique democracy in the Philippines: Origins and dreams. *New Left Review* 169 (May-June).

———. 1990. *Language and power: Exploring political cultures in Indonesia.* Ithaca, N.Y.: Cornell University Press.

———. 1994. *Imagined communities: Reflections on the origin and spread of nationalism.* London: Verso.

———. 1996. Elections and participation in three Southeast Asian countries. In *The politics of elections in Southeast Asia*, edited by R.H. Taylor. New York: Woodrow Wilson Center Press and the Press Syndicate of the University of Cambridge.

Anderson, Lisa. 1986. *The state and social formation in Tunisia and Libya, 1830–1980.* New Jersey: Princeton University Press.

Anderson, Malcolm. 1996. *Frontiers: Territory and state formation in the modern world.* Cambridge, UK: Polity Press.

Anderson, Perry. 1989. *Lineages of the absolutist state.* London and New York: Verso.

Annual Report of the War Department, 1 September 1904. 1904. In *Report of the Philippine Commission*, 30 June. Vol. 12, part 2. Washington: General Printing Office.

Anonymous. 1949. Confidential letter to Pres. Elpidio Quirino, 4 December. In Elpidio Quirino Papers.

Anonymous. n.d. Biography of Datu Piang. In Joseph Ralston Hayden Collection. Box 28–24.

*Araw ng Dabaw.* 1969. 32nd Anniversary souvenir program. 16 March.

Arcilla, Jose S. 1989–1990. The Philippine revolution and the Jesuit missions in Mindanao, 1896–1901. *The Journal of History* (Philippine National Historical Society) 14–15, 1–2 (January-December).

Asani, Abdurasad. 1979. Appeal of the Bangsa Moro people to the International League for the rights and liberation of peoples, 10 June.

Ang ating walong taong pakikibaka sa Mindanaw, 1971–1979. 1992. Manuscript most likely written by a member of the Communist Party of the Philippines-Mindanao Commission.

Azarya, Victor and Naomi Chazan. 1987. Disengagement from the state in Africa: Reflections on the experience of Ghana and Guinea. *Comparative studies in society and history* 29.

Azarya, Victor. 1988. Reordering state-society relations: Incorporation and disengagement. In *Precarious balance: State and society in Africa*, edited by Donald Rothchild and Naomi Chazan. Boulder: Westview Press.

Baclagon, Uldarico S. 1952. *Philippine campaigns*. Manila: Graphic House.

———. 1988. *Christian-Moslem guerrillas of Mindanao*. Manila: Lord Avenue Printing Press.

Bacon, Robert 1926. Remarks in the House of Representatives. In Joseph Ralston Hayden Collection. Box 28–24. 9 February.

———. 1926. Speech. In *U.S. Congressional record*. Vol. 67, part 8, 69th Cong., 1st sess., 6 May.

Badie, Bertrand and Pierre Birbaum. 1983. *The sociology of the state*. Chicago: University of Chicago Press.

Balakrishnan, Gopal, ed. 1996. *Mapping the nation*. New York and London: Verso.

Bautista, Filomeno M. 1939. *Glimpses of Mindanao: The land of promise*. Manila: Tong Cheong Sons.

Bayart, Jean Francois. 1993. *The state in Africa: The politics of the belly*. London and New York: Longman.

Beckett, Jeremy. 1982. The defiant and the compliant: The datus of Magindanao under colonial rule. In *Philippine social history: Global trade and local transformation*, edited by Alfred W. McCoy and Ed. de Jesus. Quezon City: Ateneo de Manila University Press.

———. 1993. Political families and family politics among the Muslim Maguindanaon of Cotabato. In *An anarchy of families: State and family in the Philippines*, edited by Alfred W. McCoy. Quezon City: Ateneo de Manila University Press and Madison, Wisconsin: University of Wisconsin Center for Southeast Asian Studies.

Bell, Jasper (chairman, House Committee on Insular Affairs). 1945. *Rehabilitation of the Philippines*. Washington: General Printing Office.

Benda, Harry J. 1968. The Japanese interregnum in Southeast Asia. New Haven: Yale University Southeast Asia Studies Reprint Series No. 26.

———. 1972. *Continuity and change in Southeast Asia*. New Haven: Yale University Southeast Asia Studies, Monograph no. 18.

Bentley, G. Carter. 1985. Dispute, authority and Maranao social order. In *Dispute processing in the Philippines*, edited by Resil Mojares. Quezon City: Bureau of Local Governments Supervision, Ministry of Local Government.

———. 1989. Implicit evangelism: American education among the Muslim Maranaos. *Pilipinas: A Journal of Philippine Studies* 12 (Spring).

Bliss, Tasker. 1903. The government of the Moro Province. In Report of the Philippine commission, *Annual report of the War Department,* 30 June, Vol. 5. Washington: General Printing Office.

———. 1909. The government of the Moro Province and its problems. *Mindanao Herald*, 3 February, 4.

Bodnar, John. 1992. *Remaking America: Public memory, commemoration, and patriotism in the twentieth century*. Princeton: Princeton University Press.

Boissevain, Jeremy (chief). 1953. CARE Mission. Marbel Report I. 3 June. United States, Department of State central files: The Philippine Republic, internal and foreign affairs.

Boyce, William. 1914. *United States colonies and dependencies.* Chicago and New York: Rand McNally.

Brass, Paul R. 1991. *Ethnicity and nationalism: Theory and comparison.* New Delhi: Sage.

Breuilly, John. 1993. *Nationalism and the state.* Chicago: University of Chicago Press.

Brown, David. 1988. From peripheral communities to ethnic nations: Separatism in Southeast Asia, *Pacific Affairs* 61, 1.

*Bulletin of the American Historical Collection.* Various issues, 1970–1990.

Bureau of Insular Affairs File No. 4865–150. 14 November 1923.

Bureau of Non-Christian Tribes Scholarship Fund. 1935. In Joseph Ralston Hayden Collection. Box 29–24.

Buttinger, Joseph. 1967. *Vietnam: A dragon embattled.* New York: Praeger.

Cabañero-Mapanao, Ruth. 1985. Maguindanao 1890–1913: The life and times of Datu Ali of Kudarangan. Master's thesis, University of the Philippines.

Canoy, Reuben. 1989. *The quest for Mindanao independence.* Cagayan De Oro City: Mindanao Post Publishing.

Caoili, Manuel A. 1986. The Philippine Congress and the political order. *Philippine Journal of Public Administration* 30, 1 (January).

Carano, Paul and Pedro S. Sanchez. 1964. *A complete history of Guam.* Rutland, Vermont and Tokyo: Charles E. Tuttle Co.

Carpenter, Frank W. 1915. Department of Mindanao and Sulu, Report to the governor-general, Philippine Islands, 1915. In *Report of the governor-general of the Philippine Islands to the secretary of war.* Washington: General Printing Office.

———. C 1915. House Document 1378, part 3, $64^{th}$ Cong., 2nd sess.

———. 1917. Department of Mindanao and Sulu. Report to the governor-general, Philippine Islands, 10 January. In *Report of the governor-general of the Philippine Islands to the secretary of war.* Washington: General Printing Office.

———. 1919. Department of Mindanao and Sulu. Report to the governor-general, Philippine Islands, 15 March. In *Report of the governor-general of the Philippine Islands to the secretary of war.* Washington: General Printing Office.

Casambre, Napoleon. 1975. The Harrison Administration and the Muslim Filipinos, *Mindanao Journal* 1 (4).

Cayongat, Al-Rashid I. 1986. *Bangsa Moro in search of peace.* Manila: The Foundation for the Advancement of Islam in the Philippines.

*Census of the Philippine Islands.* 1903. Vol. 2. Washington: U.S. Bureau of Census.

*Census of the Philippines: Population and housing.* 1954. Manila: Bureau of Printing.

*Census of the Philippines: Population and housing.* 1960. Manila: Bureau of Printing.

*Census of the Republic of Philippines.* 1959. Manila: Government Printing Office.

*Census of the Republic of Philippines.* 1961. Manila: Government Printing Office.

Che Man, W.K. 1990. *Muslim separatism: The Moros of southern Philippines and the Malays of southern Thailand.* Quezon City: Ateneo de Manila University Press and Singapore: Oxford University Press.

Coats, George Yarrington. 1968. The Philippine Constabulary, 1901–1927. Ph.D. diss., Ohio State University.

Cody, Cecil E. 1959. The Japanese way of life in prewar Davao. *Philippine Studies* 7, 2 (April).

Cole, Fay-Cooper. 1913. *The wild tribes of Davao district, Mindanao.* Field Museum of Natural History Publication: Anthropology Series 12, 2 (September).

Collier, Kit. 1992. The theoretical problems of insurgency in Mindanao: Why theory? Why Mindanao? In *Mindanao: Land of unfulfilled promise*, edited by Mark Turner, R. J. May and Lulu Respall Turner. Quezon City: New Day Publishers.

Commission on Elections 1962. *Report to the President of the Philippines and the Congress on the manner the elections were held on 14 November 1961.* Manila: Bureau of Printing.

*The Commonwealth Advocate.* Various issues, 1930–1935.

Committee on National Minorities. 1971. Report on the deteriorating peace and order conditions in Cotabato. April.

Conditions in the Philippine Islands: Report of the special mission to the Philippine Islands to the secretary of war, U.S. Congress, House document no. 325, 67th Cong., 2nd sess., 1922.

Conference held by His Excellency, President Manuel L. Quezon, with the municipal presidents of the Mindanao special provinces. 1938. In *Speeches, interviews, statements, reports and proceedings,* series VII. Manuel L. Quezon Papers, Box No. 83. 24 February.

*Congressional records.* 1969. House of Representatives. Republic of the Philippines. Manila: General Printing Office.

Connolly, Michael J. 1992. *Church lands and peasant unrest in the Philippines: Agrarian conflict in 20$^{th}$-century Luzon.* Quezon City: Ateneo de Manila University Press.

Constantino, Renato and Leticia Constantino. 1992. *The Philippines: A continuing past.* Quezon City, Tala Publishing.

Corcino, Ernesto. 1968. *Davao: An introduction to its history and people.* n.p.

———. 1969. Davao: Its history and growth. *Araw ng Dabaw*, 32nd Anniversary souvenir program. 16 March.

———. 1981–82. Pioneer entrepreneurs in Mindanao. *Mindanao Journal* 8.

———. 1992. Japan in Davao: Ventures in partnership. *Araw ng Dabaw 55th Anniversary.* Davao: n.p.

Corpuz, Onofre D. 1957. *The bureaucracy in the Philippines.* Manila: University of the Philippines Institute of Public Administration.

———. 1997. *An economic history of the Philippines.* Quezon City: University of the Philippines Press.

Correspondence relating to the war with Spain, including the insurrection in the Philippine Islands and the China relief expedition, 15 April 1898 to 30 July 1902, Vol. 2. 1993. Washington, D.C.: Center of Military History.

Costello, Michael. 1984. Social change in Mindanao: A review of the research of the decade. *Kinaadman: A Journal of the Southern Philippines* 6.

Cowen, Myron. 1945–1949. American embassy, Manila, to the secretary of state, subject: the November 1949 elections—their results and implications for the future. Dispatches No. 614, 6 July 1949. United States State Department central files.

———. 1950a. U.S. Embassy, Manila, to the Department of State, 20 January. U.S. State Department central files: The Philippine Republic.

———. 1950b. American Embassy, Manila, to secretary of state. 7 February. U.S. State Department central files. The Philippine Republic.

———. 1950–54a. Letter to the secretary of state. 4 April 1950. U.S. Department central files: The Philippine Republic, internal and foreign affairs.

———. 1950–54b. To the secretary of state, U.S. Department of State, No. 3522, 9 and 18 April 1952. United States, Department of State central files: The Philippine Republic, internal and foreign affairs.

Cullinane, Michael. 1971. Implementing the "new order": The structure and supervision of local government during the Taft era. In *Compadre colonialism: Studies on the Philippines under American rule,* edited by Norman G. Owen. Ann Arbor: Michigan Papers on South and Southeast Asia.

———. 1981. Manuel L. Quezon and Harry Bandholtz: The origins of the "special relationship." *Bulletin of the American Historical Collection* 9 (January-March).

———. 1989. *Ilustrado* politics: The response of the Filipino educated elite to American colonial rule, 1898–1907. Ph.D. diss., University of Michigan.

———. 1992. Patron as client: Warlord politics and the Duranos of Danao. In *An anarchy of families: State and family in the Philippines,* edited by Alfred W. McCoy. Quezon City: Ateneo de Manila University Press and Madison, Wisconsin: University of Wisconsin Center for Southeast Asian Studies.

Cushner, Nicholas P. 1976. *Landed estates in the colonial Philippines.* New Haven: Yale University Southeast Asia Studies.

Cuthell, David C. (American consul, Cebu). 1952. Philippine economic review for the year 1951. 11 March. United States, Department of State central files: The Philippine Republic, internal and foreign affairs.

Dabbay, Gloria P. 1987. *Davao City: Its history and progress.* Davao City: Regency.

*The Daily Mirror.* Various issues, 1950–1972.

Dans, Jose P. 1937. *Annual report of the director of lands, for the period 1 January to 31 December 1936*. Manila: Bureau of Printing.

———. 1939. *Annual report of the director of lands, for the period 1 January to 31 December 1938*. Manila: Bureau of Printing.

Davis, Geo. 1902. Letter to adjutant-general, 24 October 1901. In *Annual report of the war department.* Washington: General Printing Office.

Davis, Leonard. 1987. *The Philippines: People, poverty and politics*. New York: St. Martins.

Davis, Ray E. 1952–57. *Land settlement and title clearance: Final report.* November 1952-February 1957. United States of America Operations Mission to the Philippines.

Davis, W. 1900–1902. Letter of the commanding general, Department of Mindanao and Sulu, to the adjutant general, Division of the Philippines. In *Affairs of the Philippine Islands: Hearings of the senate committee on the Philippines*, Washington: General Printing Office. 10, 24 October 1901.

De Dios, Aurora, et al., eds. 1988. *Dictatorship and revolution: Roots of people's power.* Manila: Conspectus.

De Guzman, Nicolas (chief inspector). 1930. Report to Serafin Hilado, director of lands, 8 December. In Joseph Ralston Hayden Collection. Box 12–17.

De Guzman, Raul. 1969. Reorganizing local government. In *Perspectives in government reorganization*, edited by Jose Veloso Abueva. Manila: University of the Philippines College of Public Administration.

De Jesus, Alejandro Y. 1951. Memorandum to Pres. Elpidio Quirino. In Elpidio Quirino Papers.

———. 1952. Memorandum to Pres. Elpidio Quirino. In Elpidio Quirino Papers.

De los Santos, F. 1961–1962. Progress report, series II, to Mr. Gabriel Kaplan, CDCS. Subject: The Philippine community development program, period covered 4 December 1961–4 January 1962. In Milton Barnett Papers. Kroch Library, Cornell University.

Demegillo, Eugenio. 1979. Mindanao: Development and marginalization. *The Philippines in the Third World Papers,* 20.

Department of Mindanao and Sulu. 1915–1920. Various reports.

Detalles sobre lo del hari-hari de Malita. n.d. Letter of Tirso Coronado, superintendent-at-large, Bureau of Non-Christian Tribes, to the director, Bureau of Non-Christian Tribes, n.d. In Joseph Ralston Hayden Collection. Box 30–17.

*Development potentials of northern and eastern Mindanao: A report for the Maryknoll missionaries.* 1969. Manila: Asian Social Research Institute.

Dimaporo, Ali. 1950. Speech and interpellation. *Congressional Records*, 2nd Cong., 1st regular sess. 1, 34. House of Representatives. Republic of the Philippines, 9 March.

———. (Lanao del Sur). 1970a. Speech. In Proceedings and debates of the seventh session. In *Philippine Congressional Record* 1, 35. House of Representatives. 1 April.

———. 1970b. Islam and socioeconomic development. Speech delivered at the inauguration of the Supreme Council for Islamic Affairs of the Philippines, Inc. (SCIAP), Mindanao State University 24–27 December.

Division of Philippine Affairs, Department of State. 1945–49. Summary of developments in connection with Philippine affairs, 1–31 July 1944. In U.S. State Department central files: The Philippine Republic, internal and foreign affairs.

Dogan, Mattei and Ali Kazancigil, eds. 1994. *Comparing nations: Concepts, strategies and substance*. Oxford and Cambridge: Blackwell.

Doronila, Amando. 1992. *The state, economic transformation and political change in the Philippines*. Singapore: Oxford University Press.

Dougherty, Joseph L. 1953. Dispatch No. 997, to the Department of State. Subject: Damage for 1953–54 crops by rats in Cotabato, Mindanao. 9 November. United States, Department of State central files: The Philippine Republic, internal and foreign affairs.

Early, John Chrysostomom. 1930. Memorandum to the governor-general on Japanese and Filipino pioneers in Davao, 28 August. In Joseph Ralston Hayden Collection. Box 28–1.

———. n.d. Profile of Sebastian Generoso, provincial governor. In Joseph Ralston Hayden Collection. Box 30–17.

———. Collection. Bentley Historical Collection, University of Michigan.

Economic Development Foundation, National Power Corporation. 1970. *The Mindanao economy: The growth and need for power.* 1 January.

Elarth, Harold Hanne. 1949. *The story of the Philippine Constabulary*. Los Angeles: Globe.

Elayda, Jose. 1939. Letter to S. Artiaga, Davao city mayor. 30 October. In J. C. Early Collection.

Elequin, Eleanor. 1981–82. The impact of American education in Mindanao and Sulu. *Mindanao Journal* 8, 1–4.

Elliot, Charles Burke. 1917. *The Philippines to the end of the commission period: A study in tropical democracy*. Indianapolis: Boobs-Merrill.

Elpidio Quirino Papers. Ayala Museum, Makati City.

*Employment problems and policies in the Philippines*. 1969. Geneva: International Labour Office.

Evans, Peter, Dietrich Reuschmeyer and Theda Skocpol. 1985. *Bringing the state back in*. Cambridge: Cambridge University Press.

Farolan, M. 1935. *The Davao problem*. Manila: M. Farolan.

*Fifth annual report of the executive secretary of the governor-general, covering the period from 1 July 1905 to 30 June 1906*. 1906. Manila: Bureau of Printing.

*The Filipino People*. Various issues, 1907–1912.

Finin, Gerard Anthony. 1991. Regional consciousness and administrative grids: Understanding the role of planning in the Philippine Gran Cordillera. Ph.D. diss., Cornell University.

Forbes, Cameron. 1928. *The Philippine Islands*. Vol. 2. Boston and New York: Houghton Mifflin.

Ford, Henry Jones. 1913. Report to the President. MSS. Division of Territories and Island Possessions, Department of Interior.

*Forging unity towards development: Caucus of Development NGO Network*. 1991. University of the Philippines. 4 December.

Foster, Clinton B. 1950. Confidential report on the unrest in Mindanao and comments thereon by Mr. Edward Kuder. U.S. Embassy (Manila), to the Department of State Department central files: 17 November 1950. The Philippine Republic, internal and foreign affairs.

Francisco, G.G. 1950. Memorandum to Pres. Elpidio Quirino, 24 November. In Elpidio Quirino Papers.

Friend, Theodore. 1965. *Between two empires: The ordeal of the Philippines, 1929–1946*. New Haven and London: Yale University Press.

Fry, Howard T. 1978. The Bacon Bill of 1926: New light on an exercise in divide-and-rule. *Philippine Studies* (Third Quarter).

Funtecha, Henry Florida. 1979. *American military occupation of the Lake Lanao region, 1901–1903: An historical study*. Marawi: University Research Center, Mindanao State University.

Furiya, Reiko. 1993. The Japanese community abroad: The case of prewar Davao in the Philippines. In *The Japanese in colonial Southeast Asia*, edited by Saya Shiraishi and Takashi Shiraishi. Ithaca, New York: Cornell University Southeast Asia Program.

Furnivall, John S. 1939. The fashioning of leviathan: The beginning of British rule in Burma. *Journal of the Burma Research Society* 29, 1 (April).

Garchitorena, Mariano. 1938. *The Philippine abaca industry*. Manila: Bureau of Printing.

Garcia, Leon. Annual report of the mayor, Davao City, to the Department of Interior 1946–47. 1 July 1946–30 June 1947.

Garcia, Mauro, comp. 1944. More documents on the Japanese occupation of the Philippines: Mindanao. As reprinted by *Historical Bulletin* 10, 4, (December 1966).

Garfield, Jones O. 1920. Our mandate over Moroland. *Asia* 20 (July).

Gellner, Ernest. 1983. *Nations and nationalism*. Ithaca, NY: Cornell University Press.

George, T.J.S. 1980. *Revolt in Mindanao: The rise of Islam in Philippine politics*. Kuala Lumpur: Oxford University Press.

Glang, Alunan. 1969a. Modernizing the Muslims. *Solidarity* 4, 3.

———. 1969b. *Muslim secession or integration?* Quezon City: R.P. Garcia.

———. 1972. Why the shooting won't stop. *Solidarity* 2, 4.

Gleeck, Lewis E. 1974. *Americans on the Philippine frontier*. Manila: Carmelo and Bauerman.

———. 1984. *The American half-century (1898–1946)*. Manila: Historical Conservation Society.

———. 1986. *The American governors-general and high commissioners in the Philippines: Proconsuls, nation-builders and politicians*. Quezon City: New Day Publishers.

———. 1989. American planters and the tribes in Mindanao. *Bulletin of the American Historical Collection* 12, 2 (April-June).

———. 1991. Achievement and tragedy: The life of Frank W. Carpenter. *Bulletin of the American Historical Collection* 14, 1 (January-March).

Golay, Frank H. 1961. *The Philippines: Public policy and national economic development.* Ithaca, NY: Cornell University Press.

———. 1998. *Face of empire: United States-Philippine relations, 1900–1946.* Quezon City: Ateneo de Manila University Press and Madison: University of Wisconsin Center for Southeast Asian Studies.

Goodman, Grant K. 1967a. *Davao: A case study in Japanese-Philippine relations.* Kansas: The University of Kansas Center for East Asian Studies.

———. 1967b. *Imperial Japan and Asia: A reassessment.* New York: East Asian Institute, Columbia University.

Gopinath, Aruna. 1987. *Manuel L. Quezon: The tutelary democrat.* Quezon City: New Day Publishers.

———. 1989. Muslim Filipinos under the Commonwealth government, 1935–1941. *Pilipinas: A Journal of Philippine Studies* 12 (Spring).

Government of the Philippine Islands. 1904. *Official register of officers and employees in the civil service of the Philippine Islands.* Manila: Bureau of Printing.

Gowing, Peter. 1979. *Muslim Filipinos: Heritage and horizon.* Quezon City: New Day Publishers.

———. 1980. Moros and Indians: Commonalities of purpose, policy and practice in American government of two hostile subject peoples. *Philippine Quarterly of Culture and Society* 8.

———. 1983. *Mandate in Moroland: The American government of Muslim Filipinos, 1899–1920.* Quezon City: New Day Publishers.

———. 1988. *Understanding Islam and the Muslims in the Philippines.* Quezon City: New Day Publishers.

——— and Robert D. McAmis, eds. 1974. *The Muslim Filipinos.* Manila: Solidaridad Publishing House.

Grindle, Merilee. 1977. *Bureaucrats, politicians and peasants in Mexico: A case study in public policy.* Berkeley: University of California Press.

———. 1996. *Challenging the state: Crisis and innovation in Latin America and Africa.* New York: Cambridge University Press.

Grunder, Garel A., and William E. Livezy. 1951. *The Philippines and the United States.* Norman, Oklahoma: University of Oklahoma Press.

Guerrero, Amado. 1971. *Philippine society and revolution.* Hong Kong: Ta Kung Pao Publications.

Guingona, Teofisto. 1919. Report of acting governor, Department of Mindanao and Sulu, 1919. In *Report of the governor-general of the Philippine Islands to the secretary of war.* Vol. 3. Washington: General Printing Office.

———. 1935. Annual report of director, Bureau of Non-Christian Tribes, to the secretary of interior, 11 March. In Joseph Ralston Hayden Collection. Box 28–22.

Guinto, Leon. 1934. Memorandum of acting director, Bureau of Non-Christian Tribes, to the secretary of interior, 23 June. In Joseph Ralston Hayden Collection. Box 30–5.

Gullick, J.M. 1958. *Indigenous political systems of Western Malaya*. New York, Humanities Press.

Gutierrez, Dionisio. 1934. Report of the provincial governor to the director of Bureau of Non-Christian Tribes, 10 August 1934. In Joseph Ralston Hayden Collection. Box 27–31.

Hackenberg, Robert A. n.d. The poverty explosion: Population growth and income decline in Davao City, 1972. Boulder Institute of Behavioral Science, University of Colorado.

Hagedorn, Hermann. 1969. *Leonard Wood: A biography*. Vol. 2. [1931] Reprint, New York: Kraus Reprint Co.

Haggerty, Edward S.J. 1964. *Guerrilla padre in Mindanao*. New York: Longmans.

Hancock, H. Irving. 1912. *Uncle Sam's boys in the Philippines, or following the flag against the Moros*. Philadelphia: Henry Altmus.

Hardie, Robert S. 1951. Philippine land tenure reform: Analysis and recommendation. United States of America Special Technical and Economic Mission to the Philippines. 23 October.

Harrington, Julian F. 1951. Chargé d'affaires, to Department of State, 5 June 1951. Department central files: The Philippine Republic, internal and foreign affairs.

Harrison, Francis Burton. 1922. *The cornerstone of Philippine independence: A narrative of seven years*. New York: The Century Co.

Hartendorp, A.V.H. 1961. *History of industry and trade of the Philippines: The Magsaysay administration*. Vol. 1. Manila: Philippine Education Company.

———. 1967. *The Japanese occupation of the Philippines*. Vols. 1 and 2. Manila: Bookmark.

Hartley, Douglas Thompson Kellie. 1983. American participation in the economic development of Mindanao and Sulu, 1899–1930. Ph.D. diss., James Cook University of North Queensland.

Hashiya, Hiroshi. 1993. The pattern of Japanese economic penetration of the prewar Philippines. In *The Japanese in colonial Southeast Asia*, edited by Saya Shiraishi and Takashi Shiraishi. Ithaca, New York: Cornell University Southeast Asia Program.

Hayase, Shinzo. 1984. Tribes, settlers, and administrators on a frontier: Economic development and social change in Davao, southeastern Mindanao, the Philippines, 1899–1941. Ph.D. diss., Murdoch University.

Hayden, J. R. 1935. Confidential radio message to secretary of war, Washington, no. 85, regarding the Rodriguez investigation of Davao Japanese landholdings, 23 February. In Joseph Ralston Hayden Collection. Box 28–4.

———. 1942. *The Philippines: A study in national development*. New York: Macmillan.

Heffington, J.J. 1934. Letter of the provincial governor, Lanao province, to the governor-general, Philippine Islands, 6 March. In Joseph Ralston Hayden Collection. Box Box 27–31.

Henderson, James. 1949. Memorandum of conversation with Mr. Bernardo Teves, mayor, City of Davao. 18 May. American consulate, Cebu-Philippines.

Hernandez, Carolina Galicia. 1979. The extent of civilian control of the military in the Philippines, 1946–1976. Ph.D. diss., State University of New York at Buffalo.

Hester, E.D. 1950. Report of counselor of Embassy for Economic Affairs, to Department of State on Abaca Development: NAFCO-Marsman Agreement. 17 January. Department central files: The Philippine Republic, internal and foreign affairs.

Hobbs, Colonel Horace P. 1962. *Kris and krag: Adventures among the Moros of the southern Philippine Islands.* Privately printed.

Hobsbawm, Eric J. 1990. *Nations and nationalism since 1780.* Cambridge: Cambridge University Press.

Hobsbawm, Eric J. and Terence Ranger, eds. 1983. *The invention of tradition.* Cambridge: Cambridge University Press.

Horn, Florence. 1941. *Orphans of the Pacific: The Philippines.* New York: Reynal and Hitchcock.

Hunt, Chester L. 1957. Ethnic stratification and integration in Cotabato. *Philippine Sociological Review* 5, 1.

Huntington, Samuel. 1968. *Political order in changing societies.* New Haven: Yale University Press.

Hurley, Vic. 1936a. *Men in sun helmets.* New York: Dutton.

———. 1936b. *Swish of the kris: The story of the Moros.* New York: Dutton.

Hutchcroft, Paul. 1991. Oligarchs and cronies in the Philippine state: The politics of patrimonial plunder. *World Politics* 43, 3.

———. 1992. The political foundations of booty capitalism. Paper presented at the 1992 Annual Meeting of the American Political Science Association, 3–6 September.

———. 1993. Predatory oligarchy, patrimonial state: The politics of private domestic banking in the Philippines. Ph.D. diss., Yale University.

Ileto, Reynaldo Clemeña. 1971. *Magindanao 1860–1888: The career of Datu Uto of Buayan.* Southeast Asia Program data paper no. 82. Ithaca, NY: Department of Asian Studies, Cornell University.

Jayme, Vicente R. 1961. The Mindanao Development Authority: A new concept in Philippine economic development. *Philippine Journal of Public Administration* (October).

Jenista, Frank Lawrence. 1987. *The white apos: American governors on the Cordillera central.* Quezon City: New Day Publishers.

Joint United States Military Advisory Group to the Republic of the Philippines, (JUSMAG). 1958. Subject: Narrative statement of MAP guidance for the Republic of the Philippines, Section V. Philippine Constabulary Forces. 24 November.

Jones, Gregg R. 1989. *Red revolution: Inside the Philippine guerrilla movement.* Boulder: Westview Press.

Joseph Ralston Hayden (JRH) Collection. Box 29–5. Bentley Historical Collection, University of Michigan.

*Journal of the constitutional convention of the Philippines* 3, 4. 1934. (Reprinted in Manila: East Publishing Co., 15 January 1962). 18 September.

*Journal of the Philippine commission*, being a special session and the first session, 1911. 28 March 1910 to 19 April 1910 and 17 October 1910 to 3 February 1911, respectively, of the Philippine Legislature. 1911. Manila: Bureau of Printing.

———. Second session. 1912. 16 October 1911 to 1 February 1912, and a special session, 2 February 1912 to 16 February 1912. 1912. Manila: Bureau of Printing.

Jubaira, Ibrahim. 1960. No peace, no progress in the land of the Muslims. *Progress.*

Kalaw, Maximo M. 1919. *Self-government in the Philippines.* New York: The Century Co.

———. 1931. The Moro bugaboo. *Philippine Social Science Review* 3, 4 (September).

Kasilag, Maricar. 1938. Policy of the commonwealth government towards the non-Christians in Mindanao and Sulu. In *The development of Mindanao and the future of the non-Christians,* edited by Maricar Kasilag. Manila: Philippine Council, Insitute of Pacific Relations.

Kathirithamby-Wells, J. 1993. Restraints on the development of merchant capitalism in Southeast Asia before c. 1800. *In Southeast Asia in the early modern era: Trade, power and belief,* edited by Anthony Reid. Ithaca and London: Cornell University Press.

Kathirithamby-Wells, J. and John Villiers, eds. 1990. *The Southeast Asian port and polity: Rise and demise.* Singapore: Singapore University Press.

Kaviraj, Sudipta. 1995. Crisis of the nation-state in India. In *Contemporary crisis of the nation state?* edited by John Dunn. Oxford, UK and Cambridge, U.S.A.: Blackwell.

Kazancigil, Ali and Mattei Dogan, eds. 1994. *Comparing nations: Concepts, strategies and substance.* Oxford and Cambridge: Blackwell.

Keats, John. 1963. *They fought alone.* Philadelphia and New York: Lippincott.

Kerkvliet, Benedict J., ed. 1974. *Political change in the Philippines: Studies of local politics preceding martial law.* Honolulu: Asian Studies Program, University of Hawaii.

Kerkvliet, Benedict J. Tria and Resil B. Mojares, eds. 1991. *From Marcos to Aquino: Local perspectives on political transition in the Philippines.* Quezon City: Ateneo de Manila University Press.

*Kislap Graphic Magazine.* Various issues, 1946–1972.

Kohli, Atul. 1990. *Democracy and discontent: India's growing crisis of governability.* Cambridge: Cambridge University Press.

Koo, Hagen, ed. 1993. *State and society in contemporary Korea.* Ithaca and London: Cornell University Press.

Krinks, Peter. 1970a. Peasant colonisation in Mindanao. Ph.D. diss., Australian National University.

———. 1974b. Old wine in a new bottle: Land settlement and agrarian problems in Southeast Asia. *Journal of Southeast Asian Studies* 5.

Laarhoven, Ruurdje 1990. Lords of the great river: The Magindanao port and polity during the seventeenth century. *In The Southeast Asian port and polity: Rise and demise*, edited by J. Kathirithamby-Wells and John Villiers. Singapore: Singapore University Press.

Laitin, David. 1985. Hegemony and religious conflict: British imperial control and political cleavage in Yorubaland. In *Bringing the state back in*, edited by Peter Evans, Dietrich Reuschmeyer, and Theda Skocpol. Cambridge: Cambridge University Press.

Lande, Carl H. 1964. *Leaders, factions and parties: The structure of Philippine politics*. New Haven: Yale University Southeast Asia Studies Monograph no. 6.

Lane, Lyle F. 1965. American consul, Cebu, to the Department of State. Pre-election survey of Mindanao, 19 October 1965. United States, Department of State central files: The Philippine Republic, internal and foreign affairs.

———. 1965. American consul, Cebu, to the Department of State. Assessment of election results in southern Philippines, 19 November 1965. United States, Department of State central files: The Philippine Republic, internal and foreign affairs.

Lao, Mardonio M. 1985. *Bukidnon in historical perspective*. Musuan, Bukidnon: Central Mindanao University.

———. 1987. The economy of the Bukidnon plateau during the American period. *Philippine Studies* 35.

Laurel, Jose P. 1933. Letter to Bureau of Lands. 25 October. In Jose P. Laurel Papers Collection (microfilm). Kroch Library, Cornell University.

Legislative Council of the Moro Province. 1904. Act No. 35, an act to amend act no. 82 of the Philippine Commission, entitled, the municipal code, as amended, in its application to the Moro Province, enacted 27 January 1904, and approved, 27 April 1904.

Leuchtenburg, William E. 1952. Progressivism and imperialism: The progressive movement and American foreign policy, 1898–1916. *The Mississippi Valley Historical Review* 24 (December).

Lewin, Moshe. 1985. *The making of a Soviet social system: Essays in the social history of interwar Russia*. New York: Pantheon.

Liang, Dapen. 1970. *Philippine parties and politics: A historical study of national experience in democracy*. San Francisco: The Gladstone Company.

Licaros, Gregorio S. 1959. Economic development of Mindanao. *Crescent Review* 3, 3 (March).

Limerick, Patricia Nelson. 1987. *The legacy of conquest: The unbroken past of the American West*. New York and London: Norton.

Local Government Research Team. October 1970. *Report on the Davao City government*. Local Government Center, University of the Philippines College of Public Administration. October.

Lockett, Thomas A. 1948. Letter of American Embassy, Manila, to secretary of state. Subject: Views of Senator Pendatun with regard to possible final Quirino-Avelino split. 15 December.

Lunaria, D.O. 1975. The Americans: Their role in the development of Mindanao, 1899–1913. Master's thesis, University of Santo Tomas.

Madale, Nagasura. 1984. The future of the Moro National Liberation Front (MNLF) as a separatist movement in Southern Philippines. In *Armed separatism in Southeast Asia,* edited by Joo-Jock Lim and S. Vani. Singapore: Institute for Southeast Asian Studies.

Magsalin, Pedro. 1948a. Report of technical adviser to Elpidio Quirino, President of the Philippines. 5 October. In Elpidio Quirino Papers.

———. 1948b. Report of technical adviser to Pres. Elpidio Quirino. 29 October. In Elpidio Quirino Papers.

Majul, Cesar Abib. 1973. *Muslims in the Philippines.* Quezon City: University of the Philippines.

———. 1976. Some social and cultural problems of the Muslims in the Philippines. *Asian Studies* 14, 1 (April).

———. 1985. *The contemporary Muslim movement in the Philippines.* Berkeley: Mizan Press.

Malcolm, George A. 1936. *The commonwealth of the Philippines.* New York and London: D. Appleton-Century.

Mamdani, Mahmood. 1996. *Citizen and subject: Contemporary Africa and the legacy of late colonialism.* New Jersey: Princeton University Press.

*The Manila Bulletin.* Various issues, 1946–1972.

*The Manila Chronicle.* Various issues, 1946–1972.

*The Manila Times.* Various issues, 1946–1972.

*The Manila Tribune.* Various issues, 1946–1950.

Manalaysay, M.O. 1966. Quantifying the growth potentials and economy of the Mindanao region. *The Philippine Statistician* 15, 3–4 (September-December).

Manrique, P. 1938. Confidential efficiency report of Davao acting chief of police, Davao City. 18 June to 31 December. J.C. Early Collection.

Maramba, Felix D. 1952. Mindanao development. *Philippine Agricultural Engineering Journal* (First Quarter).

Mariano, Juan, et al. 1953. *Soil survey of Davao province, Philippines.* Manila: Bureau of Printing.

Marking, Agustin. 1950. Confidential report of special technical adviser to Pres. Elpidio Quirino, 30 November. In Elpidio Quirino Papers.

Martin, Salamen. 1964. Annual report of the agricultural and rural development division. Proposed committee on land policy, rural development. Republic of the Philippines, Commission on National Integration. In Milton Barnett Papers. Box 2, Kroch Library, Cornell University.

Mastura, Michael. 1984. *Muslim-Filipino experience: A collection of essays.* Manila: OCIA Publications.

May, Glenn. 1989. Civic ritual and political reality: Municipal elections in the late nineteenth century. In *Philippine colonial democracy*, edited by Ruby R. Paredes. Quezon City: Ateneo de Manila University Press.

Mayall, James and Mark Simpson. 1992. Ethnicity is not enough: Reflections on protracted secessionism in the Third World. In *Ethnicity and nationalism*, edited by Anthony D. Smith. Leiden and New York: E.J. Brill.

Mayo, Katherine. 1925. *The isles of fear: The truth about the Philippines*. New York: Harcourt, Brace.

McCoy, Alfred W. 1985. *Southeast Asia under Japanese occupation*. New Haven: Yale University Southeast Asia Studies Monograph No. 22.

———. 1989. Quezon's commonwealth: The emergence of Philippine authoritarianism. In *Philippine colonial democracy*, edited by Ruby R. Paredes. Quezon City: Ateneo de Manila University Press.

———. 1993. *An anarchy of families: State and family in the Philippines*. Quezon City: Ateneo de Manila University Press and Madison, Wisconsin: University of Wisconsin Center for Southeast Asian Studies.

———. Forthcoming. *Lives at the margins: Biographies of obscured Filipinos*. Quezon City: Ateneo de Manila University Press.

McCoy, Alfred W. and Ed. de Jesus, eds. 1982. *Philippine social history: Global trade and local transformation*. Quezon City, Ateneo de Manila University Press.

McDougald, Charles C. 1987. *The Marcos file: Was he a Philippine hero or corrupt tyrant?* San Francisco: San Francisco Publishers.

McKenna, Thomas. 1992. Martial law, Moro nationalism and traditional leadership in Cotabato. *Pilipinas* 18 (Spring).

Mednick, Melvin. 1965. *Encampment of the lake: The social organization of a Moslem-Philippine (Moro) people*. Chicago: Philippine Studies Program Research Series No. 5, Department of Anthropology, University of Chicago.

*The memoirs of Elpidio Quirino*. 1990. Manila: National Historical Institute.

Mercado, Eliseo. 1984. Culture, economics and revolt in Mindanao: The origins of the MNLF and the politics of Moro separatism. In *Armed separatism in southeast Asia*, edited by Joo-Jock Lim and S. Vani. Singapore: Institute of Southeast Asian Studies.

Merrill, Thomas. 1951. Report of agricultural attaché, U.S. Embassy (Manila) to the Department of State, 19 September 1951. Central files: The Philippine Republic, internal and foreign affairs.

Meskill, Johanna Menzel. 1979. *A Chinese pioneer family: The Lins of Wu-feng, Taiwan, 1729–1895*. Princeton: Princeton University Press.

Migdal, Joel. 1987. Strong states, weak states: Power and accommodation. In *Understanding political development,* edited by Myron Weiner and Samuel P. Huntington. Boston: Little, Brown.

———. 1988. *Strong societies and weak states*. Princeton: Princeton University Press.

Migdal, Joel, Atul Kohli and Vivienne Shue, eds. 1994. *State power and social forces: Domination and transformation in the Third World.* New York: Cambridge University Press.

*Military notes on the Philippines.* 1898. Washington: General Printing Office.

*The Mindanao Cross.* Various issues, 1949–1972.

Mindanao Development Authority. 1965a. Summary of five-year plan, 1965–1970, Davao City.

———. 1965b. A survey of resources and potentialities, social conditions, values, institutions are regional problems of Mindanao, Sulu and Palawan. July. Part 1. Davao City July.

———. 1970a. Brief on Mindanao, Sulu and Palawan and the Mindanao Development Authority, parts I–III. Davao City.

———. 1970b. A draft of a five-year program for the social and economic development of Mindanao, Sulu and Palawan, FY 1965–1966 to FY 1969–1970. Davao City. July.

———. 1968. Progress attained by the Mindanao economy, parts 1 and 2. Davao City.

*The Mindanao Herald.* Various issues, 1906–1910.

*The Mindanao Times.* Various issues, 1946–1972.

Misuari, Nur. 1980. The Bangsamoro right to self-determination. Address at the International Islamic Conference on Prophet Muhammad and His Message, Tripoli, Libya.

Mojares, Resil, ed. 1985. *Dispute processing in the Philippines.* Quezon City: Bureau of Local Governments Supervision, Ministry of Local Government.

Molloy, Ivan. n.d. *The conflict in Mindanao: Whilst the revolution rolls on, the Jihad falters.* Monash: University Centre for Southeast Asian Studies.

Monk, Paul M. 1990. *Truth and power: Robert S. Hardie and land reform debates in the Philippines, 1950–1987.* Australia: Centre for Southeast Asian Studies, Monash University.

Mora, Anacleto. 1963. 104th PC Company, Task Force Braco, to the chief of staff, Armed Forces of the Philippines, Camp Murphy, Quezon City. Subject: The Bilaan tribe, its problems and its conversion to Christianity. 12 March.

Morison, Samuel Eliot. 1963. *The liberation of the Philippines, Luzon, Mindanao, the Visayas, 1944–45.* Boston: Little, Brown.

Murphy, Frank. 1937. Message of his excellency, the governor-general to the Philippine legislature in its final session, 14 November 1935. In *The first annual report of the United States high commissioner to the Philippine Islands covering the period from 15 November 1935 to 31 December 1936.* Washington: General Printing Office.

National Abaca and Other Fibers Corporation and J.H. Marsman. 1950. Operating and development agreement. 6 January.

National Economic Council. 1960. Industrial survey report of the province of Davao. November. Manila.

Nowak, Thomas Claus. 1974. Class and clientelist systems in the Philippines: The basis for instability. Ph.D. diss., Cornell University.

Nowak, Thomas Claus and Kay A. Snyder. 1974. Economic concentration and political change in the Philippines. In *Political change in the Philippines: Studies of local politics preceding martial law*, edited by Benedict J. Kerkvliet Honolulu: Asian Studies Program, University of Hawaii.

Ocampo, Romeo B. 1971. Technocrats and planning: Sketch and exploration. *Philippine Journal of Public Administration* 15, 1 (January).

Ockey, James Soren. 1992. Business leaders, gangsters and the middle class: Societal groups and civilian rule in Thailand. Ph.D. diss., Cornell University.

Office of Strategic Services (OSS), Research and Analysis Branch. 1945. Prominent Moros of Mindanao and Sulu, R and A No. 2825. 15 February. Washington, D.C.

Office of Strategic Services. 1944a. The government of the new Philippines: A study of the present puppet government of the Philippines. Report no. 1752. 15 May.

———. 1944b. The programs of Japan in the Philippines. Assemblage No. 33, Supplement No. 1, Research and Analysis Branch. 29 July.

Official roster of officers and employees in the civil service of the Philippine Islands. 1929. Manila: General Printing Office.

Ombra, Amilbangsa. 1936. Memorandum to Manuel L. Quezon, 26 October. In Joseph Ralston Hayden Collection. Box 27–2.

Onorato, Michael Paul. 1975. Governor-General Francis Burton Harrison and Filipinization. *Bulletin of the American Historical Collection* 3, 3 (July).

Oosterhout, A. Von. 1983. Spatial conflicts in rural Mindanao, the Philippines. *Pacific Viewpoint* (May-June).

O'Shaughnessy, Thomas J. 1975. How many Muslims has the Philippines? *Philippine Studies* 23 (Third Quarter).

Owen, Norman G. 1984. *Prosperity without progress: Manila hemp and material life in the colonial Philippines*. Quezon City: Ateneo de Manila University Press; Berkeley and London: University of California Press.

Pacis, Salvador L. 1930. *Davao: Its progress and future*. Davao: Southern Islands Publishing.

Paderanga, Cayetano Jr. 1987. A review of land settlements in the Philippines, 1900–1975. *Philippine Review of Economics and Business* 24, 1–2.

Paguia, Antonio. 1948. Letter of National Land Settlement Authority general manager, to Pres. Elpidio Quirino. 29 March. In Elpidio Quirino Papers.

Paredes, Ruby R., ed. 1989. *Philippine colonial democracy*. Quezon City: Ateneo de Manila University Press.

Pelzer, Karl J. 1945. *Pioneer settlement in the Asiatic tropics: Studies in land utilization and agricultural colonization in Southeast Asia*. New York: American Geographical Society.

Pendatun, Salipada. 1935a. Memorandum to his excellency, the honorable acting governor-general J.R. Hayden, Malacañang.

———. 1935b. Memorandum for Honorable Teofisto Guingona, director of the Bureau of Non-Christian Tribes.

Pendatun, Salipada K. 1950. Memorandum to his excellency Elpidio Quirino. 17 October. In Elpidio Quirino Papers.

———. 1952. Memorandum to his excellency Elpidio Quirino. 8 May. In Elpidio Quirino Papers.

———. 1961. Biography of Speaker Pro-Tempore Salipada K. Pendatun. Liberal Party Information Office.

Pernia, Ernesto, et al. 1983. *The spatial and urban dimensions of development in the Philippines.* Manila: Philippine Institute for Development Studies.

Pershing, John. 1916. Report of the governor of the Moro Province. In *Annual report of the war department.* Zamboanga: *Mindanao Herald.*

Petition of the Association of Muslims to Manuel Quezon, signed by its president Alawadan Bandon, 1935. 4 August. In Joseph Ralston Hayden Collection. Box 27–32.

Pfanner, Margaret Ruth. 1958. Postwar land colonization in the Philippines. Master's thesis, Cornell University.

Philippine Alien Property Administration. 1949. Vested real property in the city of Davao, 1948. United States State Department central files. The Philippine Republic, internal and foreign affairs.

Philippine Alien Property Agreement pursuant to section 4 of the United States Public Law No. 485, 79th Cong., 2nd sess., 1948.

Philippine Commission Act 2408. 1914. An act providing for a temporary form of government for the territory known as the Department of Mindanao and Sulu, making applicable thereto, with certain exceptions, the provisions of general laws now in force in the Philippine Islands, and for other purposes. 23 July.

Philippine Commission Act No. 787. 1903–1904. An act providing for the organization and government of the Moro Province, 1 June 1903 and 1 September 1904.

*Philippine News Digest,* 5 August 1960.

*The Philippine policy of the United States.* 1939. New York: Institute of Pacific Relations.

Philippine Research and Information Section. 1945. Conditions affecting domestic order in the Moro Provinces of Mindanao and Sulu. 1945. Counter-Intelligence, GHQ, AFPAC, APO 500, 28 August—Confidential. In Joseph Ralston Hayden Collection. Box 42–20.

*Philippine Statistical Review* 2, 3 (1935).

*The Philippines Free Press.* Various issues, 1912–1972.

*The Philippines Herald.* Various issues, 1946–1972.

Phin-keong, Voon. 1977. *American rubber planting enterprise in the Philippines, 1900–1930.* London: Department of Geography Occasional Papers, School of Oriental and African Studies.

Piang, Abdullah. 1926. Interview. In Joseph Ralston Hayden Collection. Box 28–24.

———. 1933. Legislative speech. In the *Philippines Free Press.* 1 October.
Pier, Arthur S. 1971. *American apostles in the Philippines.* Freeport, NY.
Pintoy, Climaco. 1950. Confidential report of provincial commander, Philippine Constabulary, Davao, to the adjutant general, GHQ, PC Camp Crame, Quezon City. Subject: Attempt to squat Bago-Oshiro, Furukawa and Arakaki plantations by veterans. 16 November. In Elpidio Quirino Papers.
Pohl, James William. 1967. The general staff and American military policy: The formative period, 1898–1917. Ph.D. diss., University of Texas.
Pomeroy, Earl S. 1947. *The territories and the United States, 1861–1890: Studies in colonial administration.* Seattle and London: University of Washington Press.
Porter, Gareth. 1989. Strategic debates and dilemmas in the Philippine communist movement. In *The Philippines in a changing Southeast Asia: Conference papers,* edited by Steven R. Dorr and Lt. Deborah J. Mitchell. Washington: U.S. Defense Intelligence College.
*Proceedings of the Philippine Constitutional Convention, 1934–1935.* 1935. Manila: Bureau of Printing.
*Proceedings of the second national Muslim conference,* 11–16 October 1956. n.d. Marawi: Muslim Association of the Philippines.
(A) Proposed five-year integrated program for socio-economic development, 1963–1964. State of the nation message of President Diosdado Macapagal. 22 January 1962.
Putzel, James. 1992. *A captive land: The politics of agrarian reform in the Philippines.* Quezon City: Ateneo de Manila University Press.
Quezon, Manuel L. 1912. The right of the Philippines to independence. *The Filipino People* 1, 2 (October).
———. 1936a. Speech before the Philippine Assembly, 23 June. In *National Archives, Bureau of Insular Affairs.* File no. 17073.
———. 1936b. Telegram to Ombra Amilbangsa, Sulu, 26 October. In Joseph Ralston Hayden Collection. Box 27–2.
———. 1937a. Speech delivered before the Philippine Society of Japan, Tokyo, 22 February.
———. 1937b. Memorandum to the secretary of interior, 30 September. In Joseph Ralston Hayden Collection. Box 27–27.
———. 1940a. *President Quezon: His biographical sketch, messages and speeches.* Manila: Philippine Publishing Inc.
———. 1940b. *Fifth annual report of the President of the Philippines to the President and the Congress of the United States, covering the period 1 July 1939 to 30 June 1940.*
Quirino, Carlos. 1971. *Quezon: Paladin of Philippine freedom.* Manila: Filipiniana Book Guild.
———. 1984. *Chick Parsons: America's master spy in the Philippines.* Quezon City: New Day Publishers.

Ramos, Simeon. *Annual report of the director of lands, from the period 1 January to 14 November 1935.* Manila: Bureau of Printing.

Reid, Anthony. 1988. *Southeast Asia in the age of commerce, 1450–1680.* Vol. 1. *The land below the winds.* New Haven and London: Yale University Press.

———. 1993. *Southeast Asia in the early modern era: Trade, power and belief.* Ithaca and London: Cornell University Press.

Report of Special Committee on Land Settlement and Title Issuances and Clearance. 1951. Ms. In Elpidio Quirino Papers.

Report of the Commission on Elections to the President of the Philippines and Congress on the manner the election was held on 10 November 1959. 1960. Manila: Bureau of Printing.

Report of the governor of the Moro Province, 1901. 1902. In *Report of the Philippine Commission,* 360–61. Washington: General Printing Office.

———. 1904. Zamboanga, Mindanao, P.I.

———, 1905. 1906. In *Annual report of the war department.* Washington: General Printing Office.

———, 1906. 1907. In *Report of the Philippine Commission.* Washington: General Printing Office'.

———, 1906. 1907. In *Report of the Philippine Commission,* 340. Washington: General Printing Office.

———, 1907. 1908. In *Annual report of the war department.* Washington: General Printing Office.

———, 1909. 1910. In *Annual report of the war department.* Washington: General Printing Office.

———, 1909. 1910. In *Report of the Philippine Commission,* 3–4. Washington: General Printing Office.

———, 1910. 1911. In *Report of the Philippine Commission,* 21. Washington: General Printing Office.

———, 1911. 1911. In *Annual report of the governor-general, Philippine Islands.* Washington: General Printing Office.

———, 1912. 1912. In *Annual report of the War Department,* 14–15. Washington: General Printing Office.

———, 1912. 1912. In *Annual report of the governor-general, Philippine Islands.* Washington: General Printing Office.

———, 1913. 1913. In *Annual report of the governor-general, Philippine Islands.* Washington: General Printing Office.

———, 1914. 1915. In *Report of the governor of the Philippine Islands,* 124. Manila: General Printing Office.

*Report of the governor-general of the Philippine Islands to the secretary of war.* 1917. Washington: General Printing Office.

Report of the governor-general, Philippines, 30 October 1909. 1909. In *Report of the Philippine Commission*, 67. Washington: General Printing Office.

Report of the Mindanao Exploration Commission, organized under the auspices of the President's Advisory Committee on Political Refugees, Refugee Economic Corporation. 1939. 2 October.

Report of the officer commanding 5th District, Philippine Constabulary, 5 July 1905. 1906. Part 3. In *Report of the Philippine Commission.*

*Report of the Philippine Commission,* 1901, 1902. Washington: General Printing Office.

———.1905. In *Annual report of the War Department,* fiscal year ended 30 June. 1904. Vol., 11, part 1. Washington: General Printing Office.

———. 1908. Washington: General Printing Office.

Report of the Senate Committee on National Minorities. 1960. Manila.

*Report of the special congressional committee on land grants.* 1931. 6 November.

*Report to the President of the United States by the economic survey mission to the Philippines.* 1950. 9 October. Washington: General Printing Office.

*Reports to the President of the Philippines and the Congress.* Various years. Commission on Elections. Republic of the Philippines.

Republic of the Philippines, Department of Finance. 1953. Farm landholdings of 50 hectares or more. 31 December.

*Rereading Frederick Jackson Turner: The significance of the frontier in American history and other Essays.* 1994. New York: H. Holt.

Reyes-Churchill, Bernardita. 1983. *The Philippine independence missions to the United States, 1919–1934.* Manila: National Historical Institute.

Rivera, Juan. 1953. Confidential memorandum to Pres. Elpidio Quirino, regarding the present Constabulary set-up in Mindanao and Sulu. 30 March. In Elipidio Quirino Papers.

Rodil, Rudy. 1961. Davao's conquest, government and economy, 1847–1898. *Mindanao Historical Journal* 41 (August).

———. 1990. Davao's conquest, government and economy, 1847–1898.

Rodriguez, Eulogio. 1938. *The economic development of Mindanao.* Occasional paper no. 7, Institute of Pacific Relations, 12 October.

Rodriguez, Filemon. 1985. *The Marcos regime: Rape of the nation.* Quezon City: Moed Press.

Roth, Fred. 1935. Letter to A.V. Hartendorp, editor, *Philippine Magazine,* 19 May. In Joseph Ralston Hayden Collection. Box 5.

Roth, Russel. 1981. *Muddy glory: America's 'Indian wars' in the Philippines, 1899–1935.* Massachusetts: Christopher Publishing House.

Rothchild, Donald and Naomi Chazan, eds. 1988. *The precarious balance: State and society in Africa.* Boulder, CO: Westview Press.

Saber, Mamitua. 1962. The Muslim minority in the Philippines. Typescript. Kroch Library, Cornell University.

———. 1974. The contact between the traditional and legal authority in a Muslim setting. In *On the codification of Muslim customary (Adat) and Quranic laws*, edited by Alfredo Tiamson. Davao City: Ateneo University and Mindanao State University.

Saleeby, Najeeb. 1913. The Moro problem: An academic discussion of the history and solution of the problem of the government of the Moros of the Philippine Islands. Manila: n.p.

Salgado, Geoffrey. 1989. Development politics for Muslim Mindanao in the pre-martial law period (1955–1971). *The Journal of History* 34–35, 1–2 (January-December).

Samson, Melody. 1957. Land settlement program in the Philippines. Business research paper, University of the Philippines College of Business Administration.

———. 1953. Jr. The Philippines: Quarterly economic and financial review. Report to the Department of State, 12 January 1953. United States, Department of State central files: The Philippine Republic, internal and foreign affairs.

Sandoval, Pedro R. 1957. Socioeconomic conditions of settlers in Kidapawan, Mindanao. *Philippine Agriculturist* 11, 9.

Saniel, Josefa. 1963. Four Japanese: Their plans for the expansion of Japan to the Philippines. *Asian Studies* 1, 53 (April).

———. 1966. The Japanese minority in the Philippines before Pearl Harbor: Social organization in Davao. *Asian Studies* 4 (1), 125–26.

Santos, Joel de los. 1975. The "Christian problem" and the Philippine south. *Asian Studies* 13, 3 (August).

Santos, Paulino (Lt. Col.) and Prof. Inocencio Elayda. 1934–35. A tentative plan for the development of agricultural colonies under the new colonization law.

Sarmiento, A.R. 1953. Department of Agriculture and Natural Resources, to Henry Townes, Mutual Security Agency, 23 February. 1953. United States, Department of State central files: The Philippine Republic, internal and foreign affairs.

Sawyer, Frederick H. 1900. *The inhabitants of the Philippines*. New York: Charles Scribners and Sons.

Scaff, Alvin. 1954. Class stratification in the EDCOR communities. *Philippine Sociological Review* 1, 2 (July).

———. 1955. *The Philippine answer to communism*. Stanford, CA: Stanford University Press.

Scott, James C. 1985. *Weapons of the weak: Everyday forms of peasant resistance*. New Haven and London: Yale University Press.

Senate Committee on the Philippines Hearing: Testimony of Manuel L. Quezon. 1916. *The Filipino People* 3, 10 February.

*Seventh and final report of the high commissioner to the Philippines, covering the period from 14 September 1945 to 4 July 1946*. 1946. Washington: General Printing Office.

Shefter, Martin. 1987. *Political crisis/fiscal crisis: The collapse and revival of New York City*. New York: Basic Books.

———. 1994. *Political parties and the state: The American historical experience*. Princeton: Princeton University Press.

Shiraishi, Saya and Takashi Shiraishi, eds. 1993. *The Japanese in colonial Southeast Asia.* Ithaca, New York: Cornell University Southeast Asia Program.

Shue, Vivienne B. 1988. *Reach of the state: Sketches of the Chinese body politic.* Stanford, CA: Stanford University Press.

———. 1994. State power and social organization in China. In *State power and social forces: Domination and transformation in the Third World,* edited by Joel Migdal, Atul Kohli and Vivienne Shue. New York: Cambridge University Press.

Sidel, John Thayer. 1995. Coercion, capital and the postcolonial state: Bossism in postwar Philippines. Ph.D. diss., Cornell University.

Silva, Rad. 1979. *Two hills of the same land: Truth behind the Mindanao problem.* Mindanao: Mindanao-Sulu Studies and Research Group.

Silverstein, Josef., ed. 1966. *Southeast Asia in world war II: Four essays.* New Haven: Yale University Southeast Asia Studies Monograph No. 7.

Simkins, Paul D. and Frederick L. Wernstedt. 1971. *Philippine migration: The settlement of the Digos-Padada valley, Davao province.* New Haven: Yale University Southeast Asia Studies Monograph no. 16.

Sinsuat, Duma. 1950–1951. Reports of the governor of Cotabato to the Office of the President. In *Historical Data Papers, Cotabato.*

———. 1952. Confidential letter to Pres. Quirino. 23 February. In Elpidio Quirino Papers.

———. circa 1953. Annual report of the governor of Cotabato to the President of the Philippines for the years 1952–1953.

*Sixth annual report of the United States high commissioner to the Philippine Islands, 1 July 1941 to 30 June 1942.* 1943. Washington: General Printing Office.

Skocpol, Theda. 1979. *States and social revolutions: A comparative analysis of France, Russia and China.* Cambridge: Cambridge University Press.

———. 1994. *Social revolutions in the modern world.* New York: Cambridge University Press.

Skocpol, Theda and Jeff Goodwin. 1994. Explaining revolutions in the contemporary Third World. In *Social revolutions in the modern world.* Cambridge: Cambridge University Press.

Skowronek, Stephen. 1982. *Building a new American state: The expansion of national administrative capacities, 1877–1920.* Cambridge: Cambridge University Press.

Smith, Anthony D. 1981. *The ethnic revival.* Cambridge: Cambridge University Press.

Smith, Cornelius C. 1977. *Don't settle for second: The life and times of Cornelius C. Smith.* California: Presidio Press.

Smith, Michael J. 1969. J. Henry L. Stimson and the Philippines. Ph.D. diss., Indiana University.

Smith, Warren D. 1990. The pearl of the eastern seas: A record of experiences of an American geologist in the Philippines, 1905–1922. *Bulletin of the American Historical Collection* 13, 4 (October-December).

Sorongon, Arturo. 1955. *A special study of landed estates in the Philippines.* Manila: ICA.

Southard, Milton I. 1878. Speech (Democrat, Ohio). Congressional record, 45th Cong., 2nd sess. Washington: General Printing Office.

Spence, Hartzell. 1979. *Marcos of the Philippines.* Manila: Ferdinand Marcos.

Spencer, J.E. 1952. *Land and people in the Philippines: Geographical problems in rural economy.* Berkeley and Los Angeles: University of California Press.

Springer, John E. 1904. Letter of attorney of the Moro Province to the Philippine Commission, 1 October. Exhibit G, *Report of the Philippine Commission.*

Stanley, Peter W. 1974. *A nation in the making: The Philippines and the United States, 1899–1921.* Cambridge, MA: Harvard University Press.

Starner, Frances Lucille. 1961. *Magsaysay and the Philippine peasantry.* Berkeley and California: University of California Press.

Stauffer, Robert. 1975. *The Philippine congress: Causes for structural change.* Series no. 90–024. Beverly Hills and London: Sage Publications.

Stewart, James. 1977. People of the flood plains: The changing ecology of rice farming in Cotabato. Ph.D. diss., University of Hawaii.

———. 1988. The Cotabato conflict. In *Understanding Islam and the Muslims in the Philippines*, edited by Peter Gowing. Quezon City: New Day Publishers.

Sturtevant, David R. 1976. *Popular uprisings in the Philippines, 1840–1940.* Ithaca and London: Cornell University Press.

Suazo, Amadeo. 1961. Davao under the American regime. *Mindanao Historical Journal* 1, 1 (October-December).

*The Sunday Times Magazine.* Various issues, 1960-1970.

Tadem, Eduardo. 1980. *Mindanao report: A preliminary study on the economic origins of social unrest.* Davao: AFRIM Resource Center.

———. 1992. The political economy of Mindanao: An overview. In *Mindanao: Land of the unfulfilled promise*, edited by Mark Turner, R. J. May, and Lulu Respall Turner. Quezon City: New Day Publisher.

Taft, William Howard. 1908. Special report of the secretary of war to the President of the United States, 23 January 1908. In *Report of the Philippine Commission,* vol. 9. In *Annual report of the War Department.* Washington: General Printing Office.

Tan, Samuel K. 1977. *The Filipino Muslim armed struggle, 1900–1972.* Manila: Filipinas Foundation.

———. 1982. *Selected essays on the Filipino Muslim.* Marawi City: Mindanao State University Research Center.

———. 1989. *Decolonization and Filipino Muslim identity.* Quezon City: Department of History, University of the Philippines.

———. 1993. *The critical decade, 1921–1930.* Quezon City: University of the Philippines College of Social Science and Philosophy Publications.

Tate, Merze. 1965. *The United States and the Hawaiian kingdom: A political history.* New Haven and London: Yale University Press.

*The third annual report of the United States high commissioner to the Philippines covering the calendar year 1938 and the first six months of 1939.* 1943. Washington: General Printing Office.

Thomas, Ralph Benjamin. 1971. Muslims but Filipinos: The integration of the Philippine Muslims, 1917–46. Ph.D. diss., University of Pennsylvania.

Thompson, Carmi A. 1926. Conditions in the Philippine islands together with suggestions with reference to the administration and economic development of the islands, 22 December. U.S. Senate Document 180, 69th Cong., 2nd sess.

Thompson, Mark R. 1995. *The anti-Marcos struggle: Personalistic rule and democratic transition in the Philippines.* New Haven and London: Yale University Press.

Thompson, Wayne W. 1975. Governors of the Moro Province: Wood, Bliss and Pershing in the southern Philippines. Ph.D. diss., University of California, San Diego.

Tiamson, Alfredo, ed. 1974. *On the codification of Muslim customary (Adat) and Quranic Laws.* Davao City: Ateneo University and Mindanao State University.

Tiglao, Rigoberto. 1981. *The Philippine coconut industry: Looking into coconuts (export oriented agricultural growth).* Davao City: ARC Publications.

———. 1988. The consolidation of dictatorship. In *Dictatorship and revolution: Roots of people's power,* edited by Aurora de Dios et al. Manila: Conspectus.

Tilly, Charles. 1975. *The formation of national states in western Europe.* New Jersey: Princeton University Press.

———. 1984. *Big structures, large processes, huge comparisons.* New York: Russell Sage Foundation.

———. 1990. *Coercion, capital and European states, AD 990–1190.* New York: Basil Blackwell.

Townes, Henry. 1953. Memorandum to Ray G. Johnson, director, Mutual Security Agency, regarding the rat situation in Cotabato. 4 March 1953. United States, Department of State central files: The Philippine Republic, internal and foreign affairs.

Trinidad, Teodosio. 1935. Confidential report of inspector, Bureau of Lands (Davao).

Turner, Frederick Jackson. 1921. *The frontier in American history.* New York: H. Holt.

Turner, Mark. 1995. Terrorism and secession in the southern Philippines: The rise of Abu Sayyaf. *Contemporary Southeast Asia* 17, 1.

Turner, Mark, R.J. May and Lulu Respall Turner, eds. 1992. *Mindanao: Land of unfulfilled promise.* Quezon City: New Day Publishers.

U.S. Embassy, Manila, to the Department of State. 1951a. Confidential report on congressional proposal to make mayors, vice-mayors and municipal board members in the Philippine chartered cities elective. 11 May. Department of State central files: The Philippine Republic, internal and foreign affairs.

———. 1951b. Report on the abaca situation in Davao, 24 August 1951. Department of State central files: The Philippine Republic, internal and foreign affairs.

U.S. Embassy, Manila, to Department of State. 1953a. Telegram 2785. 13 March. United States, Department of State central files: The Philippine Republic, internal and foreign affairs.

———. 1953b. Subject: The June 1951 abaca situation, 31 July 1953. United States, Department of State central files: The Philippine Republic, internal and foreign affairs.

———. 1971. The 1971 elections—results from the south, 22 November. United States, Department of State central files: The Philippine Republic, internal and foreign affairs.

Valdepeñas, Vicente B., Jr. and Germelino Bautista. 1977. *The emergence of the Philippine economy*. Manila: Papyrus Press.

Valenzuela, Wilfredo P. 1968. *Know them: A book of biographies.* Vol. 2. Manila: Dotela Publications.

Veloso, Ismael. 1950. Privilege speech. Philippine House of Representatives, *Congressional Records* 1, 62. 24 April.

———. 1953. Privilege speech. In *Congressional Record* 4, 58. 12 March. House of Representatives.

Villafuerte, Fundador. 1950. Letter to Pres. Elpidio Quirino. 8 August. In Elpidio Quirino Papers.

Villiers, John. 1990. Makassar: The rise and fall of an East Indonesian maritime trading state, 1512–1669. In *The Southeast Asian port and polity: Rise and demise*, edited by J. Kathirithamby-Wells and John Villiers. Singapore: Singapore University Press.

Warren, James F. 1977. Sino-Sulu trade in the late eighteenth and nineteenth centuries. *Philippine Studies* 25 (First Quarter).

Wernstedt, Frederick L. 1957. *The role and importance of Philippine interisland shipping and trade.* Ithaca, NY: Cornell University Southeast Asia Program, Data Paper 26.

Wernstedt, Frederick L. and Paul D. Simkins. 1965. Migration and settlement of Mindanao. *Journal of Asian Studies* (November).

White, Richard. 1991. *It's your misfortune and none of my own: A history of the American West.* Norman and London: University of Oklahoma Press.

Wiebe, Robert. 1975. *The segmented society: An introduction to the meaning of America.* New York: Oxford University Press.

Wilkinson, R.J. 1923. *A history of the peninsular Malays, with chapters on Perak and Selangor.* Singapore: Kelly and Walsh Ltd.

Williams, Daniel R. 1913. *The odyssey of the Philippine Commission.* Chicago: A.C. McClurg & Co.

Wolters, O.W. 1982. *History, culture and region in Southeast Asian perspectives.* Singapore: Institute of Southeast Asian Studies.

———.1994. Southeast Asia as a Southeast Asian field of study. *Indonesia* 58.

Wurfel, David Omer Drury. 1960. The Bell report and after: A study of the political problems of social reform stimulated by foreign aid. Ph.D. diss., Cornell University.

———.1988. *Filipino politics: Development and decay.* Quezon City: Ateneo de Manila University Press; Ithaca and London: Cornell University Press.

Young, Crawford. 1994. *The African colonial state in comparative perspective.* New Haven and London: Yale University Press.

Youngblood, Robert L. 1966. A study of the 1963 mayoralty election in Jolo, Philippines. Master's thesis, University of Hawaii.

Yu-Jose, Lydia N. 1992. *Japan views the Philippines, 1900–1944*. Quezon City: Ateneo de Manila University Press.

Zartman, I. William, ed. 1995. *Collapsed states: The disintegration and restoration of legitimate authority*. Boulder, CO: Lynne Rienner.

# INDEX